W9-BFY-082

Praise for
The Real History Behind the Templars

"[An] indispensable companion to current popular works."

—*Library Journal*

"In a series of concise, highly informative chapters, Sharan Newman sets forth the story of the Templars and everything associated with them in a logical, chronological progression. The result is a book that you'll not only understand, but enjoy, no matter how familiar (or unfamiliar) you may be with Templar history." —About.com

"*The Real History Behind the Templars* is a useful resource for separating fact from fiction about this controversial medieval order. As the author of a series of medieval mystery novels and someone with an advanced degree in medieval studies Sharan Newman has the skill to take modern scholarship and package it for a popular audience."

—*Catholic World Report*

"This smart and engaging book will make readers who are familiar with the array of pseudo-histories think twice. Newman writes simply yet eloquently. Her prose is lucid and poised and her observations succinct, which makes this tome difficult to put down. She is unafraid to examine the primary sources anew and has the talent to summarize a stack of convoluted material in a few concise sentences. But the popular historian's real accomplishment is that she is fundamentally exact, bright and interesting." —*Independent Weekly of Australia*

Praise for
The Real History Behind The Da Vinci Code

"If, like Sam Cooke sang, you 'don't know much about history,' Newman's encyclopedic, A-to-Z look at the topics ranging from 'Aprocrypha' to 'Wren, Christopher' provides perspective and insight."

—Pittsburgh Tribune-Review

"Witty and charming, but nonetheless rational in explanation and complete in background research, *The Real History Behind The Da Vinci Code* seeks not so much to refute the novel but to elucidate on the truth, and not so much to disparage the mistakes of Mr. Brown but to make readers realize that the history is bigger than any one person, popular novelists included."

—Business World

"The book . . . gives the truth about topics used in Brown's fiction . . . well written and precise, it is the work of a woman who writes what she knows."

—Statesman Journal (Oregon)

"For fans of Dan Brown's popular *The Da Vinci Code*, Sharan Newman's *The Real History Behind The Da Vinci Code* is a must-have companion."

—The Sunday Oregonian

"Newman has arranged her discussion of the people, places, and events in *The Da Vinci Code* in an encyclopedic format, creating a book that is both accessible and fun to read."

—Library Journal

The Real History of the
END OF THE
WORLD

SHARAN NEWMAN

BERKLEY BOOKS, NEW YORK

THE BERKLEY PUBLISHING GROUP
Published by the Penguin Group
Penguin Group (USA) Inc.
375 Hudson Street, New York, New York 10014, USA
Penguin Group (Canada), 90 Eglinton Avenue East, Suite 700, Toronto, Ontario M4P 2Y3, Canada
(a division of Pearson Penguin Canada Inc.)
Penguin Books Ltd., 80 Strand, London WC2R 0RL, England
Penguin Group Ireland, 25 St. Stephen's Green, Dublin 2, Ireland (a division of Penguin Books Ltd.)
Penguin Group (Australia), 250 Camberwell Road, Camberwell, Victoria 3124, Australia
(a division of Pearson Australia Group Pty. Ltd.)
Penguin Books India Pvt. Ltd., 11 Community Centre, Panchsheel Park, New Delhi—110 017, India
Penguin Group (NZ), 67 Apollo Drive, Rosedale, North Shore, 0632, New Zealand
(a division of Pearson New Zealand Ltd.)
Penguin Books (South Africa) (Pty.) Ltd., 24 Sturdee Avenue, Rosebank, Johannesburg 2196,
South Africa

Penguin Books Ltd., Registered Offices: 80 Strand, London WC2R 0RL, England

While the author has made every effort to provide accurate telephone numbers and Internet addresses at the time of publication, neither the publisher nor the author assumes any responsibility for errors, or for changes that occur after publication. Further the publisher does not have any control over and does not assume any responsibility for author or third-party websites or their content.

Copyright © 2010 Sharan Newman

Cover design by Richard Hasselberger
Book design by Tiffany Estreicher

All rights reserved.
No part of this book may be reproduced, scanned, or distributed in any printed or electronic form without permission. Please do not participate in or encourage piracy of copyrighted materials in violation of the author's rights. Purchase only authorized editions.
BERKLEY® is a registered trademark of Penguin Group (USA) Inc.
The "B" design is a trademark of Penguin Group (USA) Inc.

PRINTING HISTORY
Berkley trade paperback edition/ April 2010

Library of Congress Cataloging-in-Publication Data

Newman, Sharan.
   The real history of the end of the world : apocalyptic predictions from Revelation and Nostradamus to Y2K and 2012 / Sharan Newman.—1st ed.
      p. cm.
   Includes bibliographical references and index.
   ISBN 978-0-425-23253-8
   1. End of the world—History of doctrines.   2. Prophecies—History.   I. Title.
   BL503.N49 2010
   202'.309—dc22

                                                           2009050669

PRINTED IN THE UNITED STATES OF AMERICA

10 9 8 7 6 5 4 3 2 1

This book is dedicated to all the Chicken Littles among us, who are sure that the sky will soon fall. Someday you will be right.

And for Rebecca Hill and John Parks, who shared the load.

Acknowledgments

Deborah Adams, for urging me to send in the proposal for this book when I was just going to delete it.

Erika Johnson Bayless, for telling me how to put it all together.

Jennifer Johnson Bell, for teaching me how to make a table.

Dr. Eddie Chan, for finding esoteric groups for me to study.

Professor Armin Geertz, Aarhus University, Denmark, for proofing my section on the Hopi.

Professor Susan D. Gillespie, University of Florida, for directing me to references on the Mayan calendar.

Professor Salima Ikram, American University of Cairo, Professor Aidan Dodson, Bristol University, and Dr. Barbara Mertz for references on ancient Egyptian eschatology and making sure I didn't spell *Osiris* as if he were a Roman.

Morgan Kay, for taking time from her dissertation to check my information on Merlin.

Steven Lavoie, of the Oakland Library, for sending me references to the Doomsealers.

Connie L. F. Terwilliger, for suggesting the proper group to dedicate this book to.

As always, any mistakes in this book are mine alone.

Contents

PART SEVEN:
Still Waiting for the End

The Beginning of the End

It may seem strange, if not impossible, to write a history of something that hasn't happened yet. I could point out that if I wait until it does, there will be very few readers to benefit from my work. But it makes more sense to explain that this is really a history of how people all over the world and through time have thought about the end of the world and how they have dealt with the concept.

Very few people have actually believed that the whole world will end. But almost every culture has some belief or folk myth that tells how the gods or God renew an earth that has become morally corrupt. It seems that people everywhere have looked around at the chaos caused by nature or humanity and at some point just have thrown up their hands, too overwhelmed with the problem to see a way to fix it.

But how could the world be fixed? Some cultures see time as cyclical; nothing ends, but now and then a new cycle begins. In many cases the birth of the cycle is painful and most of the corrupt world is lost in the transition. In other traditions time is linear. Western society, under the influence of Judaism, Christianity, and Islam, tends to view history as moving along a straight track from beginning to end. Whether the start was the Garden of Eden or the Big Bang doesn't matter. The direction is the same.

When I began work on this book, I didn't think I would find much on the end in cultures with cyclical viewpoints. I was mistaken. Just as I could find few traditions that the world would end completely in linear societies, I discovered there were groups within Chinese, Hindu, and other societies with cyclical worldviews that shared end-time ideas that were much the same as the Western picture of the Apocalypse.

Which brings me to the tricky topic of terminology. There are several words and phrases used by people who study the end times (*end times* is one). Some of them are just different ways of saying the same thing. Some are technical terms, like *eschatology*, an academic term for study of the idea of the end times. Still others have picked up new meanings over the years. For my purposes, *Apocalypse* means everything ending with a bang: war, fire, flood, etc. Even though it means the same thing as Revelation, too many people see them as different. I will use *Revelation* to refer to the book of the New Testament attributed to John of Patmos, although sometimes that is also called the Apocalypse. Okay?

Millennium is the happy time during which the saved or the elect will live in peace before the final grand reckoning. Some Christians think that Jesus will return at the beginning of the Millennium, some think it won't be until the end. This return of Jesus is expressed in many ways: Second Coming, Second Advent, Parousia (my favorite).

I will try to explain these terms as they appear in the text but, just in case, there is also a short glossary at the end of the book. It's for my benefit, too, because there are some words I have to look up every time I run across them.

At times it seemed to me as if everyone who had ever picked up a quill or pen or stylus had written about the end of the world. Everywhere I looked, someone was either predicting the end or at least describing the events that would precede it. But, after a while I began to see that almost all of the movements fell into categories, although the categories often overlapped. For instance, there were those who were interested in predicting the end as a mathematical exercise, using primarily the biblical books of Daniel and Revelation. This includes Isaac Newton and William Miller. The difference between the two is mainly that Miller felt he should warn people. Newton seemed to think everyone was on his own.

Most of the millennial movements, as distinct from individual date-setters, are tied to a belief that only a few people can be saved from the coming destruction. I thought that this was just a Christian phenomenon but then found it in non-monotheistic societies, like the Chinese Yellow Turbans and the Hopi. So perhaps the belief in an imminent end coupled with the salvation of the elect believers is either very ancient or universal common sense. It's difficult for people to imagine their own end, even if everything else goes up in a cataclysm. There are hard-nosed scientists, who know that one day the sun will use up its fuel, who still hypothesize that humanity will figure out a way to colonize another planet before that happens.

Therefore I have selected representative groups and influential writers or leaders of apocalyptic or millennial movements, such as people who believed their leader to be the Messiah, or a prophet, who would build a heaven on earth or give them a free pass to the real heaven; those who thought that the thousand years of happiness would start if they helped it along with military force; and those who thought that we were at the end of the thousand years and braced themselves in various ways to survive the horrors of the final battles and breakdown of society before the final judgment.

The reader may be surprised to know how many mainstream religions today began as millennial movements that later adapted their dogma to living in a world that didn't end when expected.

I also included some people and groups that fascinate me. Although most of them did not leave lasting memorials or establish religions that still exist, they reflect the myriad ways that humans have interpreted their own times as apocalyptic. It is also intriguing to consider why most people muddle on through good times and bad without ever assuming that the end is upon them while a small but intense segment of society feels compelled to fix the time and prepare for it, sometimes in terribly destructive ways.

However, this is not a book of sociology or psychology. I looked at a number of theoretical studies on the reasons behind millennial movements, charismatic leaders, and doomsday cults. I would always find exceptions to the conclusions. So as a historian, I've simply tried to record, as accurately as possible, how humankind has anticipated the end of the world in various ways.

Here and there in this work, I mention the upcoming prediction that the world will end on the winter solstice of 2012. I did some work on the ideas that the poles will flip, or that there will be catastrophic solar flares, or that a galactic alignment will occur that will signal some great upheaval. I haven't found a clear explanation for what. None of these things seems to be of serious concern.

For instance, the magnetic poles wander about all the time within a certain radius, never far from the geographic pole.[1] But they don't move together. The North Pole is moving toward Siberia at about fifty kilometers a year. The South Pole is heading northwest at about five kilometers. I have been assured that they will not end up making snow in Ethiopia.[2] I love the idea of independent poles, each setting out on its own adventure. What is even more amazing is that the movement of the magnetic poles has been known since the 1600s. It's only recently that the fact has been dragged out to join the list of scary things that might happen in 2012. Now, some people say that the poles aren't just going to wobble; they'll reverse, so south will be north and north will be south. Birds won't know where to migrate; planes won't be able to navigate. It does seem that north and south trade places every so often. But there's a lot of debate about when, where, and how long it would take, never mind what the effects might be. It's not high on my list of worries.

Solar flares can be a problem with power plants and other technology, and scientists are saying we may have a lot of them around 2012, but the last round was just a few years ago and the world didn't end then. But there's no point in trying to refute each of these 2012 end-of-world theories individually because there's always a new one coming up. However, I do make a point of giving the background on the Maya, the Hopi, and Nostradamus, whose supposed prophecies tend to be cited most often. I heard the other day that the Mother Shipton, invented by a journalist in the eighteenth century, had predicted the end in 2012. I hadn't even considered writing about her since she, like the Greek tradition of the Sibyl, is basically a franchise. There never was a Mother Shipton. Publishers just hired writers to put together new prophecies every few years in her name.

A word on footnotes. As I have said in my earlier books, I believe in using them. I know that seeing lots of footnotes can be intimidating. You don't have to read them. There will not be a test. But, if you want to check my facts or find out more about something, the information is there so you can find it. Also footnotes keep writers honest. It is all too tempting just to write down what you want to be true without being certain that it is. Several of the books that I looked at, both ones that stated a theory and ones that debunked it, have suffered from this problem. I don't want to add to the confusion.

Anyway, research is fun. Many of the things I found surprised me and fascinated me. I hope you agree.

---

1 J. Hospers, "Rock Magnetism and Polar Wandering," *The Journal of Geology* 63, no. 5 (1955): 59.

2 Sid Perkins, "North by Northwest: The Planet's Wandering Magnetic Poles Help Reveal History of Earth and Humans," *Science News*, December 22–29, 2007, pp. 392–394.

PART ONE:

Before the Common Era

CHAPTER ONE

Nothing but Humankind
and the Stars

The idea that the world will end some day makes a lot of sense. People are born and die, plants grow and wither, floods and volcanoes change the landscape with terrifying suddenness. The people living thousands of years ago must have been brilliant to take the uncertainties of life and create systems that would make sense of why they were on this planet.

With fire, flood, drought, predatory animals, and disease to contend with, it must have been a comfort to look at the stars and realize that they formed a constant pattern that could be used to signal the coming of spring and times to plant and harvest. It's no wonder that early cultures like the Vedic Hindus, Maya, and Egyptians got a bit carried away, measuring the stars, sun, and moon from every conceivable angle throughout the years. The belief that stars could predict the future must have begun shortly after the patterns were recognized.

Theories about the beginning of the world must have been an amusing speculation for an evening around the campfire or during those three-thousand-mile migrations our ancestors made as they spread across the world. Imagining the end seems to have come later.

The earliest known stories of the end of the world come from the Indo-European tradition. Many of these cultures use the same image of the cyclical ages of the world, from a Golden Age, in which people are happy and live almost forever, down (in the case of Daniel, literally) to an Iron Age, the present, in which humanity has declined. In the Mediterranean world the influence of the Greek author Hesiod, writing in the eighth century B.C.E., was strong. He was decidedly pessimistic, feeling that his age would be the last. The signs of the end include a shortening of lifespan, until babies are born with gray hair.[1] Hesiod believed that humanity can stave off the end, though. All we need to do is live just and moral lives.[2] Hesiod's ideas are part of an intertwined tradition of very similar stories from all over the Mesopotamian, Indian, and Egyptian worlds. The similarity among them indicates that they may have come from even older traditions that were passed on only orally.

In this first section I look at some of the earliest end stories I could find. Often they are part of an epic cycle of stories of gods and heroes. For the most part, the end is not the main thrust of the story. To use a cliché, it's the journey that matters. But in those stories are the seeds of our current obsession with the end of all things.

---

1 Ludwig Koenen, "Greece, the Near East and Egypt: Cyclic Destruction in Hesiod and the Catalogue of Women," *Transactions of the American Philological Association (1974–)* 124 (1994): 6.
2 Ibid., 10.

CHAPTER TWO

Akkadians, Babylonians, and Hittites, Oh My!

Has some living soul escaped? No man
was to survive the destruction!

—*Epic of Gilgamesh* (the God Enlil on learning that Atrahasis
and his household have escaped the Great Flood)

The name of the original Noah started out as Atrahasis, which in later versions became Utanapishtim. One can see how a mouthful like that would be changed. In Hebrew, he is called Noach, meaning "rest" or "comfort." But it is as Atrahasis, Utanapishtim, or sometimes Ziusuddu (which is almost as bad) that the leader of the sole survivors of the first destruction of the world appears. The fact that he has so many names indicates that there probably was a flood once and that similar stories were told of it in several traditions.[1]

There are many versions of the story of the Great Flood in Mesopotamia. They almost certainly predate written history, which began in Babylonia (now Iraq and bits of adjoining countries) about 4000 B.C.E. Evidence of a complex society there has been dated by archaeologists to around 5000 B.C.E. The area was inhabited by two different groups, which joined eventually to become the Babylonians. In the north were the Akkadians, who were Semitic. In the south were the

Sumerians. Their language has been deciphered, but it doesn't seem to be related to any other known language, so where they came from is uncertain. However, their invention of cuneiform writing was revolutionary and acclaimed from the start, especially by merchants who needed to keep track of inventory. Cuneiform was adapted for other languages and used for nearly two thousand years.[2] The language was lost well before the Common Era and deciphered again only in the nineteenth century. It came as a major shock to linguists and an even bigger one to theologians when one translation turned out to be a flood story that paralleled Noah's, down to the measuring of the Ark, but which predated the Bible by two thousand years.[3]

The story of the flood is first found in the "Myth of Atrahasis," which was discovered in its entirety by Iraqi archaeologists when they unearthed a library at Ninevah in 1986. It is around 1800 years older than the earliest known rendition of the *Epic of Gilgamesh* in which it was incorporated.[4] In it, the reason for the flood is not the wickedness of humankind but the noise made by so many people carrying on with their lives. According to the Atrahasis, there were once two levels of divinity. The lesser gods had to do all the work for the higher gods. So some lesser god had the bright idea of inventing people to take over the hard jobs. But the gods didn't take into account how quickly people procreate. The god Enlil, who was one of the upper echelon, couldn't get to sleep for all the nighttime activity. He decided that creating a humanity eager to reproduce had been a mistake. When plague and famine didn't work in slowing them down, he sent the flood.[5]

This theme is also found in Sumerian poems of lamentation. One grieves over the devastation Enlil's storm caused:

> . . . *no tears could change the baleful storm's nature,*
> *The reaping storm was gathering in the country*
> *The storm was ravaging floodlike the city*
> *The storm that annihilates countries stunned the city*

The Flood Tablet. Neo-Assyrian, 7th BCE. From the palace library of King Ashurbanipal (r.669-631 BCE), Nineveh, northern Iraq. 15.24 x 13.33 cm. Inv.:K.3375. © *The Trustees of the British Museum / Art Resource, New York*

> *The storm ordered by Enlil in hate, the storm gnawing away*
> *   at the country*
> *Covered Ur like a cloth, veiled in like a linen sheet.*[6]

Gilgamesh is the oldest known epic saga of a hero's journey. It is a story of battles, friendship, and a man's search for the meaning of life.

There are several versions, all found on pieces of clay that are rarely in one piece (Figure 1). It is estimated that about 40 percent of the Gilgamesh story is still missing. However, the section about the flood is almost an interlude in the narrative because it was already a folk tale and was used in the epic to emphasize Gilgamesh's quest for immortality.

In it Utanapishtim (Noah) tells Gilgamesh how he and his wife became immortal. When Utanapishtim was warned of the coming inundation, he took his family, retainers, and the people who built his ark into it with him, thereby establishing a good base for repopulating the earth. For this forethought, the gods allowed him to live forever.

There is also an element of bargaining in the story. When the gods realized that they had done away with all their workers, they promised Utanapishtim and humanity that they would never destroy them by a flood again. But they insisted on some changes. People's lives would have to be shorter. Clans would fight rather than care for each other and live in peace. There would be more dangers from nature: snakes, scorpions, lions, and wolves, for instance. The gods weren't going to put up with overpopulation again just because they had sworn not to destroy the world.[7]

The only exceptions to these conditions were Utanapishtim and his wife. After the flood, a repentant Enlil boarded the ship and touched their foreheads, saying, "Hitherto Utanapishtim has been but human, Henceforth Utanapishtim and his wife shall be like unto us gods."[8] Gilgamesh, hearing the story, realized that he wasn't likely to be granted immortality in that way and resumed his quest.

So, if one asked a Sumerian or Akkadian about the end of the world, they would probably say that it had already happened. There was a Golden Age, then the flood, and that was it.[9] While they were intensely interested in the future and studied astrology in the hope of predicting it, the prophecies were focused on concrete things. Would the king be a just ruler? Would the crops fail? One group of Akkadian prophecies cycles through a series of kings. Under some there will be abundance, under others "revolution calamity and chaos."[10]

But, whatever happens to Akkadians, Sumerians, or Babylonions, the world doesn't end. They have the gods' word on that.

1 This may be one of the reasons most people think they'll survive the Apocalypse. We're hard-wired for it.

2 Alfred Burns, *The Power of the Written Word: The Role of Literacy in Western Civilization* (New York: Lang, 1989), 16. This, I am sure, has been noted by the "alien seed" theorists.

3 Daniel F. Fleming, "After the Gods Abandoned Us," *The Classical World* 97, no. 1 (2003): 13.

4 A. R. Millard, "A Sign of the Flood," *Iraq* 49 (1987): 65.

5 Ibid., 65.

6 Fleming, 15.

7 Benjamin R. Foster, "Mesopotamia and the End of Time," in *Imagining the End*, ed. Abbas Amanat and Magnus T. Bernhardsson (London: Tauris, 2002), 27.

8 "The Epic of Gilgamesh," trans. E. A. Speiser, in *Religions of the Ancient Near East*, ed. Isaac Mendelsohn (New York: Liberal Arts Press, 1955), 106.

9 Foster, 26.

10 Robert H. Pfeiffer, "Akkadian Prophecies," in *Religions of the Ancient Near East*, 205–207.

CHAPTER THREE

Ancient Egypt

Keeping the World in Balance

It flows through old hushed Egypt and its sands
Like some grave mighty thought threading a dream,
And times and things, as in the vision seem
Keeping along it their eternal stands.

—James Henry Leigh Hunt, "The Nile"

There are two ways of looking at the Egyptian view of the end of the world. Either it must not have been of much importance, for there are no descriptions of the end, or it must have been of vital concern because the rites performed by the kings and priests were all that kept the Egyptian world from total collapse.

"The state religion was primarily established to secure, through ritual offerings, the continuation of the universe, the prosperity of Egypt, and the gods' acceptance of the king."[1] This seems to have been the reason for the temples of the kings in every part of Egypt from at least 3000 B.C.E. At some point in prehistory it was recognized that the king was the only one who could actively interact with the gods. He took on aspects of the hero god Horus, and so the symbols of Horus, the sun and the falcon, became part of the regalia of kingship.[2]

To the Egyptians the world was originally balanced and in harmony but when the god Seth killed his brother Osiris, the balance, which the Egyptians called *ma'at*, was disrupted. In order for the universe to remain together, a just king, one who "caused Right to exist," had to constantly tend to the gods. It was essential that this king and his representatives, the priests, offer up the Right to the sun god, Ra, every day to prevent the disintegration of the universe.[3] "Because of the continual vulnerability of order to fall into chaos, Egyptians needed to conceive of creation not as a single past event but as a series of 'first times,' of sacred regenerative moments."[4]

For the Egyptians, the gods were not independent of humanity; they couldn't regenerate alone. They had to be fed and washed and given wine or beer each day. The gods seem to have preferred concrete evidence of the fidelity of their people rather than emotional commitment. However, there is a line in the "Instructions to Mekerre," written about 2000 B.C.E., in which the god says, "More acceptable is the character of the straightforward one than the ox of the evil-doer."[5] While this indicates that it's better to come empty-handed than with a wicked heart, the instructions continue, "Act for God, that he may do the like for you, with offerings for replenishing the altars and with carving."[6]

These instructions were first written after an impious king had ordered the sack of a cemetery in which gods were buried. The king responsible for the desecration, Akhtoy, composed them as a remembrance to his son of all that Ra has given them and of all that they owe Ra in return.[7]

The continuation of the universe was a burden that likely affected average people as well as rulers and priests. It would also be easy, I think, for people to interpret disasters of any sort to the failure of the leaders to perform their duties properly. The pressure of constant observance of ritual could also encourage the cult of the king because, ultimately, it was he and not his subordinate priests who dealt with heaven. Putting all the stress on the king allowed people to get on with daily life. The cult was "part of a cosmic pact in which the king offered up to heaven the fruits of the earth, in exchange for channeling down to earth the blessings of heaven."[8] "Offerings were more than gift giving; they were reciprocal creation."[9]

Many religions have a clear or cloaked system of giving something to the gods or God in return for prosperity, health, or victory in battle. But if the Egyptians failed, the gods themselves might die. The ancient Mayans also believed that the only way to keep doom away was to make offerings to the gods; they were much more dramatic about it and seemed to fear that the world might be destroyed but never the gods. At least the Egyptians were able to maintain cosmic order with bread and beer instead of a constant flow of blood.

The only other religion I know of that put the onus of continued existence on humankind was that of the Zoroastrians, whose god created them in order to swing the balance in favor of goodness against the dark god.

The cult of each Egyptian king generally lasted only as long as the king lived. Although there seems to have been some belief in the power of dead rulers to intercede on behalf of their descendants, the one with the real power, the one who continued the necessary rituals, was the living king.

There are some ancient warning and prophecy poems in Egyptian literature that promise the eventual coming of a new king who will restore *ma'at* to a world out of balance. *The Admonitions of Ipuwer* from about 1300 B.C.E. is typical of these.[10]

The preservation of the universe is not the same as the preservation of individual souls. The Egyptians were extremely concerned about the solitary journey after death, as the *Book of the Dead* demonstrates. The book gives step-by-step directions for passing the tests of the gods so the soul can ascend into a paradisiacal afterlife. There are numerous versions of this book, and other guides, such as *The Book of Two Ways*, and texts from various sources found written on coffins of people from all levels of society. The care taken to preserve the body with grave goods also speaks to a rich tradition of a full afterlife.

It seems like a contradiction that a people so seemingly obsessed with the next world have no tales of the end times for the earth. But there appears to be no Apocalypse, no collective final judgment. Perhaps the ancient Egyptians had faith that their descendants would continue to keep the world stable. So far, they have been right.

1 Rosalie David, *The Experience of Ancient Egypt* (London: Routledge, 2000), 25.
2 Leonard H. Lesko, "Ancient Egyptian Cosmologies and Cosmogonies," in *Religion in Ancient Egypt* ed. Byron E. Shafer (Ithaca, NY: Cornell University Press, 1991), 93.
3 Stephen Quirke, *Ancient Egyptian Religion* (London, British Museum Press, 1992), 70.
4 Dieter Arnold, Lanny Bell, Ragnhild Bjerre Finnestad, Gerhard Haeny, and Byron E. Shafer, *Temples of Ancient Egypt* (Ithaca, NY: Cornell University Press, 1997), 2.
5 Quoted in Lesko, 103.
6 Ibid.
7 Ibid., 102. This may mean that the king was tomb robbing.
8 Quirke, 81.
9 Dieter et al., p. 24.
10 Ludwig Koenen, "Greece, the Near East and Egypt: Cyclic Destruction in Hesiod and the Catalogue of Women," *Transactions of the American Philological Association (1974–)* 124 (1994): 15.

CHAPTER FOUR

Thus Spoke Zoroaster

The Ancient Persian Cosmos

This, too, it says, that this earth becometh an iceless, slopeless
plain; even the mountain whose summit is the support of the
Kinvad Bridge, they press down, and it will not exist.

—*Bundahis*, c. XXX, 33

Z oroaster was a mysterious prophet who appeared in what is now
northern Iran in the sixth century B.C.E. He may have been an
exile from the area around Tehran. In a civilization that worshipped
many gods, all of whom needed to be propitiated, Zoroaster preached
a stark religion in which there was only one decision: Be on the side
of good or the side of evil. In his books, the *Gatha*, written in an early
form of Persian, the nature of the struggle is explained.

In the beginning, according to the books, there was nothing in
the universe but the god Ohrmazd, all-good and all-knowing. Then
he slowly became aware that there was also another god, Ahiram, who
was Ohrmazd's evil opposite.[1] Ohrmazd realized that he needed to
destroy Ahiram but could not do it in the unchanging timeless universe in which they existed. So Ohrmazd created seven divine helpers
to fight Ahiram. He also created the earth, like an island in the ocean.
"On it stood one bull, one plant and a single human."[2]

Ahiram saw this and, in response, created his own set of demons to aid him in battling Ohrmazd.

At first Ahiram seemed to be winning the battle. He polluted the water; brought darkness to the earth; and destroyed the first plant, bull, and man. But from their seed, all other living things arose, and since Ohrmazd could create nothing evil, his creations were good and began to fight back against Ahiram's evil.[3]

But Ohrmazd knew that the struggle would never be over if the good and evil were always evenly matched so the eternal souls of human beings, the *fravashi*, were invited to enter the world and were given moral choice. Thus good and evil became mixed, and humans must choose between them. The Zoroastrian texts indicate that good can't triumph without the active participation of humanity.[4]

This is the foundation of the Zoroastrian religion, begun three thousand years ago and still in existence today. Many of the beliefs that are basic to the teachings of Zoroaster infiltrated later religions, such as Judaism, Christianity, and Islam, and affected the development of nontraditional forms of Buddhism and Taoism in China.

The god Ohrmazd was not imagined as a human form, like the deities of the Greeks, Hindus, and Egyptians. He was a spirit that could not be represented by an image, but he was sometimes compared to a flame, which led to the idea among outside groups that the Zoroastrians were fire worshipers.[5] They did see the sun as something worthy of reverence and even worship but did not, apparently, consider it a god. It was more like an avatar of Ohrmazd.

In later centuries, the worship of Ohrmazd mingled with that of the earlier god Mithra, whose symbol was a bull, and with other pre-Zoroastrian traditions. However, the central dogma of life being a struggle between good and evil, truth and lie never changed.

The *Avesta*, later Zoroastrian books written in Old Persian, give detailed instructions for living an ethical life. Since there is complete free will, the decisions a person makes affect his or her final fate in the afterlife. Hell is described in terrifying, graphic images. Heaven, by contrast, is less clearly visualized, simply being a place of immortality and well-being.[6]

The *Avesta* also tell of a savior who will come at the end of time, wage a final battle, and pronounce a final judgment.

The savior is called Saoshyant. He will appear to raise the dead and reunite the soul with the body. Those who died as adults will be resurrected as forty-year-olds (thereby driving another nail into the popular myth that people in ancient times were old at thirty). Those who died as children will return at about the age of fifteen.[7]

The Saoshyant is aided in this resurrection by a powerful entity in the form of a plant. One of the probable leftovers from earlier religious beliefs is the story of Haoma (Soma in Hindu). Haoma is both a god and a plant that is presumed to have mind-altering properties. Scholars have tried to identify the actual plant, perhaps a mushroom of some sort, but have not yet come to agreement.[8] Haoma is almost certainly the rebirth of a cult that Zoroaster had tried to suppress at least a part of. The plant was harvested ritually, made into a liquid, and drunk by the priests in a ceremony called *Yasna*. This was accompanied by the sacrifice of an animal.[9] It was the joy that people apparently displayed as the animal was painfully slaughtered that offended Zoroaster in the first place.[10] Haoma has been identified with the Indo-Iranian Vedic gods of the ancient world.

As transmuted into the Zoroastrian tradition, the Haoma plant was ritually burned, mixed with the fat of the sacrificial animal, and ingested, first by the priests and then by the congregation, during the day-long *Yasna* ceremony. The plant was believed to give spiritual immortality. "The sacrament on earth, however, is only in anticipation of the final sacrifice of the bull Hadhayans performed by the Soshyant, the eschatological savior who, in the last days, will rise up from the seed of Zoroaster to restore the whole of the good creation. From the fat of this ultimate sacrificial victim the white Haoma will be prepared, the drink of immortality, by which all men are made anew, perfect and whole in body and in soul."[11]

This eating of the sacrifice has resonances in Christianity, for the Haoma was also believed to be the son of Ohrmazd who willingly became the plant and the sacrifice for the salvation of the believers. "The plant is identical with the son of God: he is bruised and mangled in the mortar so that the life-giving fluid that proceeds from his body may give new life in body and soul to the worshipper."[12] But the sacrifice of Haoma does not just ensure personal salvation but also the welfare of the society as a whole. He gives health, makes herds of cattle multiply, protects from the attacks of wild beasts, and maintains the balance of the world.[13]

The story of the Saoshyant begins with the account of three virgins who swim in a lake in which Zoroaster has left some of his seed. Each of them becomes pregnant and one of these virgins becomes the mother of Soshyant. As he grows up, he gathers around him many others who fight demons and liars. He is also the one who resurrects the dead with the Haoma and is the final judge.[14] However, he does this only with the permission of Ohrmazd because the Soshyant is the son of Zoroaster and not divine in himself.

Sometime around 500 B.C.E., the Zoroastrians developed a linear view of time that was expressed as a cosmic year of twelve millennia, ending with the time of the Soshyant. This is similar to later monotheistic divisions of the ages of the world. The Zoroastrians may have borrowed the idea from the Greeks. Interesting ideas tend to float about with trade routes and get adopted by a variety of cultures that find them attractive.

Zoroastrians were persecuted from the time of the conquests of Alexander the Great until, in the third century C.E., the Sassanian Empire in Persia made Zoroastrianism the state religion. At that time, the *Avesta*, the holy books of the religion, had to be reconstructed because most had been lost during the centuries of suppression. Many have never been found. This renaissance lasted until the Muslim invasions of 651, at which time many Zoroastrians converted, fled, or died.

While Zoroaster apparently intended the wicked to be totally destroyed at the end of the world, in the Sassanian tradition, "there will be a mighty conflagration, and all men will have to wade through a stream of molten metal which will seem like warm milk to the just and be in very truth what it is to the wicked. The sins of the damned are, however, purged away in this terrible ordeal and all creation returns to its Maker in joy."[15] So the concept of redemption for even the worst sinners had been introduced.

Today, the majority of the Zoroastrians in the world are the Parsi of India. They are the descendants of those who fled first from Alexander the Great and then from the armies of Islam.

An ancient story about Zoroaster is that he was born laughing.[16] At what, no one knows, but perhaps he expected his life to be one of joy living together with all those on the side of Truth and Goodness.

---

1 Philip G. Kreyenbrock, "Millennialism and Eschatology in the Zoroastrian Tradition," in *Imagining the End: Visions of the Apocalypse from the Ancient Middle East to Modern America, ed.* Abbas Amnanat and Magnus T. Bernhardsson (London: Tauris, 2002, 34. Ohrmazd is also called Avestan and Ahura Mazda, or Lord Wisdom. Ahriman goes by Angra, or Evil Spirit.

2 Ibid.

3 Ibid., 35.

4 Ibid.

5 Miles Menander, *The Ethical Religion of Zoroaster* (New York: Macmillan, 1931), 13.

6 R. C. Zaehner, *The Dawn and Twilight of Zoroastrianism* (New York: Putnam, 1961), 60.

7 Ibid., p. 62.

8 R. Gordon Wasson, "The Soma of the Rig-Veda, What Was It?," *Journal of the American Oriental Society* 91, no. 2 (1971): 169–187, opts for a mushroom.

9 René Dussaud, *"Ancien bronzes de Louristan et les cultes iranien,"* *Syria* 2, no. 3.4 (1949): 205–207.

10 Zaehner, 87.

11 Ibid., 90.

12 Ibid., 91.

13 Dussaud, 218.

14 John R. Hinnells, "Zoroastrian Saviour Imagery and Its Influence on the New Testament," *Numen* 16, no. 3 (1969):167.

15 Zaehner, 58.

16 James R. Russell, "On Mysticism and Esotericism among the Zoroastrians," *Iranian Studies* 26, no. 1–2 (1993): 76. This is even reported by the Roman historian Pliny.

CHAPTER FIVE

India

The Great Mandala

Even though its tradition is that the world is cycling though time, Hinduism does have a concept of the decay of the earth and the inhabitants on it as the end of a major cycle approaches. The time between regenerations is known as a *kalpa*, or "Day of Brahma." This day is divided into one thousand *mahayuga* made up of four *yuga* of twelve thousand divine years each. A Day of Brahma is 4,320,000 years.[1] So, even though we are presently in the final *yuga* there is probably a good long time before everything is destroyed and remade.

Of course, this final age, the *kali yuga,* is marked by a decline in virtue and in the length of human lives. In the earlier ages, virtue reigned, and people lived four hundred years. Now the best we can manage is one hundred years, and virtue can barely hobble about.[2] Still, some believe that the end of this *kalpa* won't arrive until the average human life span goes down to ten years.[3]

When the Day of Brahma ends, everything in the world, but not the earth itself, will be destroyed. As the dawn of Brahma's new day arrives, creation will occur again. It is only when a hundred years of these days are over that Brahma himself will die and everything with him. The total for this has been reckoned as 311,040,000,000,000 solar years.[4] Therefore, the people of ancient India were more optimistic about the length of the universe than most scientists today.

One *kalpa* is also described as the time it takes the universe to make one revolution. Of course, if one wants to measure it, it's necessary to mark a starting point. The creators of the *Vedas* were phenomenal at astronomical mathematics, just as the Maya and Egyptians were. It has been suggested that the temples at Angkor Wat, in Cambodia, were built for astronomical observations, and archaeoastronomers have found that the measurements of the buildings correspond to both the turning of the seasons and to the cycles of the *yuga*, with the *kali yuga* being the shortest.[5]

But even with this sophisticated computational ability, the Hindu scholar never pinpointed an exact day for the ending of the current *kalpa*.

The theme of the *pralaya*, or dissolution of the world at the end of each *yuga*, makes up a good part of the Hindu epics: the *Mahabharata*, the *Upanishads* and the *Bhagavad-Gita*. All have scenes of the destruction of the world, often in the form of a final battle. Even without a specific apocalyptic ending, the gods of the end are referenced throughout the *Mahabharata*. For instance, referring to a warrior, the epic states, "He was like Antaka at the end of time, destroying all things."[6]

The *Mahabharata* actually begins with signs of the approaching end. It is announced that trees are blossoming in the wrong seasons and animals are having monstrous young. There are earthquakes, comets, rivers flowing backward, dust storms, and even antelopes and parrots are warning of evil times to come.[7] Also, people of low caste are laughing and dancing, a sure sign of something wrong with the world.

The *kali yuga* has been described in the epics in terms that may sound familiar to us now. In interviews with people of all levels, Professor Lance Nelson found that many people in India today interpret contemporary droughts, deforestation, and other disasters as being

A battle scene from the *Mahabharata*. *Réunion des musées nationaux / Art Resource, New York City*

part of the *kali yuga*. They point out one of the other signs of the degeneration of the age, the lack of *dharma*, or just behavior. One man insisted, "The *kali yuga* has come one hundred percent. People used to be very happy and generous, but now they are misers. It used to be if I had grain and saw a hungry person I would give, and even if only women were home and one had no grain, she could borrow from another and clean it and grind it and make bread so no one could go to bed hungry."[8]

Like many people across the world, those interviewed in India saw the problems of climate change and lack of care for others as signs of the approaching end. In the case of Sanskrit tradition from over three thousand years ago, the *kali yuga* is expressed in ecological terms: There is no rain for a hundred years, the world dries up, the water to unfit to drink.

When I began this study, I thought I would find nothing in

Hindu tradition that would compare with Western beliefs in the End Times. But it is clear that within the cycles of eternal renewal there is the sense that the present time, whenever that may be, is the end of the age.

There is also the judgment and promise of heaven. And there is, as in most religions, a ray of hope. Even during the *pralaya*, while individual bodies or whole worlds die, their souls will remain with the Brahma to be reborn in the next creation.[9]

And we still have trillions of years to get our *dharma* in order and make the world a wonderful place in which to live.

---

1 Ananda K. Coomaraswamy, "Time and Eternity," *Artibus Asiae Supplementum* 8 (1947): 40.

2 Ebeneezer Burgess, "Translation of the Surya-Siddhanta, A Textbook of Hindu Astronomy," *Journal of the American Oriental Society* 6 (1858–1860): 154.

3 Hubert Seiwart, *Popular Religious Movements and Heterodox Sects in Chinese History* (Boston: Brill, 2003), 128.

4 Burgess, 155.

5 Robert Stencel, Fred Gifford, Eleanor Moron, "Astrology and Cosmology at Angkor Wat," *Science* new ser. 193, no. 4250 (1976): 181–187. It's easier to understand with lots of pictures, but I can't manage that. Check out the article.

6 Quoted in Lynn Thomas, "The Identity of the Destroyer in the Mahabhrata," *Numen* 41, no. 3 (1994): 257.

7 *Mahabharata*, book 6, *Bhisna parva*, sec. 3.

8 Quoted in Lance E. Nelson, *Purifying the Earthly Body of God: Religion and Ecology in Hindu India* (Albany: State University of New York Press, 1998), 181.

9 S. Radhakrishnan, *The Brahma Sutra: The Philosophy of Spiritual Life* (New York: Harper & Brothers, 1960), 99.

CHAPTER SIX

The Book of Daniel

For understanding the Prophecies, we are, in the first place, to
acquaint ourselves with the figurative language of the Prophets.
This language is taken from the analogy between the world
natural, and an empire or kingdom considered as a world politic.

—Isaac Newton, *Observations upon the Prophecies of Daniel
and the Apocalypse of St. John*

The Book of Daniel is one of the major sources for the symbols
and the predictions of the coming end of the world that have
been used by Christians and Jews up to the present day. It is written partially in Hebrew and partially in Aramaic. In it, a number of
prophetic dreams are interpreted. In some, the dreamer is the Babylonian king Nebuchadnezzar; in others, Daniel, his servant/slave, is the
dreamer. The influence of earlier Greek and Babylonian myths about
the ages of the world is obvious in Daniel but there are additions to
the tales that are unique.

In the Christian Bible, the Book of Daniel is placed with the
other prophets, such as Ezekiel and Jeremiah. In the Jewish Tanakh
Daniel belongs between the Books of Esther and Ezra, creating a
more chronological order.

The first six chapters of Daniel tell the story of how Daniel was
taken from Jerusalem to the court of King Nebuchadnezzar, where he

and three other Jewish boys were trained to serve the king. In chapter two, Nebuchadnezzar is troubled by dreams that his magicians and wise men can't interpret. The king orders all his advisers killed due to their incompetence, including Daniel and his friends (Daniel 2:12). In a night vision, Daniel received not only the meaning of the king's dream but also the content, even though he hadn't heard the specifics of the dream before.

Daniel told Nebuchadnezzar that he had dreamed there was a huge statue of a king. It was made of many elements, starting with gold at the head, then silver, bronze, iron, and finally at the feet, iron mixed with clay. In the king's dream a stone struck the statue and destroyed it, after which the stone grew to become a mountain. Daniel, tactfully, tells the king that he is the gold head but that after him there will be kingdoms of decreasing worth. The mountain meant that "in the days of those kings the God of heaven will set up a kingdom that shall never be destroyed" (Daniel 2:44).[1]

Nebuchadnezzar liked this interpretation and rescinded the order to kill all the wise men of the kingdom. He gave Daniel and his friends increased responsibility at court, and put Daniel in control of the wise men, something anyone could have guessed would turn out badly.

Nebuchadnezzar seems to have forgotten how impressed he was with the Hebrew God and His prophecies. In chapter three, the king has a gold statue made, and commands all his people to worship it. The wise men, annoyed at having been upstaged by an outsider, tell Nebuchadnezzar that the Jews won't comply with the public adoration of the statue. Daniel's three companions, Shadrach, Meshach, and Abednego, are thrown into a fiery furnace when they refuse. With the aid of a divine presence, the three walk safely through the flames (Daniel 3:19–27).

Apparently Nebuchadnezzar was hard to convince even with this miraculous proof. Therefore, God sees that his life takes a downturn. He has more dreams, goes mad, and spends seven years grazing like an ox before he finally comes to his senses and praises God. Upon his death, his son, Belshazzar, takes over.

Belshazzar must have also been a slow learner or had not paid attention to his father's experiences with the god of the Jews. One day he decided to have a feast and use the ritual gold and silver vessels that Nebuchadnezzar had looted from the Temple in Jerusalem. While he and the court were all eating and drinking, a hand appeared in the air and began writing on the wall next to the lamp stand.[2] Daniel interpreted the words *mene, mene, tekel parsin* to mean doom for Belshazzar (Daniel 5:5–29). That night, the king is killed, and Darius, the Mede, takes over the kingdom.

Darius has no trouble with dreams, just bad advisers. Again Daniel is punished for not praying to the gods of the Medes and Persians and is punished by being thrown into a lion's den. The lions don't eat him, and his accusers and their families become the lions' breakfast instead.

Darius finally caught on that Daniel's god was a force to be reckoned with and issued a proclamation that everyone in his kingdom "should tremble and fear before the God of Daniel" (Daniel 6:28). And high time, too. After this, Daniel lived out his days in peace.

Now, in my opinion, all of this has just been prologue to show that Daniel is a good Jew and a deserving prophet. The second half of the book of Daniel is very different. Instead of a king, the dreamer is Daniel, and large parts of the story are told in first person. Chapters seven through twelve are decidedly apocalyptic, with many-horned monsters and other warnings of the end. Daniel is terrified and puzzled by his dreams and enters into them to ask what they mean. At one point, he needs to be visited by the angel Gabriel, first in the dream and then in reality, for the visions to be explained. The style of this section is very different from the first part, and many scholars have suggested that the second half of the book was written separately from the first.[3]

While the mystery of who actually wrote the prophecies and when is important in biblical scholarship, it makes little difference in a history of how people viewed the upcoming end of the world.

Most scholars now think that chapter eleven, particularly the image of "king of the north," referred to the Greek invader Antiochus. The following chapter is seen as foretelling his defeat by the Maccabees, as is commemorated every year by the festival Hanukkah, and the visions in the second half of Daniel are believed to have been written in the second or third century B.C.E. and after the fall of Antiochus. That hasn't kept many others, including John of Patmos, from seeing the visions of Daniel as specific to their own time.[4]

Daniel's first dream is one of the most bizarre and popular among doomsday seekers. In it, Daniel saw four beasts rise out of a wind-tossed sea. The first was a lion with the wings of an eagle. As Daniel watched, its wings were plucked; it was made to walk on two feet and given a human mind. The second beast was a bear with three tusks that was told to devour many bodies. The third beast was sort of like a leopard, except it had four heads and four wings. It was given dominion over the earth.

The fourth beast is the one that captured the imagination of centuries of interpreters. It had iron teeth that destroyed everything around it. It also had ten horns. Daniel was staring at these when another horn began to grow, uprooting three others to make room. This horn had human eyes and a mouth that spoke arrogantly (Daniel 7:1–8).

Just as the vision was at its worst, Daniel saw a celestial court ruled over by the Ancient of Days, which destroyed the fourth beast and diminished the power of the other three. An attendant at the court explained to him that the first three beasts were kingdoms that would submit to God but that the fourth would then arise and "devour the whole earth" (Daniel 7:23). This kingdom would last "for a time, two times and half a time" before finally being overthrown, after which all the kingdoms of the world would be given to "the people of the holy ones of the Most High" (Daniel 7:25–27).

The view of most biblical scholars is that the four kingdoms in Daniel's dream were Assyria, Persia, Greece, and Rome. Other scholars have suggested that the kingdoms are actually those created by the break up of the empire of Alexander the Great.[5]

This section of the dream had resonance for downtrodden people that continues to the present day. The identity of the "little horn" has been speculated on with as much intensity as the search for the Antichrist. Sometimes the two have been combined. People suffering under oppression must have found great comfort in the promise that the beast would be destroyed.

The date of the end is suggested several times in Daniel. The first time is with the enigmatic phrase "for a time, two times and half a time." Of course, the problems have always been just how much "a time" is and when does it start. Newton and the Millerites are among the many who have tried to figure these out.

Added to this quandary is the next, and final, section of the book. After Daniel has spent several days in prayer and fasting, the angel Gabriel comes to him to give him wisdom and understanding as well as the "book of truth." First he tells Daniel that the Jews will have to wait seventy weeks to finish atoning for their transgressions. Then the angel tells Daniel in great and confusing detail about the rise of the "anointed one" and the battles that will lead to the end of the world (Daniel 9–11).

Gabriel ends by saying that a great prince named Michael will come and everyone whose name is in the book, including those who have already died, shall be saved. He adds that Daniel is "to keep the words secret and the book sealed" until just before the end (Daniel 12:4).[6] The angel repeats the need for secrecy, and then Daniel sees two men on either side of a river, one dressed in linen. The man in linen tells the other man that it would be "a time, two times and a half" until the end, reinforcing Gabriel's prophecy.

However, Gabriel then adds that "from the time that the regular burnt offering is taken away and the abomination that desolates is set up, there shall be one thousand two hundred ninety days. Happy are those who persevere and attain the thousand three hundred thirty-five days" (Daniel 12:11–12).

The confusion that these two numbers created is responsible for centuries of disappointment for millennial mathematicians.

Daniel's prophecies were interpreted by Jews in the first centuries before and after the Common Era as foretelling the end of foreign domination of Israel. The image of the leader who would destroy the evil kingdoms was very powerful to those suffering under the yoke of Rome and it fed their expectations of a warrior Messiah.[7] Later Jewish commentators used Daniel both to support their messianic expectations and to refute Christian insistence that the Messiah had already come.

Saadia ben Joseph (892–942), Gaon of Sura, in Persia, was one of the preeminent medieval Jewish scholars. Saadia wrote that Daniel predicted the end of both the Roman Empire and the Islamic one. He fixed the date for this by working out the three time periods as three ways of calculating the same date. The "time, two times and half a time" he worked out to total 1335, the second number given by Gabriel. For the number 1290, Saadia counted from the time of the "removal of the daily sacrifice," which he figured at forty-five years after the building of the Second Temple. Starting from two different points, he arrived at the same number 4725 by the Hebrew calendar, or 965.[8] Two hundred years later, the scholar Rashi, born Solomon ben Isaac (1040–1105), started with the time of the Exodus to predict the end in 1352.[9]

The early Christians, coming from the Jewish tradition, took the Book of Daniel as a prophecy of Christ's return. At the end of the first century, a document known as the Epistle of Barnabas used the Book of Enoch and Daniel's "little horn" in its plea for new Christians to turn away from Jewish customs because Christ would soon return.[10]

The third-century writer Julius Africanus worked out a chronology of the Bible, including leap years. He was determined to prove that Jesus was the savior Daniel foretold, who would come at the

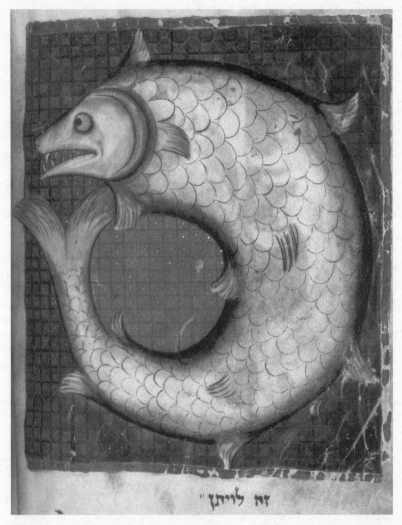

זה לויתן "

Leviathan c1280. Fish curving round to form a circle. The Leviathan was, according to Talmudic sources, one of the mythical creatures that would be consumed at the messianic banquet awaiting the virtuoso in the world to come. From the "North French Miscellany," a Hebrew manuscript written by Benjamin The Scribe. Location: British Library, London, Great Britain. *HIP / Art Resource, New York* end of seventy weeks—that is, 490 years.[11] Africanus started from the twentieth year of the reign of Artaxerxes of Persia, which signaled the return from the Babylonian Captivity. His computations are impressive, including reconciling the years of the Persian Empire, the Olympiads (Jesus was born in the year of the 202nd Olympiad, by the way), and the Jewish calendar as well as changing the date from solar to lunar measurements.[12] Africanus didn't predict the end; he just wanted to reconcile all the dates.

The prophecies of Daniel are part of Islam as well. Some apocalypses written in the first few centuries after the death of Muhammad draw on Daniel's visions. Other apocalyptic Muslim authors use Daniel as a character to give their own visions more credibility, proving that he was respected as a prophet in Islamic tradition, too.[13]

In the seventeenth century, Daniel's dreams were the basis for the militant millennial movement in England known as the **Fifth Monarchy.** Daniel's four kingdoms seem to have had a universal popularity for that era. The Portuguese Jesuit António Vieira, wrote in his *História de Futuro* that Brazil would be the fifth kingdom.[14] Isaac Newton spent many hours studying the Book of Daniel, both to reconcile it with the Book of Revelation and to compute the end of the world.[15]

In any study of apocalyptic predictions, Daniel must be included as a major influence and as the chief contributor to the game of "When will the world end?" We shall hear of his visions many times in this book.

---

1 Holy Bible, New Revised Standard Version.

2 I never understood this. Was it to be sure everyone understood that the problem with interpreting the writing wasn't lack of light?

3 George A. Barton, "The Composition of the Book of Daniel," *Journal of Biblical Literature* 17, no. 1 (1898): 62–86, gives an overview of theories from Spinoza and Newton to his own time.

4 That the Book of Daniel as a source for the Book of Revelation is well established and is discussed in the section on John.

5 R. B. Y. Scott, "I Daniel, the Original Apocalypse," *The American Journal of Semitic Languages and Literature* 47, no. 4 (1931): 296. Isaac Newton, among others, agreed.

6 John of Patmos builds on this in his vision in which the sealed book is opened.

7 Salo Baron, *A Social and Religious History of the Jews,* vol. 2, 2nd ed. (New York: Columbia University Press, 1952), 58–61. See also the section on the other Jewish apocalypses.

8 Joseph Saracher, *The Doctrine of the Messiah in Medieval Jewish Literature* (New York: Hermon Press, 1968), 37–41.

9 Ibid., 59.

10 "Epistle of Barnabas," in *Apostolic Fathers, vol. 1, trans* Kirsopp Lake (Cambridge, MA: Harvard University Press, 1912), 349–350.

11 Julius Africanus, "The Five Books of the Chronography of Julius Africanus," in *The Ante-Nicene Fathers, vol. 6, rpt. ed.* (Grand Rapids, MI: Eerdmands, 1997), 134–135.

12 It wasn't just the Maya who were obsessed with calendars.

13 David Cook, "An Early Muslim Daniel Apocalypse," *Arabica* 49, no. 1 (2002): 55–56.

14 Carole A. Myscofski, "Messianic Themes in Portuguese and Brazilian Literature in the Sixteenth and Seventeenth Centuries," *Luso-Braziliam Review* 28, no. 1 (1991): 89.

15 I. Bernard Cohen and George E Smith, eds., *The Cambridge Companion to Newton* (Cambridge, UK: Cambridge University Press, 2002), 409–421. See also the section "Founders of Modern Science."

PART TWO:

The First Five Centuries of the Common Era

Defining the End

CHAPTER SEVEN

Apocalypses Everywhere

But if you believe that . . . the races of men perished in blazing
fires or that the cities fell in a great upheaval of the world,
or that . . . devouring rivers spread all over the earth and
drowned the towns, so much the more must you . . . admit
that destruction awaits the earth and sky, too.

—Lucretius, *De Rerum Natura* V, ll. 339–341[1]

When Lucretius, a pagan Roman, wrote the words in the epigraph in the first century c.e., he was simply repeating common speculations about how the world had ended many times before, only to be remade by the gods, and how humans had to begin all over again, basically reinventing the wheel. Lucretius took this to its logical conclusion.

He wasn't alone in this among the people of his time. Even though no one knew that they were living on the cusp of the first millennium of the Common Era, there was definitely something apocalyptic in the air at the time. In Judea, the revolt of the Maccabees in 168–164 B.C.E., which had given conservative Jews hope, turned out to be a temporary victory. Over the next one hundred years, power in Judea passed back and forth between the Jewish Hasmonean kings and the Persian Selucids. Finally in 64 B.C.E., the two warring parties went to the Roman general Pompey for mediation. Not a smart move.

Soon after, Judea became a Roman colony.

Well before this happened, a group of strict Jews with a strong apocalyptic bent escaped the whole situation to form a community in the desert. Two thousand years later, the discovery of the Dead Sea Scrolls, left by these Essenes, gave an expanded look at how deep their feeling was that they were facing the end of the world.

The Essenes were mentioned in the works of Philo, Josephus, and Hippolytus, but what they thought of themselves and the world weren't known until the twentieth century. They had apparently removed themselves from mainstream Judaism in about 140 B.C.E., when a Hasmonean king, not of the priestly caste, named himself high priest in Jerusalem.[2] The group survived until they were destroyed by the Romans in the Jewish War of 68 C.E., making them one of the longest-surviving apocalyptic communities. Like later such communities, they had a core group who, in this case, lived in the desert and a number of urban supporters who visited them and brought provisions.[3]

Their writings include some of the oldest known copies of books of the Bible, many with commentaries that reveal that the Essenes were positive that they were living in the end times. One document is the halakhic letter, which was written mainly to point out the differences between the Essenes and the priests in Jerusalem. After listing these, the letter tells the recipients that "we recognize that some of the blessings and curses which are written in the Book of Moses have come to pass and that this is the End of Days."[4]

Almost everything that has been found in the Dead Sea Scrolls is either messianic or apocalyptic. The Essenes expected at least two messiahs: a priest and a king. But they expected to do their part in the upcoming battle at the end as well. The War Scroll is a history before the fact that tells the world what is going to happen. At the appointed time the (Essene) Sons of Light will go to war with the *kittim* or Sons of Darkness. The war will last nearly forty years, and its progression is given in detail, along with which families will fight and against whom. There are also several passages detailing the trumpets, standards, and weapons, with instructions as to what should be written on each one. God and Israel will triumph eventually over Satan and everyone else.

It seems that the Romans attacked the Essenes before they had finished writing all the posters or inscribing all the weapons. The battle led by the Messiah seems to have happened only in the scrolls.

The Romans, like Lucretius, were also feeling apocalyptic at that time. The Republic had suddenly become a dictatorship, then an empire. While their conquest of the known world would continue, there would also be civil war. Romans increasingly became involved in "mystery" religions, in which only the initiates knew all the rituals and dogma that promised to explain the turmoil occurring in their society.

In the first centuries of Christianity there were numbers of apocalypses flying about. While Daniel and Revelation were the only ones to make the Bible, the others were read widely, as the next section will discuss.

---

1 Trans. and ed. Monica R. Gale (Oxford, UK: Oxbow Books 2009), 38–39.

2 Helmut Koester, *History, Culture and Religion of the Hellenistic Age* (New York: de Gruyter, 1982), 234–235.

3 Geza Vermes, *The Dead Sea Scrolls in English* (Hammersmith, UK: Penguin Books, 1962), 17.

4 Quoted in Lawrence H. Schiffman, "Origin and Early History of the Qumran Sect," *The Biblical Archeaologist* 58, no. 1 (1995): 38–39.

CHAPTER EIGHT

The First Christians

These are the seven signs before the ending of this world. There
shall be in all the earth famine and great pestilence and much
distress: then shall all men be led captive among all nations and
shall fall by the edge of the sword.

—Apocalypse of Thomas (fourth century c.e.)[1]

The very first Christians knew when the world would end—
immediately, if not sooner. They expected the swift return of
Jesus along with the establishment of a heaven on earth for the faithful. The belief is most strongly stated in the Gospel of Mark, thought
to be the earliest of the four, "the sun will be darkened and the moon
will not give its light and the stars will be falling from heaven and
the powers in the heavens will be shaken. Then they will see 'the
Son of Man coming in clouds' with great power and glory. He will
send out the angels and gather his elect from the four winds, from
the ends of the earth to the ends of heaven" (Mark 13:24–27). Thus the
concept of the end of the world was built into the religion.

Before the end of the first century, evangelists such as Paul were
reminding the fledgling Christian communities: "I consider that the
sufferings of this present time are not worth comparing with the glory
about to be revealed to us" (Romans 8:18). In his first letter to the
Thessalonians, Paul makes it clear that the Second Coming will be

soon. "[T]he dead in Christ will rise first. Then we who are alive, who are left, will be caught up in the clouds together with them to meet the Lord in the air; and so we will be with the Lord forever" (1 Thessalonians 4:16–17).[2]

The fundamental belief that Jesus was the Messiah, and that he would return at the impending end time was the essential dogma that set Christianity apart from Judaism. But from the beginning, there was also confusion. At first, many Jews who followed Jesus were convinced that he was the Messiah of the Tanakh who would physically lead an army to defeat the Roman Empire and establish a kingdom on earth that would be governed according to Mosaic Law. Others were convinced that Jesus' kingdom would be in heaven and, as Paul said, all believers, living and dead, would be taken bodily to the skies and life everlasting.

These two views of the Parousia[3] have existed within Christianity throughout its history. They have been expressed in different ways but ultimately derive from the earliest days of the religion. And throughout time, some have merged the two beliefs to assume that, at the Second Coming, Jesus would descend to lead a real army.[4]

But even by the time of Paul, in the late first century, people were beginning to think that they needed a back-up plan in case the Second Coming took a bit longer than they had thought. Most of Paul's letters are on how to conduct a Christian life while waiting for the end. The admonition to those "living in idleness" (2 Thessalonians 3:11) may well be a reminder to Christians who felt that there was no reason to work since the final days were at hand.

So, from the beginning, Christianity was being pulled in two directions. There were those who believed that Christ would return soon so that there was no need to earn a living, marry, or save. There were even those who courted martyrdom in order to ensure a direct route to heaven without waiting for the Second Coming.[5] Ignatius, the third bishop of Antioch, who was reported to be a disciple of the Apostle John, was eager to be killed for the faith. "Let fire and the cross; let the crowds of wild beasts; let tearings, breakings, and dislocations of bones; let cutting off of members; let shatterings of the whole body; and let all the dreadful torments of the devil come upon me: only let me attain to Jesus Christ."[6]

Ignatius got his wish. When the Emperor Trajan came to Antioch, he obligingly ordered the bishop to be bound and sent to Rome to be fed to the beasts. On the way, Ignatius seemed to have considered the journey a triumphal procession. He must not have been guarded very closely, for at Smyrna, he dropped in to see his old friend Polycarp (who would also be happily martyred). He then wandered about the Near East, seeing other friends and writing to churches he couldn't get to. He hoped to have a sightseeing jaunt at Puteoli, where Saint Paul had been, but a storm, not the Roman soldiers, made it impossible to land. When he finally reached Rome, he almost missed out on his execution because the games had nearly ended. But he hurried and was thrown to the wild beasts in the amphitheater, just as he desired.[7]

Sometime later, Origen of Alexandria (c. 180– c. 250) was heartbroken because he didn't get to be a martyr. When his father was arrested and sentenced to death, Origen was determined to join him. His mother was having none of that. When her tears and pleading didn't work, she hid his clothes and forbade him to leave the house.[8] It seems to have strained relations between them for some time.

Like Origen's mother, most Christians were willing to let martyrdom find them, if it had to. And, despite the often repeated verse "But about the day or hour, no one knows, neither the angels in heaven, nor the Son, but only the Father" (Mark 13:32), people still wanted to find the exact date for the end. Why buy more grain than you need to? They looked for the signs listed in Mark (13:9–24): war, persecution, earthquakes, and false messiahs. None of these were hard to find, and this kept the apocalyptic enthusiasm burning.

Added to the words of Jesus in the Gospels of the New Testament, there were many apocalyptic books and letters, some attributed to the Apostles, which were also circulating at the time. The contents of neither the New Testament nor the Tanakh had been decided in the first three centuries after Christ. Therefore, many of these works were felt to be genuine and were read by Christians and Jews as authoritative predictions of the end. The second book of Esdras (or Ezra) was probably rewritten in the middle of the first century from a Hebrew or Aramaic original, to which the author added Christian elements.[9] With its references to the coming of the "Son of Man," it was considered useful for Christians who wished to prove that Jesus had been predicted by the Jews. But, in the end, the book was not accepted as canonical by either religion.

Most of Esdras is a Socratic dialogue between Ezra and the angel Uriel. Ezra wants to know why people were made, why there is evil in the world, and why the good are punished along with the bad. Uriel answers with some really quite lovely parables and analogies before they get to the end of the world and the Last Judgment. Before he can find out about the end, Ezra is instructed to pray and fast for several days, the better to receive the vision.

Ezra must have read Daniel because after days of fasting he sees "an eagle, with twelve feather-covered wings and three heads."[10] The eagle gains and loses wings, which talk, and then he has a confrontation with a lion and loses. Fortunately, Uriel is on hand to explain that the eagle represents the emperors to come and the lion is the Messiah who will defeat them. Ezra has more, rather repetitive, visions of destruction that frighten him. Uriel calms him by telling him that the righteous will be spared. "For behold, in a little while, wickedness will be removed from the earth and uprightness will reign over us."[11] Ezra keeps pushing for a date, but the angel refuses to give one, only cautioning Ezra to be prepared.

Two early apocalypses that are definitely Christian are the Apocalypse of Peter and the *Shepherd of Hermas*. The Apocalypse of Peter is from at least 150 C.E. It was considered by several early Church Fathers, such as Clement of Alexandria, to be a true vision by Saint Peter.[12] It reinforces the idea of the Antichrist. "Many shall come in my name, saying 'I am the Christ.' Believe them not. . . . For the coming of the Son of God shall not be plain . . . so will I come upon the clouds of heaven with a great host in my majesty" (Peter 1:14–16).[13] Although Peter asks him exactly when this will be, Jesus doesn't tell him, preferring to dwell on the Last Judgment.

In the first list of books considered authentic, known as the Muratorian Fragment, which was composed in the second half of the second century, the Apocalypse of Peter is considered suspect, but not definitely out. St. Jerome wrote, "We receive only the apocalypses of John and Peter, although some of us are not willing that the latter be read in church."[14] Even though it was eventually discarded as not having been written by Peter, the book continued to be read and copied for several centuries and was among those found in the Nag Hammadi library discovered in Egypt in the twentieth century.

An apocryphal Apocalypse that was popular for several centuries was that of Paul. This was rather like a spin off from Paul's second letter to the Corinthians, in which he says, "I know a person in Christ who fourteen years ago was caught up to the third heaven" (2 Corinthians 12:2). Paul doesn't say what the man, presumably Paul himself, saw there because God told him not to. This didn't stop the author of the apocalypse (not Paul) from imagining it. This book dwells mainly on the torment of the damned, always a good topic, and the rewards to the faithful. It shows elements from Revelation as well as the Apocalypse of Peter and others. It has been dated to the mid-fourth century. Although it was well known that the book was not written by Saint Paul, there was nothing in it that offended orthodoxy, so it was allowed to circulate. Some believe that Dante used passages from it or the Apocalypse of Peter in the *Inferno*.[15]

Some Christians felt the need to convince pagans that their own seers had foreseen the coming of the Messiah as well as to convince them of their version of the end of the world. Following on the work of Jewish scholars, they rewrote the Greek oracles of the Sibyl. The most famous of the sibyls was at Delphi. Her prophesies were respected by kings and commoners alike. Sometime at the end of the second century, they were given a Christian twist. The apocalypse recounted in book two of these Christian Sibylline Oracles is a mixture of Jewish and early Christian themes. In it the earth is destroyed first, "A dark mist shall cover the boundless world. . . . And then shall a great river of flaming fire flow from heaven and consume all places, the earth and the great ocean and the gleaming seas, lakes and rivers and fountains, and merciless Hades and the vault of Heaven . . . the stars shall all fall from heaven into the sea."[16]

That about covers it.

In these oracles, the angel Uriel will open the gates of hell and bring out not only people but the Titans of Greek mythology and the giants in the earth who were drowned in Noah's flood. Then God, Adonai Sabaoth, will arrive—followed by Christ, "the undying," trailed by angels and clouds of glory—to judge all. He will be followed by Moses, Abraham, and all the Hebrew Patriarchs. Then the evil will be punished and the good rewarded, as usual.[17]

The oracles end on a conciliatory note. For the saved are merciful and ask God to take the pagans out of their punishments and "remove them elsewhere, sending them for the sake of his people to another life eternal and immortal in the Elysian plain."[18] Even if pagans have persecuted them, Christians can still be kind to their enemies, they are telling the still-dominant society. But think how much better your afterlife would be if you converted?

It's not known how many pagans were swayed by this, but throughout the Middle Ages and Renaissance, the Sibylline oracles were held in high esteem by Christians, and new ones were being written all the time. They figured in many religious works of art, including those of Raphael, and the Sibyls even appear in Michelangelo's paintings in the Sistine Chapel.

So the Book of Revelation was only one of many competing Apocalypses. Therefore, how was this one chosen over all the others to become the final book of the New Testament? It's a long and twisty story that I shall summarize next.

1 J. K. Elliott, ed. and trans., *The Apocryphal New Testament* (Oxford, UK: Clarendon Press, 1993), 648. Thomas isn't heretical, just known to have been written later, and he doesn't have the pizzaz of John.

2 This line is also used for the contemporary belief in the physical rapture, although early Christians did not dwell on this passage.

3 *Parousia* is the word used in the original Greek of the New Testament. It means "arrival in person" and now is used by scholars for the Second Coming.

4 See, for instance, the seventeenth-century Fifth Monarchists.

5 E. R. Dodds, *Pagan and Christian in an Age of Anxiety* (Cambridge, UK: Cambridge University Press, 1965), 136.

6 Ignatius, *"Ad Romanum"* 5, in *The Ante-Nicene Fathers, vol. 1*, rpt. ed., ed. Phillip Schaff. (Grand Rapids, MI: Eerdmans, 1997), 56.

7 "The Martyrdom of Ignatius," ibid.

8 Eusebius, *The History of the Church* 6.2, trans. G. A. Williamson (Cambridge, UK: Cambridge University Press, 1965), 239–240.

9 "The Second Book of Esdras," in *The Apocrypha*, rpt. ed., trans. Edgar J. Goodspeed (New York: Random House, 1959). Just to keep things confused, it is also called IV Esdras and The Apocalypse of Ezra.

10 Ibid., Esdras 11:2.

11 Ibid., Esdras 16:52.

12 G. Quispel and G. M. Grant, "Note of the Petrine Apocrypha," *Vigilae Christianae* 6, no. 1 (1952), 32.

13 "Apocalypse of Peter: The Ethiopic and Akhmim Texts," in *The Apocryphal New Testament*, trans. J. K. Elliot (Oxford, UK: Clarendon Press, 1993), 600. This is a good example of the merging of the Jewish and Christian images of the Messiah.

14 Bart D. Ehrman, *Lost Scriptures: Books That Did Not Make It into the New Testament* (Oxford, UK: Oxford University Press, 2003), 333.

15 Elliot, 616; see als. Ehrman, 288.

16 "The Sibylline Oracles," in *The Apocryphal New Testament*, trans. J. K. Elliot (Oxford, UK: Clarendon Press, 1993), 613.

17 Ibid., 614.

18 Ibid., 615.

CHAPTER NINE

John of Patmos and His Revelation

Now some before our time have set aside this book . . . criticizing
it chapter by chapter and endeavoring to show it without sense
or reason. . . . They hold that it can be no sort of revelation
because it is covered with so gross and dense an ignorance. . . .
But I, . . . although I cannot comprehend it, I still suspect that
there is some deeper sense underlying the words."

—Dionysius the Great, bishop of Alexandria (d. 264 C.E.)

O f all the writings that have affected apocalyptic thought, none
has had a larger impact than the Apocalypse, also called the
Book of Revelation. Today it is the one apocalyptic book of the New
Testament. But as the last chapter showed, when it was written there
were any number of other visions and prophesies of the end times
floating around the Roman world. Why was this one chosen to be part
of the Christian holy books? Who wrote it and when? Like Bishop
Dionysius, many were puzzled by the imagery. And, like those he
mentions, some people were decidedly against it. So what is the fascination that it has held for nearly two thousand years of readers?

First, just in case it's been a while since you read it, let's review the
main points of Revelation. If you know the book by heart, feel free to
skip ahead.

It begins as many of the other New Testament epistles (letters) do, with greetings to seven churches in Asia Minor. John writes from his exile on the island of Patmos, off what is now Turkey (Revelation 1:9). His letter immediately hints that this won't be a normal chatty exhortation, for John has seen Christ in a vision. The Lord tells John that he must write to the seven churches and report all that he is about to see in a vision of the end times. First, Christ has a few words to let each church know that he means business, telling them in turn how they are succeeding or failing to maintain His faith.

In chapter four, the vision proper begins. John sees through a door into heaven where someone is seated on the throne. Around the throne are twenty-four more thrones and an "elder" is seated in each one. There are also four living creatures, "full of eyes in front and behind: the first . . . like a lion, the second . . . like an ox, the third . . . with a face like a human face and the fourth . . . like a flying eagle" (Revelation 4:6–7).

The one on the throne holds a scroll "sealed with seven seals" (Revelation 5:1). These seals will be important later and have been interpreted many ways, even though they are explained in the text.[1] Then a lamb appears "as if it had been slaughtered." It has seven horns and seven eyes (Revelation 5:6), but you don't have to worry about what that means because John says right away that they are "the seven spirits of God sent out into all the earth" (Revelation 5:6).

After some prayers and praise, the lamb opens the seven seals. The first releases a rider on a white horse wearing a crown, ready to conquer. The second seal lets out a rider on a red horse, who was permitted to "take peace from the earth" (Revelation 6:4). At the opening of the third seal, a rider on a black horse arrives with a set of scales. The final rider comes when the fourth seal is opened. He rides a pale horse and John has no problem knowing him. His "name was Death, and Hades followed with him" (Revelation 7:8). This pair was given the power to kill one quarter of the earth.

Tradition has named the Four Horsemen of the Apocalypse,

Pestilence, War, Famine, and Death. I can understand war and death but the other two seem to me like tyranny and the tax collector. But I'm writing about the way in which Revelation has been perceived by others, not my own idiosyncratic problems with interpretation.

Now, the fifth seal is a quick interlude. John sees the martyrs who cry out for vengeance. They are each given a white robe and told to wait a bit longer. The fifth seal is not a big subject for art or exegesis.

The sixth seal, by contrast, is very dramatic. This is often quoted and very popular in medieval and Renaissance art. There is a great earthquake; the sun turns black and the moon blood red. The stars fall (but not all of them because there are angels and a dragon coming to sweep some away). The sky vanishes, and mountains and islands are removed (Revelation 6:24). Some of the population must be left because the people hide in caves and among mountain rocks.

In case the faithful are becoming too terrified to read further, John takes a moment to introduce the 144,000 virgins who have been sealed with the mark of God on their foreheads and won't have to undergo the trials of the destruction on the earth. Of course, this is the beginning of the idea of the elect that has resurfaced over and over through all of Christian history and has been to blame for a lot of arrogance, anguish, and dissension.

The seventh seal is rather an anticlimax. When it is finally opened, "there was silence in heaven for about half an hour" (Revelation 8:1). People have given all sorts of theories about what that means but it's not really that important in the grand scheme of the Apocalypse.

Next, seven angels with trumpets each cause natural (or supernatural) disasters. More stars fall, a flaming mountain falls into the sea, turning one third of it to blood. The sun and moon are darkened again. The fifth angel releases a shaft into the earth and "from the shaft rose smoke like the smoke of a great furnace and the sun and the air were darkened with the smoke from the shaft" (Revelation 9:2). Twentieth-century interpreters point to this one as proof that John knew about atomic bombs.

There are a number of other plagues, wars, and disasters, but those few people who survive still don't repent. I suppose they don't like being bullied. In another interlude it is announced that the seventh trumpet will signal that the "mystery of God will be fulfilled" (Revelation 10:7). This is taken to mean the real end of everything. So the seventh angel has to wait a while longer before he can blow the trumpet because the story isn't over yet.

Two witnesses suddenly appear. They have come to prophesy for 1260 days (see Daniel), but they have to wear sackcloth, perhaps to mourn for the doomed world. These witnesses aren't named, but a later tradition makes them Old Testament prophets. After the stated time has passed, the witnesses are martyred, brought back to life and taken to heaven.

Now the seventh angel can blow its trumpet. If you think that really is the end, forget it. The Apocalypse is just revving up. In the sky, a woman appears, "clothed with the sun, with the moon at her feet, and on her head a crown of twelve stars" (Revelation 12:2). She is in the process of giving birth, and beneath her a dragon waits to snap up the newborn. The dragon is one of the two instantly recognizable villains in the vision. It is red, with seven heads and ten horns and seven diadems on his heads.

You would think that there are no more stars left after all the destruction, but the dragon still brushes down a third of them to the earth in his excited anticipation of devouring the baby. But, just as the child is born, it is snatched into heaven and safety! The woman hides in the wilderness, again for 1260 days, while there is war in heaven over the child.

The archangel Michael and his angels fight the dragon and his angels. The dragon is defeated and thrown from heaven. It will come as no surprise to the astute reader that the dragon is also known as the Devil and Satan (Revelation 12:9 and Milton's *Paradise Lost*).

But the dragon has not been destroyed, only thrown out of heaven.

So now he chases after the poor mother who has been hiding in the wilderness. She miraculously escapes, leaving the angry dragon to make war on "the rest of her children, those who keep the commandments of God and hold the testimony of Jesus" (Revelation 12:17). Throughout the Middle Ages, the woman is assumed to represent the Church.

Finally the super villain arrives, "a beast rising from the sea and on its horns were ten diadems and on its heads were blasphemous names . . . [it was] like a leopard and it's feet were like a bear's and its mouth was like a lion's mouth" (Revelation 13:2). This beast, generally considered the antichrist of John I and II, is worshiped by the few people left and is allowed to rule for forty-two months (Revelation 13:4–6). Another beast arrives as an enforcer for the first.

Those who will not worship the image of the beast are killed. Everyone else is marked with the number of the beast, which is (ready?) 666. Without this number no one can buy or sell. John then challenges his readers to figure out who the beast is. "This calls for wisdom: let anyone with understanding calculate the number of the beast, for it is the number of a person" (Revelation 13:18). So many people took the challenge that I would need a separate chapter to give even an overview of the guesses. Pretty much every king, dictator, pope, and president has made the list at one time or another.

Again John reminds the members of the seven churches that the faithful will be saved. After reassuring them, he continues his tale of the Last Days. Next, Babylon falls, but the Whore still has to make an appearance, so it must not be completely in ruins. Metaphorical grain and grapes are harvested. Seven angels appear with seven bowls "full of the wrath of God" (Revelation 15:7). Six of the angels pour out the bowls that cause plagues, which really seems like overkill since there is hardly anyone left.

The beast sends demons to gather up all the kings of what's left of the world to assemble at Armageddon for a final battle. Then the

The Whore of Babylon (Apocalypse 17:1–5), from *Commentary on the Apocalypse* (Flemish [Bruges], third quarter of the fifteenth century, M.68). *Art Resource, New York City*

seventh angel pours out the final plague, and "a loud voice came out of the temple, from the throne, saying 'It is done!'" (Revelation 16:17). But it isn't really. There's thunder, lightning, and earthquakes. Babylon falls again, and the mountains and islands vanish as they did in Revelation 6:24.

Now the great Whore of Babylon is judged. She is another popular subject for illustrated Apocalypses. She is "clothed in purple and scarlet, and adorned with gold and jewels and pearls, holding in her hand a golden cup full of her abominations and the impurities of her fornication" (Revelation 17:4). Added to this, she is seated on a scarlet beast "that was full of blasphemous names, and it had seven heads

JOHN OF PATMOS AND HIS REVELATION

and ten horns" (Revelation 17:3). There must be a nest of those beasts somewhere, presumably in the bottomless pit.

This beast "is and was and is to come" (Revelation 17:8), an angel explains to John. The seven heads are seven kings: "five have fallen, one is living and one is yet to come: and when he comes he must only remain a little while" (Revelation 17:9–10). The ten horns are more kings to come who, with the beast, will make war on the Lamb but, don't worry, they lose (Revelation 17:14).

Babylon falls once more, possibly for the last time. All the wicked kings and greedy merchants grieve but there is rejoicing in heaven. The Lamb is married, and the elect are invited to the wedding supper.

No, that's not the end, but we are getting close. The champion of God appears on a white horse, carrying his sword in his mouth, which I'm certain is a metaphor for something. He and his angels defeat the kings of the earth who have by now gathered at Armageddon. The beast and his false prophet (the other beast) are thrown into a lake of sulfur (Revelation 19:11–20).

The dragon, who has apparently been watching the destruction without participating, like a good instigator, is bound by an angel and thrown into the bottomless pit for a thousand years, "so that he would deceive the nations no more, until the thousand years were ended. After that he must be let out for a little while" (Revelation 20:3).[2]

The thousand years pass quickly, since everyone is happy, and that's no fun to write about.

Finally the good times end, and Satan is released from his prison to have one more try at corrupting the good Christians. They must be the only ones around to corrupt because all the unbelievers were done away with before the beginning of the millennium. He finds some backsliders, and together they attack the city of the faithful. But fire comes down from heaven, destroying the armies, and the dragon now joins his friends in the lake of burning sulfur for eternal torment (Revelation 20:7).

Now it is time for the Last Judgment. The Book of Life is opened, and everyone who has ever lived, except the 144,000, who are exempt, is judged. The wicked are thrown into the burning lake with Hades and Death, who have no more reason to exist.

John is shown the glories of heaven and the New Jerusalem. Instead of the number of the beast, the saved will have the name of God on their foreheads. The angel guide tells John that he has to tell his servants "what must soon take place" (Revelation 22:6). And Christ adds, "See, I am coming soon! Blessed is the one who keeps the words of the prophecy of this book" (Revelation 22:7).

John ends by assuring his readers that this was a true vision and that the angel told him, "Do not seal up the words of the prophecy of this book, for the time is near" (Revelation 22:10). This implies that John's book may be the one Daniel wasn't to open. The time wasn't right until after the coming of Christ.

At the very end of Revelation, John warns that anyone who adds or subtracts from what he wrote will lose their share in the tree of life (Revelation 22:18–19). My feeling is that John could have used a good editor to add and subtract at least a bit.

By the mid–second century, John's Revelation was known at least in the eastern Mediterranean. However, it was only one of many such visions and revealings attributed to various Apostles.

Even at the time of the Council of Nicaea, the first major gathering of bishops and leaders of the Church, Revelation was not included among the books chosen for the New Testament. The first ecumenical council that included it was at Carthage in 451.[3] For many years after that, there was still debate on whether the book had been written by John the Evangelist. Dionysius pointed out that the Greek language of Revelation is "barbarous," totally unlike the elegant language of John's Gospel. Even after it was generally accepted that the apostle John wasn't the author, most Christians accepted it as having been divinely inspired.

By that time, it really didn't matter because the story was already part of the Christian tradition along with popular but apocryphal tales like that of the veil of Veronica or the childhood miracles of Jesus. There are so many vivid images of the days of destruction. They remind Christians of what they avoid by staying true to the faith. After all, even if she wasn't created by John, the Whore of Babylon is just too wonderful a character to give up.

---

1 *The Seventh Seal* is the also the title of my favorite Igmar Bergman film, which really doesn't have much to do with John's vision, but is worth watching all the same.

2 If John were writing a screenplay, I'd assume this was to leave room for a sequel.

3 "Africanus Codex," in *Nicene and Post-Nicene Fathers of the Christian Church, vol. 14*, ed. Philip Schaff and Henry Wace (Grand Rapids, MI: Eerdmans, 1956), 454.

CHAPTER TEN

Chinese Millennial Movements I

The Yellow Turbans

For centuries, China's state religion was Confucianism, which is more a guide to living a good and balanced life in harmony with others than a fire-and-brimstone religion. But along with Confucianism the belief in the more mystical religion of Daoism was just as strong, especially among the ordinary people outside the nobility. And it is through this strain that the idea of the end of the world entered Chinese popular belief.

The founder of Daoism was the legendary Lao'zi (Old Philosopher), who may have lived in the seventh century B.C.E. His teachings were refined and organized by *Zhuang'zi* (philosopher *Zhuang*, also spelled *Chang*) in about the fourth century B.C.E. There are many forms of Daoism, but the one most influential on millennial movements in China is the *Huang-lo* (Yellow Emperor). This movement tends to be more religious and mystical than the more philosophical strain of Daoism.[1]

Daoism is not at base a millennial religion, as Christianity is. However, there are elements in it that allow for the formation of apocalyptic and messianic beliefs. This is evident in the first Daoist "church" founded by Zhang Daoling, following a vision he had about

142 C.E. He called it the Way of the Celestial Masters. At this point the Han Dynasty, which had ruled for four hundred years, was waning. It would be another four hundred years before China was again united under the Tang Dynasty (618–906).[2]

In the last days of the Han, a millennial and revolutionary group began what was known as the Yellow Turbans, from the identifying headgear they wore. Yellow was a significant color in Chinese cosmology, and it was chosen to contrast with the Han red. It also symbolized the mythical ideal Yellow Emperor.[3] Their slogan was "The blue heaven has died and the yellow heaven is about to be established."[4] The official name of the sect was the *Taiping Dao* (The Way of Great Peace).

The Yellow Turbans may have been part of or influenced by the Celestial Masters. Many of the texts used by the masters contain prophesies of the destruction of the world, ending the present cycle. They also predicted the date for the end according to the sixty-year repeating Chinese calendar. The *Lingbao* (numinous treasure) texts opted for either 382 or 442 C.E. They also promised the return to earth of Li Hong (Lao'zi) to protect and save the "seed people," believers who would repopulate the world.[5]

The Yellow Turbans consisted of two main groups, east and west. The group in the east was led by three brothers of the Zhang family. The eldest, Jue, was considered the Lord of Heaven; the middle brother, Liang, Lord of Earth; and the youngest, Pao, Lord of Man. Thus they "presented themselves to the people as symbolic embodiments of heaven, earth and man, the all-embracing triad."[6] This was in line with the Chinese three-part conception of the cosmos.

Some historians have viewed the Yellow Turban rebellion as purely a political uprising. Certainly the desire to unseat the current ruler was important, and it was rumored that the palace eunuchs, who made up the administrative branch of the government, may have encouraged the movement.[7] But the records of the Yellow Turban sect stress its Daoist and messianic nature. The Yellow Emperor that they

Amitabha with Two Attending Bodhisattvas. China, Song dynasty, 12th to 13th century. Hanging scroll, ink and color on silk, 133.5 x 79.3 cm. *The Cleveland Museum of Art. Leonard C. Hanna, Jr., Fund, 1974.35*

hoped for was associated with Lao'zi, who was expected to take on human form and appear to help defeat the Han emperor.[8]

They also pointed out that the *Lingbao* predicted natural disasters to precede the coming of the next age. The Yellow Turban leaders began preaching in around 173 C.E., a year of widespread epidemics. In 175, there was massive flooding, destroying homes and ruining crops. The next few years brought drought and more sickness.[9] The peasants, especially in eastern China, were beaten down and dispossessed. They were more than ready for a new age to come and the signs were very convincing.

The leaders of the Yellow Turbans calculated from the Daoist texts that 184, the beginning of the next sixty-year cycle, would be the time for the present world to end. They quoted from a pseudo Lao'zi, speaking through the newly written *Classic of the Transformations,* "Come quickly and join me . . . and you will be saved from danger . . . the people are suffering and illness is at its extreme. The starving are everywhere. I will change destiny. I will shake the reign of the Han . . . I have manifested myself many times for the sake of salvation."[10]

By this time there were tens of thousands of people ready to help bring about the Age of Peace. With the help of some of the palace eunuchs, they set the date for the uprising as the fifth day of the third month, which corresponds to April 4, 184. The plan was to attack the emperor's palace from within and without. But the winter before the attack, the movement was betrayed. The palace sympathizers were executed and Zhang Jue escaped in a frantic cross-country ride, during which he and his lieutenants urged their followers to rise up and attack local officials.[11]

An army was raised, and it took some time for the imperial forces to put down the rebellion. All three of the Zhang brothers died in the fighting or were executed. For several years afterward, there were sporadic attempts to revive the Yellow Turbans, with little success.

While the followers of the Zhang brothers did not enter a true new age, the rebellion did help bring down the Han Dynasty. In their desire to change the heavens, the Yellow Turban followers rejected the authority of the Confucian system. They also seemed to have rejected the standard idea of the worthlessness of women. Titles and authority within the organization were held equally by men and women.[12] By evicting the Confucian civil authorities and destroying their homes as well as Confucian temples, the Yellow Turbans cleared the way for a more progressive regime.[13]

Although Lao'zi did not descend from Heaven to save the Chinese, the belief that he would remained in popular religion. When Buddhism entered China, that religion was syncretized with the mystical side of Daoism in order to retain that millennial hope.

1 The history of Daoism summarized from Chad Hansen, "Taoism," in *The Stanford Encyclopedia of Philosophy* ed. Edward N. Zalta (2008). Available at http://plato.stanford.edu/archives/win2008/entries/taoism. Accessed November 2009.

2 David Ownby, "Chinese Millennial Traditions: The Formative Age," *The American Historical Review* 104, no. 5 (1999), 1515–1516.

3 Barbara Hendrichke, "Early Daoist Movements," in *Daoism Handbook,* ed. Livia Kohn (Leiden: Brill, 2000), 136.

4 Hubert Stewart, *Popular Religious Movements and Heterodox Sects in Chinese History* (Leiden: Brill, 2003), 38, quoted from the *Hou Hanshu* j. 31, p. 3199.

5 Ownby, 1519. It's not clear if this belief was fully developed at the time of the Yellow Turbans, but it was certainly in force by the fourth century.

6 Howard S. Levy, "Yellow Turban Religion and Rebellion at the End of the Han," *Journal of the American Oriental Society* 76, no. 4 (1956): 217.

7 Levy, 219.

8 Ownby, 1520.

9 Levy, 219.

10 Quoted in Ownby, 1521.

11 Levy, 219–220.

12 Ibid., 223.

13 Posited in Barbara Kandel, "New Interpretations of the Han Dynasty Published during the Pi-Lin -Pi-Kong Campaign," *Modern China* 4, no. 1 (1978):110–112.

CHAPTER ELEVEN

Montanism

For some persons, like venomous reptiles, crawled over Asia and
Phrygia, boasting that Montanus was the Paraclete, and that
the women that followed him, Priscilla and Maximilla, were
prophetesses of Montanus.

—Eusebius, *History of the Church,* book V, chapter XIV

T he charismatic, apocalyptic preacher Montanus was born in
Phrygia, now in central Turkey, sometime in the early second century. The sect he founded was one of the earliest apocalyptic
groups, and it managed to cover most of the beliefs and practices of all
of the Christian apocalyptic movements that came after.

Of course, the first Christians all assumed this world was about
to end. They didn't need the book of Revelation to tell them that; it
was in the essence of the religion. But most of them continued in their
normal lives all the same, at least between persecutions. However,
some Christians felt the need to be more proactive about bringing
about the Second Coming. The Montanists filled that need.

Montanus might have been a priest in one of the pagan cults before
converting to Christianity.[1] There is debate on which cult, and no one
really knows, but later writers, from the fourth century writer Epipha-
nias on, have had fun speculating. Some have thought it was that of
the god Apollo, who was associated with the Oracle at Delphi.

This association may be due to the prophetic nature of Montanus' sect. They called themselves the New Prophecy. Montanus believed that he had been filled with the Paraclete, or Holy Spirit, who was giving him instructions on the coming Apocalypse and how to prepare for it. He was joined by two women, Priscilla and Maximilla, who were also prophets.[2] Most of what we know about the sect was written by those who were opposed to it, so the information has to be taken with a grain of salt.

Eusebius, a Greek scholar and friend of the emperor Constantine, wrote a history of the Christian Church in the early fourth century. He used many documents that have been since lost. One was by a priest, whose name has not survived, who went to Phrygia and debated with Montanus and his followers. He describes Montanus's behavior, saying, "He raved, and began to chatter and talk nonsense, prophesying in a way that conflicted with the practice of the Church handed down generation by generation from the beginning."[3]

The response of the crowd in attendance does sound plausible. Some thought he was possessed and was a nuisance; others listened avidly and believed it all. The writer ends by saying that it is now thirteen years since the death of the prophet Maximilla, and none of the disasters she foretold has come to pass.[4] Maximilla was supposed to have said that the world would end immediately after her death. "After me there will be no more prophecy, but the end."[5]

The movement survived the deaths of the all the founders at the end of the second century. Like many later apocalyptic groups, the Montanists adapted to the realization that the end was not coming when it was first predicted. Their most famous convert was the theologian Tertullian (c. 160–c. 225), who lived in Carthage in North Africa. Tertullian believed that he was living in the end times, although he thought it presumptuous to name a time. "[T]wo comings of Christ having been revealed to us: a first, which has been fulfilled in the lowliness of a human lot; a second, which impends over the world, now near its close, in all the majesty of Deity unveiled."[6] So he, like other faithful Montanists, was willing to let God decide the time.

Tertullian mentions that the followers of the New Prophecy called themselves *pneumatikoi*, "spiritual persons." This is borne out by the discovery of several gravestones in Turkey that used this term.[7]

The Montanists seem to have been a sect centered on three charismatic leaders, all of whom spoke, they insisted, only as directed by a divine presence. Montanus was more likely to get into debates and shouting matches in which he may have implied that he was God himself, but that also might simply be the accusations of his enemies. Maximilla was more careful, stating, "The Lord sent me as a partisan of this task, a revealer of this covenant, an interpreter of this promise, forced, whether I will or not, to learn the knowledge of God."[8] The third prophet, Prisca (or Priscilla), caused some controversy when she told everyone that Jesus had appeared to her "as a woman clothed in a shining robe, Christ came to me [in sleep]; he put wisdom into me and revealed to me that this place is sacred and that here Jerusalem will come down from heaven."[9]

"Here" were the towns of Pepuza and Tymion in Phrygia, where the followers of the New Prophecy established themselves, renaming the area "Jerusalem," since it was well known that it was Jerusalem Christ would return to. They fasted, prayed, and abstained, as much as possible, from sexual activity. They seemed to have allowed marriage but not the remarriage of those widowed. In essence, they wanted to be ready and on the spot when Jesus returned.

The trouble for other Christians was that there was nothing in any of those activities that went counter to the beliefs of the majority of Christians. But at the time, the religion was still small and often suppressed forcefully by the government. Montanus's claim to a direct line to God probably irritated the bishops, who were trying to establish an organized church under difficult conditions. They may also have felt that the trances, speaking in tongues, and public displays made the rest of the Christians look silly.

According to Eusebius, one Apollonius wrote a polemic against the group. He accused Montanus and the women of extorting money from their followers to support a luxurious lifestyle. He also points out that Maximilla and Priscilla left their husbands to join the group, insinuating that they did this just for wild sex. He states that two of the Montanists who claimed to have been imprisoned for being Christians were actually small-time crooks, whose crimes "are filed in the record office."[10]

He finally attacks their claim to be prophets. "Tell me, does a prophet dye his hair? Does a prophet paint his eyelids? . . . Does a prophet visit the gaming tables and play dice?"[11] Montanus apparently did all these things, and so God would never sully himself speaking through such a one. Of course, we don't have a rebuttal from Montanus. Nor can we check the records office for data or go through the New Prophecy's trash looking for empty bottles of dye.

The sect outlasted its founders and took hold in Carthage, Tertullian's home. It was only after the hierarchy of the Church was better established that the Montanists were listed as heretics and accused of more than having expectations of the end and painting their eyelids.

One of the nastier charges against the Montanists, made in later centuries, was the blood libel. This is practically a subtheme in every tract against a non-mainstream religious group. Starting in the twelfth century it was used against the Jews, who were supposed to sacrifice a Christian child every Passover and bake its blood into the matzo. The communal meal and communion of the Christians opened them up for this accusation from the pagans they lived among. Cyril of Jerusalem (c. 315–386) was the first person known to use it against the Montanists. He said that they "slaughter the wretched little children of women and cut them up into unlawful meat for the sake of what among them are called mysteries."[12]

This was taken up by other writers looking for good reasons to condemn Montanists. One problem with the sect was that, except for some fuzzy logic in their claims that the Holy Spirit spoke through them, there was really nothing they believed in that was heretical. The gift of prophecy wasn't unacceptable to early Christians. Theologians were upset only when some of the pronouncements countered the fragile agreements made between theologians on matters such as the nature of the Trinity. Most Christians really didn't understand all the fine points of dogma, but killing and eating babies was clearly a Bad Thing to Do. If the Montanists did it, they were against it.

I wonder if this libel might not have been partly caused by Tertullian. In his justification of Christianity written ostensibly for all the Greek and Roman pagans, he takes up the blood libel accusation. Only Tertullian had a warped sense of humor. He writes as if Christians really did this, "Yet there is no great difference between us [Christians and pagans], only you do not kill your infants in the way of a sacred rite, nor (as a service) to God. Instead, you make away with them in a more cruel manner, because you expose them to the cold and hunger, and to wild beasts, or else you get rid of them by the slower death of drowning."[13] He continues to bait his pagan readers about the joy they take in watching people die for their sport, nothing to eating babies.

What was Tertullian thinking? Since later Christians were quite sure that they had never eaten babies, they might well have wondered if he was talking about his experiences as a Montanist, thus confirming the truth of the charge.

One of the clearest later commentaries about the Montanists wasn't written until the fourth century, by Jerome, who first translated the Hebrew Bible into Latin (with the help of several smart women). He wrote to one of them, Marcella, who had been approached by a Montanist missionary. In his letter, Jerome first says that he doesn't believe that Montanus, Maximilla, and Priscilla were prophets because the prophecy of Joel, quoted by Peter at the Pentecost (Acts 2:14–18), that in the last days there would be prophets, was fulfilled in the Pentecost at that time and couldn't happen again.[14] While he didn't obsess over it, this indicates that Jerome, too, thought the end was coming fairly soon.

His next quibble with the Montanists has to do with the nature of the Trinity. "We distinguish the Father, the Son and the Holy Spirit as three persons, but unite them in one substance. They, on the other hand, . . . force the Trinity into the narrow limits of a single personality."[15]

Because he has nothing else major to accuse them of, Jerome then chastises the Montanists for being too strict, fasting too often and not allowing forgiveness of sins. Jerome also doesn't like it that they don't consider bishops important. Finally, he is angry at the audacity of the Montanists to think that God made mistakes using Moses and Jesus and "when, by these two steps He was unable to save the world, He last of all descended by the Holy Spirit upon Montanus and those demented women Prisca and Maximilla, and that thus . . . Montanus possessed a fullness of knowledge such as was never claimed by Paul."[16] The nerve!

Jerome had heard the claims of blood libel but, to his credit, doubted them. "I prefer, I say, not to credit these: accusations of blood-shedding may well be false."[17]

So, through all the gossip and fourth-century yellow journalism, I conclude that the Montanists were a charismatic sect who believed that their leaders had received advance warning of the Second Advent of Christ, assumed it would be soon, and set up a community to make themselves ready for him. Their experience of the hope, then disappointment and scorn from outsiders would be shared by others throughout the centuries to the present. Even the accusations against them are familiar.

The sad thing for them is that one hundred years earlier, at the end of the first century, they would have been in the mainstream. But, by the end of the 190s, Christians were beginning to think that the Apocalypse wasn't showing up any time soon so, rather than being prophets, Montanus and his followers were simply an embarrassment.

1 E. R. Dodds, *Pagan and Christian in an Age of Anxiety, rpt. ed.* (Cambridge, UK: Cambridge University Press, 1990),. 63.

2 Eusebius, *The History of the Church,* trans. G. A. Williamson (Hammondswroth, UK: Penguin Books, 1965), 5.14, p. 217.

3 Eusebius, 5.16, p. 218. This was roughly five generations from the Crucifixion.

4 Eusebius, 5.16, p. 220.

5 "Montanist Fragments," Available at *http://abacus.bates.edu/Faculty/Philosophy%20and%20 Religion/rel_241/texts/montanism.html.* Accessed November 2009.

6 Tertullian, *"Apologia,"* book 21, in *Ante-Nicene Fathers,* vol. 3, rpt. ed., ed. Allen Menzies (Grand Rapids, MI: Eerdman, 1997), 200.

7 Bradford E. Hinze and D. Lyle Dabney, *Advents of the Spirit: An Introduction to the Current Study of Pneumatology* (Milwaukee, WI: Marquette University Press, 2001), 110–112.

8 "Montanist Fragments," Epiphanius, Haer, xlviii.13.

9 Ibid., xlix.1.

10 Eusebius, 18.1–5, pp. 223–224.

11 Ibid., 225.

12 Quoted in. James B. Rives, "The Blood Libel against the Montanists," *Vigiliae Christianae* 50, no. 2 (1996): 117.

13 Tertullian, *Ad Nationes,* book XV, p. 124.

14 Jerome, "Letter XLI, To Marcella," in *The Nicene and Post-Nicene Fathers,* rpt. ed., trans. W. H. Freemantle (Grand Rapids, MI: Eerdmans, 1954), 55.

15 Ibid. The distinction seems pretty slim to me.

16 Ibid., 56.

17 Ibid.

CHAPTER TWELVE

Augustine and the Apocalypse

The evangelist John has spoken of these two resurrections in
the book which is called the Apocalypse but in such a way that
some Christians do not understand the first of the two, and so
construe the passage into ridiculous fancies.

—Augustine of Hippo "Of the Last Judgment," *City of God*, chapter 7

By the end of the fourth century c.e., the debate on the time of
the Apocalypse had become extremely heated and varied. There
were those who clung to the idea that it would start at any minute
and those who were happy to accept the calculations of theologians
who put the date safely into the end of the next century. The Eastern
Church fathers were still not convinced that John's Revelation was a
canonical book, considering it as apocrypha written by an unknown
person with no apostolic authority. Some thought, with Origen, that
the book should be read as allegory. Many others sided with Lactan-
tius, who thought one should assume a literal meaning.[1]

Then something happened that made all Christians suspect that,
this time, the end really had come. In 410, the Ostragoth Alaric conquered and sacked Rome.

By this time, Rome was largely Christian. The emperor was
Christian. Therefore the persecutor had been converted, and the
Evil Empire had mutated into a city in the service of God. Further-
more, many Christians believed that Rome was the fourth monarchy

described in the Book of Daniel. Everyone knew that the fall of that monarchy signaled the coming of the end times.

Reading the reactions of the time, from both Christian and pagan authors, it's clear that the shock was devastating, shaking the foundations of world order. The pagan concept of "eternal Rome" had been taken over by many Christians who now prepared for the Parousia and the appearance of the Antichrist.

One man was determined to stem the millennial tide. His name was Aurelius Augustinus, later known as Augustine, bishop of Hippo.

Augustine was born in 354 C.E. in the town of Thagaste in North Africa in what is now in Algeria, near the border of Tunisia.[2] His father was a minor Roman official and a pagan, his mother, Monica, was a Christian. Augustine's upbringing was not devoutly Christian. He was educated in Latin rhetoric, with the intention of entering government service. When he was about eighteen, he went to Carthage to continue his education. There he converted to Manichaeism, a religion, which began in Persia, that posited a god of darkness and a god of light in constant struggle and was a descendent of Zoroastrianism. He also met a woman, never named in his memoirs, with whom he lived for fifteen years. They had a son named Adeodatus, or "gift from God."

In 383, Augustine went to Rome to teach rhetoric. The following year, he was appointed public rhetor of Milan with the assistance of the pagan senator Symmachus. The senator probably hoped that Augustine would help in the struggle with Milan's bishop, Ambrose. Despite the increasing Christianization of the empire, Symmachus wasn't going down without a fight. The Altar of Victories at which offerings were made for the welfare of the empire had been taken from the Senate House. Ambrose, who was a councilor of the emperor Valentinian II, was doing his best to block the return of the altar.[3]

Symmachus was doomed to disappointment, however, for Augustine soon fell under the spell of Ambrose, who was a powerful personality and, according to his contemporaries, an inspiring preacher. By this time Augustine was beginning his spiritual quest once more. In the meantime, his mother had sent his concubine back to Africa, over his objections, and was trying to arrange a marriage for Augustine with someone of his own class.

In his early thirties, Augustine was having an emotional crisis. In one of the more dramatic scenes of religious narrative, one evening he was sitting in a garden with his friend Alypius. From Augustine's description of it, he was close to a breakdown. He had been studying Christianity and, intellectually, was drawn to it, but part of him didn't want to give up sex and other pleasures. As he was thrashing about in spiritual agony, Augustine heard the voice of a child chanting, "Take up and read; take up and read!" He rushed back to the letters of the Apostle Paul, left open on the table, and read, "Not in reveling and drunkenness, not in debauchery and licentiousness, not in quarreling and jealousy; instead, put on the Lord Jesus Christ, and make no provision for the flesh, to gratify its desires."[4]

This providential line caused his conversion to be total. He was baptized along with his son. They set off to return to Africa, with Augustine's mother, Monica, and with friends and family members. While waiting for a ship at Ostia, Monica fell ill and died. This loss crushed Augustine, and he spent another year in Rome working through his grief. When he returned to Africa, his son, Adeodatus, suddenly died at the age of about fifteen.

Afterward, perhaps to work through his grief Augustine founded a monastic retreat where he stayed until he was ordained a priest in 389. He became bishop of Hippo in 396 and remained so until his death in 430, while a Vandal army was besieging the city.

Although in his last days Augustine may have felt that the world had to be ending, his philosophy argues that, even though the end will come, it is not possible to predict. This is most thoroughly expressed in book twenty of his monumental *City of God*.

Augustine uses his rhetorical training to present each of the main points of his argument. He begins with the statements given by Jesus in the Gospels. Starting with Matthew and the parable of the wheat and the tares, Augustine deduces that Christ has promised a day of judgment at which the dead shall rise (Matthew 13:37–43). The twelve Apostles are also told that they shall sit in judgment of the twelve tribes of Israel (Matthew 19:28). Augustine also cites several places in which the faithful are assured that the wicked shall be punished.[5]

Then Augustine departs from the still-current belief that the end will come soon by quoting from John (5:25): "The hour is coming and is now." Augustine takes this to mean that the time has come for believers, who were once dead to Christ, to be reborn in the Church. "He, therefore, who would not be damned in the second resurrection, let him rise in the first."[6]

Next Augustine tackles the millenarians, who have been driving him crazy. He thinks that the idea of a thousand years of Sabbath is not bad and admits that he once believed this himself. But many people seem to have decided that the Sabbath didn't mean going to church, praying, and appreciating creation. They thought it meant a thousand years of holiday, to party with everything one could think of to eat and drink.[7]

Patiently, Augustine explains the allegorical interpretation of the Apocalypse. We are in the millennium, he states. It began with the incarnation, at which time Satan was thrown into the abyss—that is, into the hearts of the wicked and unbelievers. He is chained and prevented from seducing the nations of the faithful. At the end of a thousand years, Satan shall be freed and gather an army to attack the Church. But Augustine is firm that the true believers shall never be fooled into following him. Some weak Christians may be swayed, but those predestined for heaven won't waver.[8]

Therefore, Augustine is a postmillennialist. He believes that we are living in the first thousand years and at the end of it will come the Second Advent. Augustine interprets Gog and Magog of Revelation to mean the nations in which the Devil was confined. He states that it's pointless to try to identify them with real places. He also admits that the Apocalypse seems to skip from literal to figurative terms. "No doubt, though this book is called the Apocalypse, there are in it many obscure passages to exercise the mind of the reader, and there are few passages so plain as to assist us in the interpretation of the others, even though we take pains; and this difficulty is increased by the repetition of the same things, in forms so different, that the things referred to seem to be different, although in fact they are only differently stated."[9]

I find it comforting that someone as brilliant and devout as Augustine couldn't make sense of the book, either.

Augustine agrees with the by then established belief that the dead shall rise bodily at the end, that the saints and sinners shall be judged, and that there shall be a blissful eternity for the elect.

By the time he finished the *City of God*, about 426, Augustine was nearly seventy. He had witnessed cataclysmic changes in the Roman Empire. However, instead of looking for omens of the end in earthquakes and wars, he insisted that the real battles were spiritual.

He was also irritated by people who constantly tried to figure out when the Second Advent would be. "A most unreasonable question," he tells them. "For if it were good for us to know the answer, the Master, God himself, would have told His disciples when they asked him."[10]

Augustine was not the first or the last to say this, but he was one of the most eloquent. His books, *Confessions, The City of God*, and *On Christian Doctrine* were tremendously influential in setting the policy of the Roman Church for the next thousand years. While people still tried to figure out the end time, since humans naturally have a need to know and control events, there were few real millennial movements until the early fourteenth century.

Augustine also considered astrology to be nonsense and did not believe that Jews should be persecuted because their ancestors had a role in the death of Christ. These ideas were too much for most of his contemporaries and later readers to accept. However, his reading of the Apocalypse helped hold down doomsday panic throughout the Middle Ages.

Then came the Reformation, and all hell broke loose, so to speak.

1 Jeffrey Burton Russell, *Satan: The Early Christian Tradition* (Ithaca, NY: Cornell University Press, 1981), 158.

2 The information on Augustine's life is drawn from his *Confessions*. He tells pretty much everything, starting from the time he was in the womb.

3 Leo C. Farrari, "Background to Augustine's 'City of God,'" *The Classical Journal* 67, no. 3 (1972): 200.

4 *Confessions,* book VIII, in *Nicene and Post-Nicene Fathers First Series,* vol. 2, ed. Philip Schaff and Henry Wace (Grand Rapids, MI: Eerdmans, 1956).

5 Augustine, *City of God,* book XX chap. V, in *Nicene and Post-Nicene Fathers First Series,* vol. 2, ed. Philip Schaff and Henry Wace (Grand Rapids, MI: Eerdmans, 1956).

6 Ibid., chap. VI.

7 Ibid l. 342. Augustine adds, "It were a tedious process to refute these opinions point by point," so he just explains the orthodox belief. I sympathize.

8 *City of God,* chap. VIII. This theory of predestination will have all sorts of interpretations later.

9 Ibid., chap. XVII, l. 1402.

10 Ibid., book XVIII, chap. LIII.

PART THREE:

The Middle Ages

CHAPTER THIRTEEN

The Calm between the Panics

Just before the third year after the millennium, throughout the
whole world . . . men began to reconstruct churches. . . . It was
as if the whole world were shaking itself free, shrugging off the
burden of the past and cladding itself everywhere in a white
mantle of churches.

—Radolphus Glaber, *Historia Libri Quinque*, book III, part 13

The image of the European Middle Ages in popular fiction and
film is generally one of dirt, superstition, and religious fanaticism. Thus people who have only that impression of the time from,
say, 900 to 1450 would expect it to be full of millennial and apocalyptic movements. That isn't the case, at least not for medieval Europe.

By the Middle Ages, people in Western Christendom had become
used to the idea of the Second Coming, Armageddon, and the Last
Judgment. Scenes of them were in art everywhere one looked. But, for
most people, the end of the world was rather like background radiation or Muzak. They knew it was there but didn't pay much attention
to it. The monk Robert of Flavigny found this distressing. "Such is
the state of the Church today that you see people of perfect faith, with
whom, if you have a conversation about the final persecution and the
coming of Antichrist, it seems as if they hardly believe it will come,
or, if they believe it, in a dreamy way will attempt to demonstrate that
it will happen after many centuries."[1]

Of course, an earthquake or a particularly nasty invasion might jolt people into wondering if this were the Big One, rather like Californians who know a monster quake is coming but assume it won't be right now. Still, whenever there's a tremor, it crosses their minds that they might have been wrong.

The years between about 1000 and 1350 were a time of expansion. The climate was mild and harvests abundant. This allowed peasants, who usually paid a fixed amount in taxes and tithes, to have enough left over to sell at markets. Many settled new villages under favorable terms from local lords. Now I don't think it was just good weather that kept medieval society from believing that the Apocalypse was imminent. But good crops, spare cash, and new frontiers do tend to make people think things aren't so bad. By the late 900s even the Vikings were settling down and learning French.

There were a few interesting apocalyptic trends, particularly toward the end of the period, when the earth entered the little Ice Age.[2] The increasing cold led to crop failure, famine, and disease. These set the stage for both political and religious upheaval.

There is another reason that there were few millennial movements in Europe during this time. It wasn't a politically sound proposition. The Roman Church had come to terms with the Book of Revelation. The end was coming, of course, but there were a lot of things that needed to be done first. One of the standard beliefs was that Christ would not return until all the Jews converted to Christianity. Now, I know that forced baptism occurred, especially in the Rhineland and in Spain. However, it was never sanctioned by Rome. The sensible reason they gave was that conversion has to come from the heart. The reason that carried more weight with the public was that, if all the Jews became Christian, then doom was at hand. Unlike the First Christians, most medieval Christians weren't all that eager for the end.

That didn't prevent them from talking about it, writing about it and painting pictures of it.

What medieval philosophers, theologians, and visionaries did was

Miniature from a Manuscript of the Apocalypse: The Fall of Babylon. **France, Lorraine, c. 1295. Ink, tempera, and gold on vellum, 12 14.2 cm.** *The Cleveland Museum of Art, John L. Severance Fund, 1983.73.1.b*

set the stage for later developments. It's at this time that the stories of what would happen at the end and of the Antichrist were developed.

This is reflected in the late-thirteenth-century picture from the Apocalypse of John shown above. The scene is the fall of Babylon, and John is on the left. Unlike similar scenes from the fourteenth and fifteenth centuries, the sense is that Babylon is a stage set from one of the religious plays staged every year by the guilds. The beasts are very much like Maurice Sendak drawings. In this and in most high medieval representations of the Apocalypse, there is no sense of terror or foreboding. It's something to make fun of because the reality is a long way off.

They knew it was a long way off because by the sixth century, when the world didn't end in 500 C.E., as predicted by some theologians, the concept of the ages of the world that the Greeks had perfected had been firmly adapted to Christian time, and while they were probably in the final age (aren't we always?), it was still early on.

IT had been suggested that the crusades were a millennial movement in the sense that returning the Holy Land to Christians was the beginning of the events that would lead to the Second Coming. It seems plausible that there were some crusaders who did think so, although not all by any means.[3] The crusaders didn't take their millennial belief from the Bible so much as the Tiburtine Sibylline Oracles. The Sybil had been keeping up her prophecies through a number of Christian interpreters (and forgers) with hardly a break since the fall of Rome. In a popular forecast, she tells of a Last World Emperor, a human king who will destroy the Muslims, establish himself in Jerusalem, and usher in a Golden Age that will prepare the world for the end.[4] Whether the conquerors of Jerusalem thought of themselves in the light of an army out to pave the way for the Last World Emperor is hard to say. In my own work on the Crusades, I don't sense that Godfroye de Bouillon, his brother Baldwin, or any of the other leaders of the armies that took Jerusalem played the millennium card in their struggles for power after the conquest.

But that doesn't mean that the rank and file among the crusaders didn't see their actions as helping the millennium along. One of their earliest efforts to end the world was to massacre the Jews in the Rhineland. Their rationale for this has always been that these were the infidels in their midst; therefore, it was only right to rid Europe of them. The vague understanding that all the Jews were supposed to be converted before Christ returned became secondary to stamping them out, although there were also a number of forced conversions.

It's possible that this persecution caused the Jews to also believe that they were living in the end times and that the Messiah would soon come. This made it all the more important for them to hold fast to the faith, even if it meant mass suicide.[5]

The trigger for the crusading movement was the conquest of Jerusalem by the Seljuk Turks in the early 1070s. Jerusalem had been governed by the easygoing Fatamid caliphs who didn't mind Christian pilgrims and were fairly tolerant toward the Jews who lived in their midst. The Seljuks were alien to the area. They dressed differently, spoke a non-Semitic language, and were recent converts to Islam. So they were much stricter with the infidels. The Jews of Jerusalem expressed their reaction to the Turkish invasion in apocalyptic terms.[6] This was reinforced by letters from Europe, particularly one written about 1096 stating that Jews from Karzaria in the Balkans were heading to Israel to meet the remnants of the lost tribes.[7]

In Salonika on the island of Cyprus the pre-crusade Jewish sense of a coming Apocalypse was particularly strong. People sold their businesses, gave away their goods, and stopped their daily activities. "They sit in their prayer shawls, they have stopped working and we don't know what they are hoping for," a Jewish observer wrote to another community.[8] It was also reported that Elijah had appeared in Egypt to announce the pending arrival of the Messiah. The leaders of the various Jewish communities tried to keep a lid on these expectations but the rumors kept circulating.[9]

Actually, while the Middle Ages saw few millenarian movements among Christians and Ashkenazic Jews (those in northern Europe), the Sephardic Jews of Spain, Italy, Africa and the Near East seemed to have been constantly on the lookout for the Messiah. In the eleventh century, there was much excitement connected with the thousandth anniversary of the fall of the Temple to the Romans. At the end of the thirteenth century, there were a number of predictions of the end coming from Spain, including one from the town of Ayllon that said "on a specified day of that year a blast of the messiah's horn would summon Jews out of their exile."[10]

In this section of the book, I discuss some of the other millenarian and messianic ideas in more depth, especially the Islamic Mahdi, the Maya, and Merlin. These all have repercussions that echo to the present.

On the whole I don't see the Middle Ages as a particularly apocalyptic time. But don't be discouraged. The traumatic fifteenth century may have produced great art, but it was also a hotbed of apocalyptic thinking and the following century was even worse.

1 Quoted in Bernard McGinn, *Antichrist: Two Thousand Years of Human Fascination with Evil* (New York: Coumbia University Press, 2000), 115.

2 This period has been variously dated as 1500–1710 or 1200–1840. However, scientists seem to agree that the worst of it was during the first part.

3 Robert Chazan, "'Let Not Remnant or a Residue Escape': Millennial Enthusiasm in the First Crusade," *Speculum* 84, no. 2 (2009): 289–313; also Norman Cohn, "Medieval Millennialism," in *Millennial Dreams in Action*, ed. Sylvia Thrupp (New York: Schocken, 1970), 33–34.

4 Cohn, 34. This prophecy would have a long life.

5 Chazan. 36 Groups pushed to the wall have resorted to this throughout history, see the sections on Russian Old Believers and the Branch Davidians.

6 Joshua Prawer, *The History of the Jews in Latin Kingdom of Jerusalem* (Oxford: Clarendon Press, 1988), 6–9.

7 Ibid., 12.

8 Ibid., 13.

9 Ibid., 12.

10 Stephen Sharot, "Jewish Millenarianism: A Comparison of Medieval Communities," *Comparative Studies in Society and History* 22, no. 3 (1980): 397.

CHAPTER FOURTEEN

The Prophecies of Merlin

More audaciously still, he [Geoffrey of Monmouth] has
taken the predictions of a certain Merlin which he has greatly
augmented on his own account, and in translating them into
Latin he has published them as though they were authentic
prophecies resting on unshakeable truth.

—William of Newburgh (c. 1180)[1]

For those who have read *The Sword in the Stone* by T. H. White
or have seen the Disney movie based on it, the idea of the cute,
befuddled wizard Merlin having anything to do with the end of the
world is ridiculous. However, for over eight hundred years, the name
Merlin was associated with prophecy, not just in England but all over
Europe. Oddly, there are even those in the twenty-first century who
have cited Merlin in their attempts to prove that all the ancient prophets foresaw the end of the world in 2012, although I have not seen any
sources for these statements.

The problem is that for all intents and purposes, Merlin is a fictional character. He was invented by a twelfth-century monk who
called himself *Galfridus Monemutensis*, or Geoffrey of Monmouth, and
who was probably the same as a *Galfridus Artur* (yes, Arthur) who was
living at Oxford from 1129 to 1152.[2] Apparently, Geoffrey wrote about
the prophecies of Merlin first, but he then incorporated that work into
his *History of the Kings of Britain*.[3] It was a runaway best-seller.

Geoffrey's book chronicles the history of Britain from its first settlement by Brutus, a Roman consul. This was a well-known myth, but Geoffrey added his own twist, in that he adds that Brutus was the grandson of Aeneas, the hero of Virgil's *Aenead,* and that before his birth there was a prophecy that Brutus would kill his own father. This came to pass in a hunting accident, and Brutus was exiled, finally ending up in Briton, which was named for him.[4] Geoffrey follows the descendants of Brutus through the centuries (including King Lear), but the heart of the story begins in book six, when Merlin enters the picture.

The Merlin that Geoffrey created was drawn from several sources. The first was the work of the eighth-century chronicler Nennius. In this work, King Vortigern in Wales wants to build a castle, but the foundations keep crumbling. The king's soothsayers tell him that the only way to fix this is to find a boy "with no father." The child must be sacrificed and his blood sprinkled on the ground around the foundation. The boy they find, named Ambrose, is not keen on this plan. He tells the king that there are two serpents in a pool under the ground that are twisting and breaking up the foundations. The building is excavated and the serpents are found. Ambrose explains that they symbolize the Britons and the Saxons and that if Vortigern gives up on building the castle on that spot he will prevail against the Saxon invaders. Vortigern thanks Ambrose, moves his castle to a new location, and gives him all the land around the serpent-infested place to be lord of.[5]

There is another tradition of a Myrddin (many spellings), a warrior who went mad in the battle of Arfderyddt in 573 and spent many years wandering around Scotland. In his madness, he is supposed to have received the gift of prophecy.[6] Poems about him may have been written as early as the tenth century. However, because all manuscripts containing these references are from the thirteenth century or later, it's difficult to be sure that the Merlin stories were in the poems originally or added later to cash in on Merlin's popularity, as happened with King Arthur.[7]

There are stories that Geoffrey tells about Merlin that have parallels in both Celtic and Latin sources. One, in which he predicts three different deaths for one person in three different disguises, only to have all of the means combine in the actual death, is told of a prophet named Lailoken in a Welsh story and also of Bishop Hildebert of Le Mans (1056—1133).[8] Geoffrey could have learned the story from either source.

Sometimes Merlin is paired with the poet Taliesin. Taliesin was a fifth-century bard and some poems attributed to him have survived. However, none contains prophecies. It is only in later folklore that Taliesin became a prophet.[9] The Welsh traditions of Merlin continue in that language independently, with Merlin being a warrior and lover as well as a poet and prophet.[10]

In his own invention of Merlin, Geoffrey expands on Nennius's story, making Merlin's father a supernatural being. He turns the serpents under the castle into dragons. Dragons always sell.[11] Later Geoffrey has Merlin magically move Stonehenge to its present spot. Finally, Merlin accomplishes his prime directive, that of arranging for the conception of King Arthur. In Geoffrey's history, that's the end of Merlin.

Except . . . Geoffrey decided to stop his account of Arthur's magical fathering to add a few pages of prophecies from his earlier book. Why waste the material because it didn't sell on its own? Geoffrey explains this digression by telling the reader that Alexander, bishop of Lincoln, gave him a book of prophecies in the British language and asked him to translate it into Latin. So Geoffrey bowed to the bishop's entreaty and inserted these prophecies, rather like a news break, into his chronicle. No copy of this book has been found, nor is it mentioned in any other source.

These prophecies are mysterious and open to many interpretations. They mainly deal with the further adventures of the dragons and how the red dragon (Wales) will suffer under the various invaders. A lot of it reads like a parody of Revelation and Daniel, both of which Geoffrey, as a cleric, would have known well. There are many references to magical women, one who will "bear in her right hand the forest of Colidon and in her left the battlements of London's walls."[12] There is an image very much like this in Revelation. There are also many astrological predictions but somehow askew, such as "Virgo will mount on Sagittarius' back and defile her virginal flowers."[13] (She probably didn't use a saddle.) There are also many mutant animals as in the Apocalypse but somewhat less impressive. Instead of horned dragons with lions' tails there are foxes with heads of asses, and deer with buffalo horns.

Geoffrey added a few lines of "prophecy" that would be understandable to most readers and help Merlin's credibility. For instance, "Two dragons will succeed, one of which will be suffocated by the arrow of envy, while the other will return beneath the shadow of a name."[14] That might actually be a veiled reference to the death of King William Rufus in a "hunting accident" and the reign of his brother, Henry I. But most of them seem to be intended as humor. For instance, "The paws of barking dogs will be cut off," "Men with curled hair will wear fleeces of varied hue," "Women will move like snakes and their every step will be filled with pride," and "All the soil will be rank, and mankind will not cease to fornicate."

Are these prophecies or observations? Of course, these observations could have been made to convince readers that the end was near since these things were clearly going on all around them.[15]

These first of a long line of prophecies of Merlin are a lot of fun to read, but I don't see how anyone could have taken them seriously. And many people didn't. Geoffrey's contemporary William of Newburgh lamented that everyone was reading about Arthur and Merlin even though they were pure fiction and no one was reading his serious history.[16]

Even Geoffrey implies that the prophecies needed reinforcement when, at the end of the history, there is a separate prophecy that one day the British (Welsh) would win back their land. To validate the prediction, the prophecies of Merlin are consulted, but the experts also check "the eagle which prophesied at Shaftsbury"[17] and the Sibyl, who could always be counted on for backup. Even for Geoffrey, Merlin's prophecies need to be supported by others.

So why did authors for centuries to come write prophecies in Merlin's name? Why did he have so much authority that some people still believe in his ability?

My answer is that Geoffrey's stories of King Arthur, which make up the second half of the *History*, were a tremendous hit. All over Europe the story was copied and expanded on. I think it is safe to compare Geoffrey's success to that of Dan Brown with *The Da Vinci Code*, minus the movie deal. There were even spin-offs. Minor characters in Geoffrey's book went on to have adventures of their own. Like Merlin's prophecies, the stories of King Arthur are fictional, gripping, and full of possibilities.

Unless you agree with me that Geoffrey was doing a take off on the Bible, there are actually no apocalyptic references in Geoffrey of Monmouth's work.

But by the thirteenth century, there were many books containing nothing but prophecies of Merlin, and some of them were very much concerned with the Millennium and the end of the world.

The Old French *Prophecies de Merlin* are typical of this genre. In them, the author has found a lost book of Merlin about a knight who was once a dinner guest along with Merlin. During dinner, the wizard told him stories of King Arthur's knights, interspersed with predictions involving the Antichrist, the dragon with seven heads, and the Whore of Babylon. It ends with a "wise cleric" opening a book that Merlin had given him, to find a prophecy that the Antichrist will be born in Barcelona and that he will make war on his neighbors, killing more than half of them with "swords and lances and big sharp knives and axes."[18]

This book, which has also been found in an Italian version, was likely written to comment on the politics of the Italian peninsula during the battle between the popes and the Holy Roman emperors. It is just one of many such stories, along with "biographies" of Merlin. Some contain prophecies; others just elaborate on other aspects of his life. In the early seventeenth century, the playwright Thomas Heywood wrote a history of Britain up to his own time, stating that it had all been foretold by Merlin.[19]

A pamphlet published anonymously in 1603 included prophecies of Merlin along with those of the Venerable Bede, Thomas Rhymer, "Sibbilla," and several others. Even in those millennial times, Merlin does not predict the end. Rather, he says, "With Hunger and Hirship on every Hill. Yet this wicked World shall last but a while."[20]

So, after spending some amount of time looking for a seriously apocalyptic prophecy by someone calling himself (or herself) Merlin, I have concluded that, like Arthur, there may have been a man named Merlin (Myrddin) in Wales or southwest Scotland in the seventh century. He may have even taken a break from sanity after a battle and made some prophecies. But, if he did exist, he didn't write any of the material published in his name, and he certainly didn't say the world would end in 2012. So, if someone tells you that he did, feel free to hand them this book.

By the way, *Myrddin* is also Welsh for the number "one thousand."[21] I'm sure that the people who try to predict the future with computers will be delighted with the one and zeroes. More predictions may soon follow.

1 P. G. Walsh and M. J. Kennedy, eds. and trans., *The History of English Affairs*, book I (Warminster, UK: Aris & Phillips, 1988), 28–29.

2 Michael D. Reeve and Neil Wright, eds. and trans., "Introduction," in *The History of the Kings of Britain*, Geoffrey of Monmouth (Woodbridge, Boydell Press, 2007), vii.

3 Ibid., viii.

4 Geoffrey of Monmouth, *History*, liber 1:6–7, pp. 7–9.

5 Nennius, 40–44.

6 A. O. H. Jarman, "The Merlin Legend and the Welsh Tradition of Prophecy," in *The Arthur of the Welsh: Arthurian Legend and Medieval Welsh Literature*, ed. A. O. H. Jarman and Rechdl Bromwich (Cardiff: University of Wales Press, 1991).

7 Rachel Bromwich, ed. and trans., *Trioedd Ynys Prydein: The Triads of the Island of Britain* (Cardiff: University of Wales Press, 2006), 458.

8 John J. Parry, "The Triple Death in the *Vita Merlini*," *Speculum* 5, no. 2 (1930): 216–217.

9 Juliette Wood, "Virgil and Taliesin: The Concept of the Magician in Medieval Folklore," *Folklore* 94, no. 1 (1983): 91–104.

10 Bromwich, 460.

11 The Saxon word *wyrm* is used for both "serpent" and "dragon," so Geoffrey could have gone either way, although he doesn't seem to have been from a Saxon family.

12 Geoffrey, *Prophecy*, liber VII, ll. 158–159: "*gestabit in dexerta sua nemus Colidonis, in sinestra vero murorum Lundoniae propugnacula.*"

13 Ibid., ll. 299–300: "*Ascendent Virgo dorsum Sagittarii et flores virgineos obfuscabit.*"

14 Geoffrey, *History*, liber VI, ll. 75–76, p. 146: "*Succedent duo dracones, quorum alter invidiae piculo suffocabitur, alter vero sub umbra nominis redibit*" (p. 147).

15 I am grateful to Morgan Kay for this point.

16 William of Newburgh, see the epigraph for this section.

17 Geoffrey, *History*, liber XI, ll. 575–576: "*prophetiis aquilae que Seftoniae prophetauit.*"

18 *Les Prophesies de Merlin* ed. Lucy Allen Paton (New York, Heath & Co. 1926) 328 p. 339.

19 Thomas Heywood, *The Life of Merlin, Surnamed Ambrosius: His Prophecies and Predictions Interpreted and Their Truth Made Good by Our English Annals*, rpt. ed. (Carmarthen: Evans, 1812).

20 Anonymous, *The Whole Prophesie of Scotland, England, & Somepart of France, and Denmark, Prophesied Bee Marvelous Merling, Beid, Bertlingtoun, Thomas Rymour, Waldhaue, Eltraine, Banester, and Sibbilla, All According in One Containing Many Strange and Marvelous Things*, (England, 1603), 11.

21 U. G. Chambers, "Elfenau Rhifyddiaeth: A Fragment," *The Mathematical Gazette* 79, no. 485 (1995): 294.

CHAPTER FIFTEEN

Setting the Clock

The Maya

Who will be the prophet? Who will be the priest
who shall interpret truly the word of the book?

—*The Book of Chilam Balam of Chumayel*[1]

Explanations of the Maya, their Long Calendar, and the end of the world in 2012 have been covered extensively in the media in the past few years. I will address that fateful date in its own section. It seemed though that it might be a good idea to find out more about the Mayans before trying to understand how or if they arrived at 2012 as an end date and what it means. I have noticed that very few of the television talking heads who tell viewers that the Maya have prophesied the end of our world actually know how to read Mayan glyphs or have degrees in archaeoastronomy. That doesn't make them wrong, just rather suspect in my mind. So I have read books and articles by people who are scholars of Mayan culture, both ancient and modern, as well as scientists who are intrigued by the intricacy of the calendars and astronomical computations.[2]

It's true that the Mayan calendar is very complex. For one thing, the Maya based their counting system on fingers and toes, instead of just fingers. So the base is twenty instead of ten. Spanish colonizers noted that in trading with them in cacao beans, the Maya counted, "by fives up to twenty, and by twenties up to one hundred and by hundreds up to four hundred, and by four hundreds up to eight thousand. . . . They have other very long counts and they extend them in infinitum."[3] And this is cacao merchants multiplying in their heads! Imagine what the priests who spent all their time studying the sky could come up with.

They also devised their calendar as most early people did, according to the seasons and the stars, trying to gauge the optimum times for planting, harvesting, and other essential occupations. But the Mesoamericans went far beyond that or any known method of dating. The reason they did this is still debated. Therefore, let's begin by looking at the Maya themselves, where they came from and what may have happened to the civilization that built the stone cities of Mesoamerica.

The Maya didn't spring from nowhere. Their predecessors were the Olmec, who may have developed the mother language, both written and oral, for the four Mayan language groups. The language of the Olmec has not yet been satisfactorily deciphered, although it's thought to be in the Zoquan language group.[4] Their writing system was adapted by the Maya, although the meaning and pronunciations of the glyphs may not be identical.

The Olmec also may have designed the first 260-day "short" calendar and, perhaps, also the Long Count Calendar.[5] Their civilization dates from around 1200 b.c.e., although that didn't appear spontaneously, either. There is pottery evidence of a developing culture that goes back another seven thousand years.[6] Recent excavations by paleobotanists indicate that people along the Gulf of Mexico were raising corn and sunflowers as early as 5000 b.c.e., although it's not known if they were the same as the people who became the Olmec.[7]

The Olmec are probably also responsible for the base twenty number system and the invention of the zero.[8] The Maya seem to have built considerably on their work.

As in many other cultures, the Maya saw time as cyclical, rather than linear. Things happened in patterns, not in exactly the same way each time, but within knowable possibilities.[9] In the *Chilam Balam*, one of the few Mayan books that survive (although written in Roman letters), this cycle is shown as a wheel. Within it are the *katunob*, "an endlessly recurring sequence of thirteen twenty-year periods, . . . each with its designation and characteristic events."[10] This is known as the Short Count Calendar. In it, a year contains 260 days. Of course, the Maya knew that the solar year is 365+ days. So there is another calendar called the *Haab*, or "vague year," of eighteen months with twenty days each, along with five "unlucky days" at the end.[11] These two calendars were used at the same time. Each day in the Short Calendar had an equivalent day in the *Haab* but, because the cycles were of different lengths, 3 *Pop* could be 3 *Kimi* in one year and 7 *Ak'bal* in another. It takes fifty-two years for the correlations to start repeating. The first day of the year, 0 *Pop*, was originally set at the winter solstice. However, because neither calendar was exact, it happened that 0 *Pop* fell on the winter solstice only every 1,507 years. This, plus archaeological evidence, has led scholars to think that this calendar was in use by 550 B.C.E.[12]

But that's only the Short Count years. For the Long Count, the Maya used another year, this time of 360 days, called a *tun;* twenty *tuns* made a *ka'tun* and twenty *ka'tuns* was a *bak'tun*, or 144,000 days.[13] The Long Count seems to have been computed starting at August 11 or 13, 3114 B.C.E. "a date on which astronomers have found no momentous celestial event to have occurred."[14]

Thirteen *bak'tuns* was the cycle that has created all the stir. According to post-conquest sources, the last creation ended in a great flood.[15] The next cycle does indeed end in December 2012. At that point, the calendar will "flip" to 13.0.0.0.0. Whether this is like a car odometer hitting a hundred thousand miles or something more momentous remains to be seen.

What did the Maya use these calendars for? It looks as if they were mainly religious in nature. The principal information on the Maya culture comes from the four books that remain from before the Spanish conquest; the observations of the conquerors, particularly Bishop Diego de Landa; and the many inscriptions on Mayan artifacts. We may have a very skewed impression of the Maya from this. As Michael Coe says, "[It's] as though all that posterity know of ourselves were to be based upon three prayer books and *Pilgrim's Progress*."[16] If someday the Great Mayan Novel turns up and there's nothing in it about the gods, then all scholarship on their culture will have to be reconsidered.

However, at least one section of Classical Maya society (400–900 C.E.) seems to have been vitally concerned with the relationship between man and the universe. How far it reached from the priests and the ruling class to the military, artisans, farmers, and others is hard to tell. But the fact that the general population tolerated, or even encouraged, the public practice of very bloody sacrifices and rites indicates that most of them were also believers.

What the Maya believed is not completely clear, either. I think they viewed the world very differently from most of us today, and so even if the tangle of gods, dates, movements of the stars and ritual were figured out, we could still not really enter into the understanding the Maya had of their place in the cosmos. Of course, that shouldn't stop anyone from trying. However, those who insist that they know exactly what the Maya believed probably haven't studied them enough.

For one thing, the Maya were not one monolithic culture. There were several cities, each with its own variation on central myths. Some of these incorporated the local ruling families into the creation stories. Others had gods, or aspects of the same gods, which were venerated only by that city. There were also gods who appeared in different forms: old, young, infant, animal, or natural force.[17] In the *Popol Voh*, one of the pre-conquest books written in Maya (but in Spanish characters), the story of the creation as known to the Quiche Maya is told.

In it, the Plumed Serpent of the sea and the Heart of Sky, with the help of other gods, created the earth, plants, and animals. The gods wanted some acknowledgment for the cleverness of their creation, but the animals only squawked or hooted or roared. So they fashioned puppet people from wood and clay, but these went about living without paying attention to the gods. Therefore the gods sent the flood to destroy them all. (In the Mayan story there are no righteous survivors.) Just to be certain, "Gouger of Faces: he gouged out their eyeballs. . . . Sudden Bloodletter: he snapped off their heads. . . . Crunching Jaguar: he ate their flesh. . . . Tearing Jaguar: he tore them open. They were pounded down to the bones and tendons, smashed and pulverized even to the bones."[18]

Added to this, their domestic animals attacked the puppet people; their pots and pans burned them; trees threw them off their branches, and caves closed before them when they tried to hide.[19] Soon, there was only a small remnant of them left, which became the monkeys.

This is what happens to a people who don't respect the hard work their gods went through to create them.

The creation of the current human race and the history and genealogy of the Quiche Maya make up the rest of the *Popol Vuh*. In the story, there is constant interaction between the people and the gods. Often the lords of the land take on the aspects of gods, changing shape, like Plumed Serpent, who could become an eagle or a jaguar or "nothing but a pool of blood."[20]

Blood was essential in most of the Mayan rites. Timing seems to have been as well. The correct sacrifice must be performed according to the season and the stars. Their calculations for the movements of Venus and Mars were particularly complicated. The Maya had charts to predict solar and lunar eclipses. The *Dresden Codex*, a book written in Mayan glyphs, contains many of these charts and calculations. Although they have been provisionally translated, the book is rather like having a manual for a machine one has never seen. The people who used it knew what it meant, but modern scholars can only guess, using inscriptions on monuments and pottery as well as remembered traditions of modern-day Maya. It does appear that they believed

A Mayan representation of the destruction of the world, from the
Dresden Codex. *Bildarchiv Preussischer Kulturbesietz /Art resource, New York*

that gods sent messages through the sky. Missing one could result in disaster.[21] Therefore the Maya had dozens of ways to observe the movements in the heavens, to measure the ecliptic and the distance of planets and stars relative to it.[22]

The need for sacrifices, particularly of blood, was deemed necessary for the continued health of the society: rain, crops, animals to hunt, and so forth. The Maya fed the gods with blood in order to be fed themselves.[23] They sacrificed captives and slaves in ways that allowed blood to flow down gutters in the altars, soaking the ground. But the Mayan priests and rulers also practiced painful rites on themselves in which men pierced their penises and women their tongues. Then they drew thorny ropes through the wounds to extract blood. The blood was mixed with incense and paper and either burned or rubbed on the stone images of the gods.[24]

The pattern of the sacrifices and other rites used only the 260-day calendar, and apparently by the end of the Classical period, the Long Count Calendar was no longer part of the calculations, although it continued to be used for other things.

It seems that the Maya, like the Egyptians, were more concerned with keeping this world going than with when it was going to end. "They had a crucial role to play in the cyclical drama, through their calendrical computations, their related rituals, and even their wars and revolts. Theirs was the task of helping the gods to carry the burden of the days, the years and the *katuns* and thereby to keep time and the cosmos in orderly motion."[25]

Only one ancient Mayan artifact has been found with a prediction by the Palequue Maya that says anything about the end of the current *bak'tun,* and that was found on an, unfortunately, broken inscribed stone. It says that "the 13th *Pik/Bak'tun* will end and . . . a god or gods called *Bolon Yokte'* will descend."[26] The unbroken section of the stone doesn't say who this god is or what he/she/they/it is going to do when he/she/they/it arrive. The Palenque Maya seem to have believed that we are not living in the last creation and that after 13.0.0.0.0 will come 14.0.0.0.1 and not the end of the world.[27]

The Mayan civilization that built pyramids and wrote astronomical texts ended in about 900 C.E. There are many theories as to what caused their cities to be abandoned, but none that dominates. It may have been a combination of wars, bad harvests, natural disasters, and disease. The Maya people, however, still exist, living in southern Mexico, Guatemala, Honduras, and Belize. They speak twenty-two languages, all descendants of that spoken by the Olmecs more than two millennia ago. Some live in cities and are fully acculturated to the dominant culture. Some live in remote villages, speak no Spanish, and follow their old religion with only a thin layer of Christianity. I have not discovered any reports that any of them are preparing for any sort of Apocalypse in the near future.

---

1 Ralph L. Roys, ed. and trans., *The Book of Chilam Balam of Chumayel* (Norman: University of Oklahoma Press, 1967), 169.

2 I am *not* going to entertain the idea that the Mayas were visited by aliens who taught them how to make computations. I believe they were smart enough to come up with the math themselves. But I'm open to any solid evidence.

3 Quoted in, Michael F. Closs, "The Nature of the Maya Chronological Count," *American Antiquity* 42, no. 1 (1977): 20.

4 John S. Justeson and Terrence Kaufman, "A Decipherment of Epi-Olmec Writing," *Science* new ser, 259, no. 5102 (1993): 1707.

5 Michael D. Coe, *The Maya*, 7th ed. (London: Thames & Hudson, 2005), 52.

6 Muriel Porter Weaver, *The Aztecs, Maya and Their Predecessors* (New York, Academic Press, 1981), 510.

7 Kevin O. Pope et al., "Origin and Environmental Setting of Ancient Agriculture in the Lowlands of Mesoamerica," *Science* new ser. 292, no. 5520 (2001): 1373.

8 John S. Justeson, "The Origin of Writing Systems: Preclassic Mesoamerica," *World Archaeology* 17, no. 3 (1986): 440–441. [And I don't think the Olmec were aliens, either.]

9 Nancy M. Fariss, "Remembering the Future, Anticipating the Past: History, Time and Cosmology among the Maya of Yucatan," *Comparative Studies in Society and History* 29, no. 3 (1987): 569–572. Westerners are not totally ignorant of this; history does repeat itself.

10 Ibid., 570.

11 Coe, 62. The idea of some days being unlucky is found in many other cultures. In medieval manuscripts, they are called "Egyptian Days."

12 Victoria R. Bricker, "The Origin of the Maya Solar Calendar," *Current Anthropology* 23, no. 1 (1982): 103.

13 Coe, 63. I think the number is just a coincidence; not a connection with the Book of Revelation.

14 Anthony F. Aveni, *Skywatchers* (Austin: University of Texas Press, 2001), 138.

15 Coe, 213. It's possible that Spanish priests influenced this, but not certain. So many cultures have a flood story.

16 Ibid., 211.

17 Ibid., 215–215.

18 *Popol Vuh,* 2nd ed., trans. Dennis Tedlock (New York, Simon & Schuster, 1996) 71–72.

19 Ibid., 72–73.

20 Ibid., 186.

21 Aveni, 17.

22 Aveni has discussed this at length for both the Maya and the Aztecs. He doesn't attempt to figure out what the purpose was, only the ways in which the sightings were done. No aliens seem to be involved.

23 John Monaghan, "Sacrifice, Death, and the Origins of Agriculture in the Codex Vienna," *American Antiquity*, 55, no. 3 (1990): 559–569.

24 Coe, 222. He mentions earlier that the Maya nobility "seemed obsessed with enemas." These might have contained drugs that helped blunt the pain.

25 Farriss, 589.

26 Mark Van Stone, "It's Not the End of the World: What the Ancient Maya Tell Us about 2012," Adobe lecture, pt. 2, Southwestern University.

27 Ibid.

CHAPTER SIXTEEN

Messiahs, the Antichrist, and the Apocalypse in Early Islam

On that day there shall be a blast on the trumpet, and
all that are in the heavens, and all that are on the earth
shall be terror-stricken, save him whom God pleaseth
to deliver; and all shall come to him in humble guise.

—The Qur'an, Sura 27:89

Islam is the last of what are known as the three great monotheistic religions. It was founded by Muhammad b. Ali, who was born in Arabia about 570 C.E. He was a merchant by trade but also a seeker after spiritual answers. He would go to a cave near Mecca, where he lived, to meditate. One day, when he was about forty, he received a vision and heard a voice telling him "Recite! Recite!" The voice, which he later learned was that of the angel Gabriel, then gave him, over a period of many years, the messages for humankind that were later written in the Qur'an. The first message, Sura 96, ends with the command, "adore and draw near to God."

It was some time before Muhammad acted on these messages, except for telling his wife and a few friends about them. Eventually, he began to preach but was not well received in Mecca. In 622, after the death of his wife, he and his followers moved to Medina. This is known as the *hegira*, and the Muslim calendar begins from this date.

Muhammad died in 10 AH/632 C.E. In his time the Qur'an was not written down, but memorized by the faithful as Muhammad received the word of God through Gabriel. When he died, it was understood that, as he was the final prophet, there would be no more revelations. There are several traditions as to when the Qur'an was put together and written down but, once it was, it was agreed that, because it had been divinely written, no changes were to be made to it, ever.

The Qur'an speaks often about the end times. In Islam, like Judaism and Christianity, there is a promise of an end to this world and a final day of judgment. But there is no one Sura (chapter) in the Qur'an that describes the end in minute detail the way that is done in Daniel or Revelation. Nor is there any hint as to the end time. Sura 53:58 is unequivocal on this, "The day that must draw nigh, draws nigh already: and yet none but God can reveal its time."[1] In short, God knows; we don't. Get over it.

Therefore Islamic scholars have not spent years trying to calculate the end, freeing them for other philosophical activities. Of course, there are always a few people who have to try. Some believed that the year 125 AH (743–744 C.E.) would be the time of *fitan* (wars) and *malahim* "apocalyptic woes and tribulations."[2]

The end of time is mentioned most fully in Sura 18:40: "And call to mind the day when we shall cause the mountains to pass away, and you shall see the earth a leveled plain, and we will gather mankind together, and not leave of them any one."[3]

In this passage, the earth is destroyed. Each person is given a book containing their deeds and misdeeds. Then a trumpet will sound, and infidels will be cast into a fiery hell. Those who believe will ascend into one of the seven heavens where there are cool drinks, soft clothing, and shade where one may recline in comfort.

By the way, in the West there is a popular notion that women don't go to heaven and men get to have unbridled sex with supernatural *houri*. However Sura 36:50 states that in paradise the saved will recline on bridal couches where "they and their spouses" will be served fruit and whatever else they need."[4] And Sura 44:70, states, "Enter [paradise] you and your wives." These say to me that women are among the saved. Even clearer is Sura 4:124. "But whoever does the things that are right, whether male or female, and he or she a believer—these shall enter Paradise."

The *houri* are a bit trickier. They are mentioned only in Sura 56. The translation I have could certainly be read that they are there for sex. But another line says that they are "dear to their spouses" (56:39). So this is something that can be open to many interpretations and has been. Islamic traditionalists have elaborated on the *houri*, describing their clothes and jewels. They are perfect women. They "do not sleep, do not get pregnant, do not menstruate, spit or blow their noses and are never sick."[5] Apart from the lack of sleep, I like it.

But many Islamic scholars interpret the *houri* differently. Some suggest that they are the women who go to paradise or that the *houri* are there to serve both men and women.[6] Others see them as allegorical, a symbol of the delights of heaven. One scholar laments that critics mock the Muslims because they think that the *houri* are there for sex as between a man and a woman. But he tells these scoffers that "the pleasure received from the *houri* in Paradise is an appearance or a representation of a supreme delight that is impossible for human comprehension."[7]

Shade and cool drinks in paradise are mentioned more times than *houri* in any case, which makes sense in a religion that began in the desert.

But what happens in heaven comes after the end of the world. Since Islam is said to be the culmination of monotheistic tradition, the Jewish and Christian books are drawn on for this as for other traditions. Muhammad never stated that his revelations were new, only that they were the most accurate. Moses and Jesus are considered prophets who are forerunners of Muhammad. None of the three is divine. Jesus, called Isa, is given an important role in the end times. He announces the "sign of the last hour" (Sura 43:61), punishes the wicked, and paves the way for God to pronounce judgment.

While not in the Qur'an, there are very early traditions of an Antichrist in Islam. He is known as the Dajjal. His coming will signal the end times. He will be a giant, blind in one eye, who rides an enormous ass: "he will be accompanied by mountains of bread, and by rivers of fire and water. He will work false miracles and claim to be God. Great numbers of Jews will follow him."[8] The story developed over time, and there are variants to it, but it is generally agreed that, until the end, Al-Dajjal is chained up in a monastery on an island in the ocean. When he is freed, he can be defeated only by Isa.[9]

All Muslims have a core belief in the Five Pillars of Islam: God is the only god and Muhammad is his Prophet, prayer must be made five times daily, the poor and needy must be cared for, during the month of Ramadan all must fast, and once in one's lifetime one must make a pilgrimage to Mecca.

The Qur'an is considered to be sacrosanct. Every word is from God. But, like the Bible, not all of it is straightforward. Some parts seem to be allegorical, others cloaked in mystical symbols. Unlike the case of Bible, no church councils or schools emerged in Islam to explain the meanings. It was, and is, up to each believer to find the meaning in the text. As happened in Europe when the Bible was made available to everyone, this resulted in many different, and sometimes opposing, views.

In the first decades after Muhammad's death, it became clear that more was needed to regulate a society according to Islam. So those who had known him began to compile a list of the Prophet's *sunna,* or "customs." They remembered things Muhammad had told them and his actions. These were put together in a collection known as the *Hadith* (Sayings). After a short time, there were thousands of apocryphal *hadith* in circulation. About two hundred years after

Muhammad, scholars set about filtering the false *hadith* from the true. There are now two collections that are considered *sahih*, or "without flaws." There are also other collections that are not as reliable but are accepted for the most part.[10] Many of the legends concerning the end of the world are in these.

As is well known, there are many sects in Islam, the two main ones being the Sunni and the Shi'ite. The division between these two came very early in the history of the religion and involved, not doctrine, but the right of leadership. But the different outlooks of the sects led to the development of a messiah-like figure, known as the Mahdi.

At the death of Muhammad, his son-in-law and cousin, Ali, was considered by some to be the leader of Islam. Others preferred Abu Bakr, an early companion of Muhammad and his father-in-law. Abu Bakr was selected by the majority, but the followers of Ali refused for some time to accept him. They felt that Ali had been passed over because when the succession was decided he had been in Medina, arranging for Muhammad's burial.[11] This would eventually lead to the Sunni, followers of Abu Bakr, and the Shi'ite, followers of the family of Ali and Fatima.

After the deaths of the first three caliphs, Abu Bakr (632–634), Umar ibn al-Khattab (634–644), and 'Uthman ibn 'Affan (644–656), Ali assumed leadership. He spent most of his time fighting the growing power of the Umayya family. When Ali was assassinated, the Umayya took over, becoming the Umayyad Dynasty. They would develop into the Sunni, whose leaders were chosen to be secular administrators, rather than religious.

Ali's son Husain tried to regain power but he died in battle against the Umayyad. He is still considered the first of the Shi'ite martyrs. It is from his line that the belief in the Mahdi would come. The Shi'ites accept only descendants of the Prophet as *imams*, through his grandsons, Husan and Husain, usually the latter. The family was hunted down and killed by the dominant Sunni, but some of them and their followers survived. In Shi'ite society the *imam* is both a religious and a secular leader, whose word is law with no chance of appeal.

The Mahdi (guided one) is mentioned in an early *hadith*, one of those compiled with the most care.[12] In it, Muhammad is said to have predicted that the Mahdi would be from his family. In other *hadith*, he states that the Mahdi will appear at the end of time, to fight Al-Dajjal alongside Jesus.

Most Sunni accept the idea of the Mahdi as a harbinger of the end of days, although some scholars consider it a folk tale.

However, in Shi'ite teaching, the Mahdi exists and is even now in occultation, hidden from view until the time is right for his return. The largest group of Shi'ites are called "Twelvers," for they believe that the twelfth *imam* after Muhammad is the one who will return. "Thenceforth, no aspect of Shi'i history has remained unaffected by the everlasting hope for the return of the Mahdi, or the rightly guided."[13]

There is only one Mahdi at the end of time, but there have been many mahdis who have appeared throughout time to revitalize Islam when its followers have deviated from the path. In Syria, one of these is known as the Sufayana, who appeared in 130 AH/752 C.E. and was defeated but is still expected to return one day.

The idea of the rightly guided savior who will clean society of its corruption is a powerful one in all cultures. Men calling themselves mahdi have appeared throughout Muslim history and continue to do so today. Many are charlatans, some are devout reformers. Whenever a ruler died without a clear heir, the mahdis seemed to appear. For instance, medieval Morocco attracted a number, when the death of the caliph al-Mansur gave rise to rumors that he would soon return as the Mahdi.[14]

So a mahdi is a messiah who might come at any time, straighten out society, and vanish until needed again, but the Mahdi is part of the Muslim Apocalypse, a savior who will fight in the final battle against evil.

As in Judaism and Christianity, millennial hopes among Muslims have fueled uprisings throughout history. We shall look at a few of them later.

---

1 *The Koran*, rpt. ed., trans. J. M. Rodwell (London, Phoenix, 1994), 359. I agree with those who say that the Qur'an should be studied only in the original but lacking classical Arabic, I have had to make do. Sorry.

2 Said Amir Arjomand, "Messianism, Millennialism and Revolution in Early Islamic History," in *Imagining the End: Visions of Apocalypse form the Ancient Middle East to Modern America*, ed. Abbas Amanat and Magnus T. Bernhardsson (London: Taurus, 2002), 107.

3 Ibid., 190.

4 Ibid., 29.5.

5 Jane Idleman Smith and Yvonne Yazbeck Haddad, *The Islamic Understanding of Death and Resurrection* (Albany: State University of New York Press, 1981), 164.

6 Ibid., 164, quoting Mawlana Muhammad 'Ali.

7 Ibid., 168, quoting Soubhi El-Saleh: "*la jouissance procure par les Houris au Paradis est une figuration ou une représentation d'un délice suprême dont la réalité et est inaccessible à la compréhension humaine.*"

8 David J. Halperin, "The Ibn Sayyad Traditions and the Legend of Al-Dajjal," *Journal of the American Oriental Society* 96, no. 2 (1976): 213.

9 Ibid.

10 Annemarie Schimmel, *An Introduction to Islam* (Albany: State University of New York Press, 1992), 52.

11 Robert Mantran, *L'Expansion Musulmane*, 4th ed. (Paris: PUF, 1991), 90.

12 *Bihar al-anwar*, 51, p. 74.

13 Seyyed Hossein Nasr, Hamid Dabashi, and Seyyed Vali Reza Nasr, *Expectation of the Millennium: Shi'ism in History* (Albany: State University of New York Press, 1989), 8.

14 Halima Ferhat, "Littérature eschatologique et espace sacré au Maroc: Le cas de Massa," *Studia Islamica* 80 (1994): 48.

CHAPTER SEVENTEEN

Joachim of Fiore

Monk, Prophet, and Superstar

It is almost evening. We have been brought
to the sunset of this life.

—Joachim of Fiore, Letter to the Abbot of Vadona

The life and experiences of Joachim of Fiore (or Flora) demonstrate the drastically different attitudes of the twelfth century toward the Apocalypse compared to those of later centuries. Joachim's radical, new interpretations were generally welcomed by popes, nobility, and commoners—that is, as much as anyone understood them.

He was born in 1135 in the Italian town of Calabria. His father, Mauro, was a notary attached to the Sicilian court, at that time one of the most diverse and open-minded in Europe. I've found no reference to prove this but, if Joachim's father was really named Mauro, it might indicate that he was a Muslim convert to Christianity. It has also been suggested that the family had converted from Judaism, mainly because of a sermon directed against Joachim by the Cistercian monk Geoffrey of Auxerre in which he accuses Joachim of having been born a Jew and hiding his Jewish identity. However, there is no evidence for either possibility, and it has been concluded that Geoffrey was just trying to discredit Joachim's writings.[1]

Under Roger II of Sicily, there was a large amount of religious toleration. Greek Orthodox Christians, Jews, and Muslims were allowed to worship as they chose. Court documents were written in both Greek and Latin.[2]

Trained to be a notary like his father, Joachim was instead converted to the monastic life. He went on a pilgrimage to Jerusalem, then in Christian hands, and received his own spiritual revelation while wandering through the Palestinian desert. He then spent the Lenten season in meditation on Mount Tabor.[3] On his return home, he became a hermit for a time, living on Mount Etna. In around 1171, he was ordained a priest and then joined the Benedictine monastery of Corazzo. By 1178, he had been made abbot of the monastery.

Prophets do not, in general, make good administrators. After fighting to change the monastery to the stricter Cistercian order, Joachim slacked in his duties. By 1183, he had left the monastery to hide out for a year to write, bringing only a few secretaries with him.[4] It was perhaps then that he wrote the books for which he is best known, the *Liber Concordiae* and the *Exposito in Apocalypsim*,[5] The first was his innovative method of seeing everything in the Old Testament as having a parallel person or event in the New Testament. He continued this idea by making history since then form a third parallel. "Everything which happened in the Old Dispensation, recorded in the Old Testament, has its own actuality in time, but is also a secret sign pointing forward to a future happening in the New Dispensation, which is, or will be, a fuller disclosure of God's purpose for humanity."[6] As Joachim put it, "According to this pattern, therefore, the persons of the Old Testament and those of the other gaze into each others' faces. City and city, people and people, order and order, war and war, act in the same way. . . . The difference is that those of the Old Testament refer more to the flesh, those of the New more to the spirit, albeit it must be recalled that there were indications of the spirit in the former, reminders of the flesh in the latter."[7] Joachim always tried to cover his bases. This three part view of the past and future led naturally to a search of the Bible for prophecies.

The second book Joachim composed was his explanation of the symbolism in the Book of Revelation. The order in which events in his life occurred after this differs from one biography to another, including the ones written by those who knew Joachim. However, it seems that about 1184 Joachim had an audience with Pope Lucius III. According to some reports, Lucius became convinced that the abbot was a genuine prophet when he explained a Sibylline oracle that had been discovered among the papers of the late Cardinal Matthew of Angers.[8] Joachim explained it, speaking "in rather veiled terms . . . of a future pope who will actively preach to convert the gentiles and the Jews, the imminence of the antichrist and the end of the world."[9] The pope was impressed and gave Joachim permission to write what he would. The next two popes, Urban II and Clement III renewed the abbot's license to write.

Joachim tried to find a place where he could work in peace. He was allowed to resign as abbot and retired to a hermitage that he named Petra-Olei. But visitors still showed up, so he moved again, founding his own monastery at San Giovanni in Fiore in 1189.[10]

But he couldn't run from fame. Nobility and clerics came to see him. In 1191, he was invited to come see Richard I of England. You don't refuse an invitation from the Lionheart as he's setting out on crusade, so Joachim went to meet Richard at Messina. It was there that Joachim told the king in the hearing of many that he believed that the Antichrist has already been born in Rome;[11] he may have derived this from the Sibylline prophecy that he had unraveled for Pope Lucius. One of the lines in it was: "A substantial cloud will start to rain since he who will change the world has been born."[12] Joachim hadn't mentioned this when he gave the first interpretation, but he may have been ruminating on the meaning in the intervening years. He also told Richard that the sixth head of the dragon of the Apocalypse was Saladin, the Turkish leader who had recently retaken Jerusalem. Joachim assured the king that God would "give you victory over your enemies."[13]

Later, in a conversation with the Cistercian abbot Adam of Persigny (which just happened to be overheard and reported), Joachim backtracked a bit, saying that he meant that the Antichrist would be born in the "celestial Babylon" not the earthly Rome. He added that he thought that the current pope, Innocent III, would be the last, implying that the end times were approaching. Joachim even said that he himself might live to see the reign of the Antichrist.[14]

In his study of the Apocalypse, Joachim continued with his theory that all of history, past and present, could be found in the Bible. One Easter as he was spending the night in meditation, "About the middle of the night's silence, as I think, . . . suddenly something of the fullness of this book and of the entire agreement of the Old and New Testaments was perceived by a clarity of understanding in my mind's eye."[15] From then on, the interpretations were easy.

For Joachim, the Book of Revelation contained within itself all the mirrored parallels that were found between the Old and New Testaments. He felt that it told both the past and the future; therefore, he blended the two in his explanation of the book.

His exposition of the dragon with seven heads includes past times of trouble for the Church as well as the troubles to come. For him the first persecutor was Herod, then Nero (a perennial favorite), then the Roman Constantius. Reflecting the fears of his own time, the next three are Muhammad, Mesmoth (thought to have been a king of Babylon), and of course, Saladin, who was not defeated by King Richard, after all.[16]

In Joachim's work, everything is seen as an allegory. He uses animals, plants, geometric forms, and natural forces, anything that he can fit in as symbol, for everything is unified and connected. In this attitude, he was right in step with other medieval thinkers and a large number of modern students of the Book of Revelation

Joachim had his own set of numbers for figuring out the

concordances within the books of the Bible. He counted the number of generations of the Patriarchs of the Old Testament, rather than adding up their ages, as most others did. From this he formed his concept of three "states." The first two were the Testaments; the third had not yet come. I am not going to try to duplicate his logic; however, the numbers three (for the Trinity), two (for the Old and New Testaments), and seven (for the days of creation and lots of other things), are favorites of his. He also was fond of twelve and five and of making diagrams that would help in understanding the connections.

One radical thing that Joachim did was to contradict St. Augustine. He would have been horrified to realize it, for Augustine was the preeminent Church Father. Joachim based his ideas of history on Augustine's work, apparently without realizing that he was negating it. From the early fifth century, when Augustine wrote, until the later Middle Ages, theologians had considered the Apocalypse to be an allegory, not a predictor of the future. The idea of the six ages of the world was well accepted. For Augustine, the sixth age started with the Advent of Christ and would continue until the end of the world. And there was no way of knowing when that would be, although he believed that society would decline until the time of Second Advent.[17]

Joachim's belief that the millennium was yet to come doesn't sound unusual now, but it made many people, especially in the following two hundred years, rethink the idea of the Apocalypse. Joachim explained it:

> *The first epoch was that in which we were under the law, the second when we were under grace, the third when we will live in anticipation of even richer grace. . . . The first epoch was in knowledge, the second in the authority of wisdom, the third in the perfection of understanding. The first in the chains of the slave, the second in the service of a son, the third in freedom. The first in exasperation, the second in action, the third in contemplation. The first in fear,*

the second in faith, the third in love. The first under slave bondage, the second in freedom, the third in friendship. The first the age of children, the second the age of youth, the third that of the old. The first in starlight, the second in moonlight, the third in full daylight. The first in winter, the second in spring, the third in summer. The first the seedling of a plant, the second roses, the third lilies. The first producing grass, the second stalks, the third wheat. The first water, the second wine, the third oil.[18]

When Joachim got on an analogy roll, nothing could stop him. But his point was that the third state or epoch was still to come. He also appeared to believe that this state would be blissful one, which would not need an organized church, for people would understand without the need of an intermediary priest. His idea seems to have been that two new orders of monks would appear to lead the world, perhaps by example, into a perfect society.[19] These new orders were foreshadowed by the appearance of the two witnesses in Revelation. He should have got in trouble for this with the papacy, but it may be that his writing was so convoluted that the authorities missed it.

Joachim seems to have worked out that the new age would begin in 1260, although this may have been an invention or misunderstanding by his followers. He also believed that the emperor at that time, Frederick II, would wreak havoc upon the Church for seventy years.[20]

Since Joachim died on March 30, 1202, at least he wasn't disappointed about the failure of the new age to arrive, although many of his followers were. The friar Salimbene (1221–1290), who wrote a chronicle of his times, was one of those so disillusioned. He was even more upset in that he had believed that the prophet, Merlin, and the Sibyl had agreed with Joachim.[21]

Joachim's influence went far beyond his life and the inaccuracy of his prophecies, however, and in ways that might have horrified him.

JOACHIM'S LEGACY

Joachim was known more by hearsay than from his writing. He was represented as one who could explain obscure prophecies, although he never claimed to be a prophet himself. His views of the Trinity were finally studied and condemned at the Fourth Lateran Council in 1215, although much of the rest of his work was allowed. He left a flourishing monastic order, the Florensians, who were not condemned at the council. These monks were instrumental in getting the work of Joachim to a wider audience.[22]

The condemnation of his ideas on the Trinity gave Joachim a posthumous reputation as a renegade with heretical tendencies. That only increased his allure for some intellectuals of the thirteenth century.

Unfortunately, what intrigued them most were his numeric prophecies. When Roger of Hovedon explained Joachim's work to the English court, they mainly wanted to know, *"Ubi est Antichristus natus? Quando erit hoc?"* (Where was the Antichrist born? When will he appear?).[23] So much for intellectual discussion.

Even the general populace became nervous as 1260 approached. In Italy, the Flagellants, a group who publicly whipped themselves to atone for the sins of the world, were out in force. "The scourging went on for many days in each city; any one abstaining was thought worse than the devil."[24] There was great disappointment when the year passed with no Apocalypse. Many years later, Salimbene was asked about those times. He admitted that he had been a believer in Joachim, "But after the Emperor Frederick died, and 1260 passed, I totally lost faith in that teaching and now I believe only what I see."[25]

However in 1255, just before the prophesied date, there was a wonderful clash at the schools of Paris when a Franciscan, Gerard of Borgo San Donnio, announced that Joachim had foretold the third epoch and that it had already started. The Old and New Testaments were to be replaced by a new book, as shown in Revelation 14:6, "And then I saw another angel flying in mid-heaven with an eternal gospel to proclaim to those who live on the earth—to every nation and tribe and language and people."

A committee sent by the pope studied Joachim's work and Gerard's preface to it.[26] Gerard, a friend of Salimbene, insisted that the Franciscans were one of the orders Joachim had predicted; that Francis of Assisi was the sixth angel of the Apocalypse; and that the eternal gospel, which superseded the other two, had been entrusted to the Franciscans.[27] After reading Joachim's genuine work, the committee made their decision. Joachim was vindicated as not being heretical, but Gerard was locked up for the rest of his life, hopefully with medication.

Not everyone was a follower of Joachim; Salimbene notes that a friend of his "cared as much for Joachim's doctrine as for the fifth wheel of a wagon."[28]

In the years after Joachim's death, other people wrote and circulated treatises under his name. Most of these were much more radical that anything the abbot had written. They took up the theme of the third epoch and elaborated on the evils of the Church, as well as the Holy Roman emperor Frederick II. These manuscripts circulated much farther than Joachim's own work had. Many of them survived into the sixteenth century and were printed both in Latin and translations.

To some, Joachim was a visionary who foresaw the Protestant Reformation, which was, of course, the real third epoch. The Catholic reformer Wycliffe quotes from what he believed were Joachim's prophecies. But, where Joachim clearly stated that the emperor was an Antichrist, Wycliffe's sources were adamant that the evil enemy was the pope.[29]

Joachim, in his afterlife, took on the image of a seer in more areas than for the end of the world. His work was known fairly early but not well understood, if the commentaries on it are anything to go by. By the middle of the thirteenth century, he was a name on a list of prophets from the ancient past.

Joachim's computations and views on the nature of the Trinity were never that much studied. It was his prophecies that made him famous. So, like Merlin, the Sybil, and other ancient prophets, new predictions written under his name eventually eclipsed the reality of his personality and his life's work.

1 E. Randolph Daniel and Joachim of Fiore, "Abbot Joachim of Fiore and the *Liber Concordi Novi et Veteris Testementii,*" *Transactions of the American Philosophical Society,* new ser. 73, no. 8 (1983): xii. Joachim and the Cistercians had a few issues.

2 For more on the Sicilian court, see Pierre Aubé, *Roger II de Sicile* (Paris: Payot, 2001).

3 Delno C. West and Sandra Zimdars-Swartz, *Joachim of Fiore: A Study in Spiritual Perception and History* (Bloomington: Indiana University Press, 1983), 3.

4 West and Zimdars-Schwartz, 4. I am so jealous.

5 Bernard McGuinn, *Visions of the End: Apocalyptic Traditions in the Middle Ages,* 2nd ed. (New York: Columbia University Press, 1998), 126.

6 Marjorie Reeves, "Joachim of Fiore and the Images of the Apocalypse According to St. John," *Journal of the Warburg and Courtauld Institutes* 64 (2001): 281.

7 Joachim of Fiore, *"Book of Figures,"* in *Visions of the End: Apocalyptic Spirituality,* trans. Bernard McGinn, (New York: Paulist Press, 1979). He may have written or revised these books after his meeting with the pope.

8 Marjorie Reeves, *The Influence of Prophecy in the Later Middle Ages: A Study in Joachism* (Oxford: Oxford University Press, 1969), 4–6, discusses this episode. The sources don't say how the prophecy landed among the papers or why the cardinal was interested in it, but the Sibyl had a long life and new oracles are still popping up today.

9 Daniel, xvi.

10 Daniel, xvii.

11 Roger of Howden, *Gesti Henrici II et Richardi I,* ed. William Stubbs (London, 1867), 151–155. For more of Joachim's thoughts on the Antichrist, see the chapter on the Antichrist. You will be aGog.

12 Joachim of Fiore, *Visions of the End: Apocalyptic Spirituality,* trans. Bernard McGinn, (New York: Paulist Press, 1979) 131.

13 Reeves, 7: *"qui dabit tibi de inimiciis tuis victoriam."*

14 Daniel, xx. The eavesdropper was Ralph of Coggleshell, who doesn't say if they had been drinking.

15 Joachim of Fiore, *Expositio in Apocalypsim* in *Visions of the End,* trans. McGinn, 130.

16 Joachim of Fiore, *Concordia,* trans. E. Randolph Daniel, in *Apocalyptic Spirituality,* McGinn, 122.

17 Robert Lerner, "Antichrists and Antichrist," *Speculum* 60, no. 3 (1985): 559.

18 Joachim of Fiore, *Concordia,* in *Joachim of Fiore, trans.* West and Zimdars-Schwartz, 17.

19 The Franciscans and Dominicans claimed to be the new orders, although they were not founded at the times Joachim predicted they would be. See Morton W. Bloomfield and Marjorie E. Reeves, "The Penetration of Joachism into Northern Europe," *Speculum* 29, no. 4 (1954), 774.

20 Lucy Allen Paton, *Les Prophecsies du Merlin*, vol. 3 (New York: Heath, 1924), 186.

21 Salimbene, *Vita* in *Transactions of the Royal Historical Society*, vol. 1, trans. tr. T. L. Kington Oliphant (1872), 268. This interesting tendency for "old" prophecies to appear in time to confirm new ones happens over and over; see the section on 2012.

22 Bloomfield and Reeves, 774.

23 Ibid., 775, my translation.

24 Salimbene, 273.

25 Salimbene: "*Sed postquam mortuus est Fredericus, qui imperator iam fuit, et annus millesimus ducentisimus sexagesimus est elapses, dimisi totaliter istam doctrinam et dispono non credere nisi que videa,*" quoted in Paton, 187, my translation.

26 Salimbene, 103.

27 David Burr, *Olivi's Peaceable Kingdom: A Reading of the Apocalypse Commentary* (Philadelphia: University of Pennsylvania Press, 1993), 17.

28 Salimbene, 262.

29 West and Zimdars-Schwartz, 107.

PART FOUR:

All Hell Breaks Loose

The Renaissance and Reformation

CHAPTER EIGHTEEN

Any Minute Now

The Millennial Renaissance and Enlightenment

> Apocalypses, or books of revelations, were not so numerous:
> but of these too there were several. One of these particularly,
> the apocalypse of St. Paul, I could almost wish that we had,
> since it pretended to relate the ineffable things he saw in the
> third heaven. But it is lost as well as others: and if that which
> we have under the name of St. John had been lost likewise,
> there might have been some madmen the fewer, and
> Christianity would not have suffered so much.
>
> —Henry, Lord Bolingbroke (1678–1751)[1]

People can't decide when the Middle Ages ended. Personally, I think we're still in them. After all, if this is the last age, then any quibbles about eras within it are rather pointless. However, there was one event of the middle of the fourteenth century that changed Europe and the Near East from being basically optimistic about the future to being frightened of it. The Apocalypse was no longer a distant event that one could laugh at in plays and stories. It walked the streets. Representations of the monsters no longer came from visions or nightmares but one's own village.

The plague had come.

In the early twenty-first century, the fear of global pandemics returned with the advent of AIDS, followed by avian and swine flus, with a shadowy worry about *Ebola*. But, while the threat is there, the pandemic hasn't actually happened yet. The response in Europe to the Black Death is a warning of how we might react.

It is not certain that the plague that hit Europe in the 1340s was bubonic plague, as has long been assumed. But that isn't important. People died between sunrise and sunset, along with their families, friends, and whole towns. It didn't spare people who were rich or pious or kind. No one was certain how it was transmitted or what to do to prevent catching it.

In their search for explanations of this disaster, it was natural to think that this disease was the first sign of the end that had been prophesied and ignored for centuries. In the twenty years after the plague, any number of supposedly ancient prophecies circulated, all showing that the plague was a harbinger of the coming of the Antichrist and the time of tribulation.[2]

I would argue that this was the end of the optimistic Middle Ages and the beginning of an age of uncertainty. While the economic recovery of Europe didn't take that long, the emotional recovery never began. The fifteenth century saw much more questioning of the order of society, especially the validity of religious authority. In the past, most heretical movements, with the exception of the Cathars, who established their own church, were intended to reform the papacy, not destroy it. After the plague, the Catholic Church split into squabbling nationalistic factions, which each elected and followed their own pope. This Great Schism lasted from 1378 to 1415. Even after the matter had been settled and there was one agreed upon pope, the papacy had lost a lot of prestige.

Added to the undermining of papal authority was the lessening of importance of the warrior class. Gunpowder had been introduced into Europe, and now it wasn't necessary to spend years developing the skill to fight with sword and lance. Even though most early cannons had a good chance of blowing up as they fired, any idiot could load one and set it off to bring down a castle wall.

Finally, the latter half of the fifteenth century, the Age of Exploration, resulted not only in the discovery of new ways to get to the wealth of India and China but in shocking revelations about the world itself. Each succeeding change in a worldview that had worked for five hundred years caused more people to wonder if this upheaval was what the Bible meant when it warned of a coming Armageddon.

Then the sixteenth century rearranged the face of Europe. There was no longer one unified Christendom in which the secular rulers used the pope as a universal arbiter. Of course, that only ever existed in theory, but it was a nice, tidy theory that helped organize society and let people get on with day-to-day activities. Now the principalities were divided and subdivided, some staying in allegiance to the papacy, others following one or another of the new splinter groups, each of which claimed to be the only true, apostolic Christians. To make things worse, some cities had been taken over by the groups and turned into theocracies. This generally didn't last long, but it was unsettling to have noble rulers replaced by charismatic religious leaders.

Added to that, it seemed there was a whole new continent that had gone unnoticed for millennia. And there were people on it! Wasn't it bad enough that the world order at home was turned upside down?

The discovery of the inhabitants of North and South America rocked the belief system of the Europeans. How did those people get there? Were they really human? Some believed that the natives were the lost tribes of Israel. In that case, their conversion would certainly mean that the end times were near. For some of the Puritan settlers in New England, the conversion of the natives was one of the essential goals intended to hasten the Millennium. Even Christopher Columbus saw his voyages in a millennial light.

The myths about Columbus having to prove the earth was round have been used to show that he was a modern Renaissance man in a dark and superstitious age. Actually, everyone knew the shape of the earth and had for some time. Columbus didn't have to prove it. What he needed to do was demonstrate that he could get to the east by sailing west without starving on the way. In his library, scholars have found marginal notes in Columbus' own hand that show he knew of Roger Bacon's thirteenth-century theories that there were Atlantic islands and maybe even another continent to counterbalance Europe, Africa, and Asia. He may have thought he could use these as stops for provisions.[3]

That he thought he was on a millennial quest is made clear in his writings as well, particularly the notes that make up his "Book of Prophecies."[4] In it, he collected quotations from biblical texts as well as from medieval Christian writers such as Nicholas of Lyra and Joachim of Fiore. In his arguments to convince King Ferdinand and Queen Isabella, Columbus stressed the eschatological importance of the mission, especially for the later voyages.

> *The overall themes of his collection were that an important stage of prophecy had been fulfilled with the discovery of new lands and new peoples and that the eschatological clock was ticking away. The next steps, he tells his monarchs, must soon begin, for the world would last only another century and a half. First the gospel message must be spread on a global scale; second, Jerusalem must be captured by the Spanish monarch and the Holy Temple on Mt. Zion must be rebuilt. These accomplishments would usher in the last days and the biblical chronology relating to them.[5]*

The Franciscan and Dominican missionaries who accompanied the Conquistadors to the new continent were on their own millennial quest. The remaking of the world as Christian and the establishment of the New Jerusalem was a cherished goal to both Protestants and Catholics.

But it wasn't just in Christian Europe that people were considering that these might be the end times. Jewish messianic figures, like Sabbatai Sevi, attracted thousands of followers. In Ismaili Islam, there continued to be those who declared they were the promised Mahdi, who would usher in the end times.

In China, the sixteenth century saw rebellions under the banner of the Pure Land White Lotus, and many expected the Buddhist Mayatreya to appear to lead their armies. And it is possible that The Aztecs were conquered so easily by the Spanish because of a world-changing prophecy in their culture.

At some point, society developed a strong undercurrent of pessimism, especially in Europe. From now on, at any given moment, someone, somewhere would be anticipating the imminent end of the world.

1 Henry St. John Bolingbroke, *The Works of Lord Bolingbroke: With a Life, Prepared Expressly for This Edition, Containing Additional Information Relative to His Personal and Public Character*, vol. 3 (Philadelphia: Carey & Hart, 1841), 477.

2 Robert Lerner, "The Black Death and Western European Eschatological Mentalities," *The American Historical Review* 86, no. 3 (1981): 533–552.

3 Delno C. West and August Kling, *The Libro de las Profecias of Christopher Columbus* (Gainsville: University of Florida Press), 11.

4 Ibid., 99–260. This edition has Latin and Spanish on facing pages to the English translation. Very useful.

5 Ibid., 29.

CHAPTER NINETEEN

The Hussites and Taborites

A Scandal in Bohemia

[Hus] replied that he had neither preached nor wished to
follow the erroneous doctrine of Wyclif or of anyone else,
as Wyclif was neither his father nor a Czech.

—Peter of Mladonovice, "The Examination and Execution of Hus"[1]

The winds of religious change swept all of Europe in the fifteenth century. Bohemia, in what is now the Czech Republic,
was no exception. One of the most influential of the leaders of the
new movements was Jan Hus (c. 1372–1415), a priest and follower of the
English reformer John Wycliffe, despite his denial of this at his trial.
Hus agreed with Wycliffe that the pope and his court in Rome should
not have the final word on matters of dogma unless they changed their
lives and returned to the poverty and humility of the Apostles.[2]

Prague already had a tradition of lay involvement in preaching
the Gospels. In 1402, two wealthy men of the town had established
the Bethlehem Chapel, a building only for preaching, with no Mass
or other sacraments.[3]

When the Church banned all of Wycliffe's writings, Hus was forbidden to preach. But Hus was both a priest and an influential master at the University of Prague. He produced tracts and pamphlets
outlining his interpretations of Wycliffe's work, often in a much less

inflammatory tone. However, his antipapal attitudes did not go unnoticed. In the late spring of 1415, he was summoned to the Council of Constance to be questioned about his beliefs.[4]

The council was held in the cathedral of Constance, in Germany. While the interrogation of Hus was an important matter, the first order of business was to decide which of three claimants was the real pope. The split in the church had occurred in 1378, and while everything was in chaos, heresy had been allowed to flourish. The hierarchy and the secular rulers realized that this was leading to a crisis of authority. In the end, two of the popes were deposed and one resigned. In 1417, a new candidate, Martin V, was given the office.

Hus, who had been imprisoned at a Dominican monastery at Gottlieben to await his trial, was brought before the council on June 5, 1415. He had apparently been promised an open interrogation as well as the freedom to return to Bohemia afterward. However, he wrote to a friend that he wasn't going to be allowed a public forum unless he paid 2000 ducats to "the servants of the antichrist."[5] He also promised his friend that if he did take back his antipapal statements, it would be "only with my mouth, but not from my heart."[6]

He was questioned for several days on his support of Wycliffe's forty-five articles of faith and on his own book, *On the Church*. Hus thought he was being clever by answering that only a pope who "sells benefices, is proud, avaricious or otherwise morally opposed to Christ,"[7] is an antichrist. A good pope would not be. I don't think he was as subtle as he thought.

The council adjourned on the morning of June 7 to watch a solar eclipse and then returned to Hus. The points on which he was questioned were mainly matters of doctrine: on the nature of Christ in the communion Host, if laypeople could have communion in both bread and wine, and whether the sacraments performed by a priest in mortal sin were valid. One question was rather intriguing. The council wanted to know if Hus had said an earthquake that took place during an earlier council in London was a sign that God agreed with Wycliffe.[8]

Hus tried to remain true to his beliefs without admitting to heresy. He also stated that many of the charges against him were due to purposely inaccurate translations of his work. He was happy to explain them. But soon the questions moved to the effects of Hus's preaching. This was the most serious accusation. If Hus not only believed in heresy but also exhorted others to believe, this was basically incitement to riot. The council gave instances of priests being attacked and other cases of civil disobedience that they put down to Hus's influence.[9]

Hus was questioned for several days before the council and assorted dignitaries, including the Holy Roman emperor. He gave enough information to convince most of them that he was indeed a heretic. Scholars are still debating the issue, but they can afford to be objective. The council saw him as a threat. Hus was told to either retract his errors or be burned at the stake. Actually, the council begged him to recant. If he did, they could lock him up somewhere and forget about him, telling his followers that he had admitted that they were right and he was wrong. Hus answered that he couldn't do that because it would be perjury against the truth.[10] So the softer punishment was out.

It was ordered that the writings of Hus be burned first, but oddly, the council didn't stop him from writing letters to his supporters, which still exist. He encouraged them to carry on the fight and expose the iniquities of the Antichrist who was very much in evidence at the council. He also said that if he had erred, it was up to Christ to correct him, not the pope and cardinals. That was heresy in itself.[11]

After a final appeal to recant failed, Hus was brought to the cathedral on July 6, 1415. The charges of which he had been convicted were read out, with some interruptions from the Czech bishops in his defense. He repeated that he had been falsely accused and that he relied on the authority of the Bible to prove him right. Hus was formally thrown out of the priesthood and turned over to secular authorities to face the flames.[12]

Hus was brought to a public square and chained to a stake. The wood was stacked around him up to his chin. The fire was lit and, a few moments later, he was choked to death by the smoke.[13]

That was the end of Jan Hus but only the beginning of the Hussite movement.

The men at the Council of Constance knew that executing Hus would provide a martyr to the cause. This was one reason why they weren't that eager to burn him. They had no idea what their decision would unleash.

Heresy was nothing new in Bohemia or in the rest of Europe. With the glaring exception of the Cathars who, like the Zoroastrians, believed in a good and an evil god, most Christian heresies were basically attempts to reform the church and return to the "pure Christianity" of the First Christians. Few of them advocated a radical change in the foundations of society; even fewer were millennial or apocalyptic in the way that the movements of the seventeenth through the twentieth centuries were.

But the world was changing. The first serious arrival of the Black Death, in the 1340s, had traumatized Europe. The Great Schism in the church weakened the authority of the popes. And, long before the printing press, the Bible had been translated from Latin into the languages spoken in the streets. More laypeople outside of the nobility were able to read, and the first book they attempted was usually the Bible. The second thing they did was read it to others.

One sect, the Waldensians, had been founded in the twelfth century on the premise that everyone should read the Bible and decide the truth for themselves. Despite two centuries of persecution, they continued to exist and even spread.[14] Many have seen Waldensian influences in the Hussite movement.

After the martyrdom of Hus, his colleagues at the University of Prague and his followers throughout Bohemia continued and expanded upon his teaching. Soon Prague was a Hussite center. The local authorities were in sympathy with the movement, and for a time, it prospered.

The Hussite leaders established four articles of faith: communion with bread and wine for both priests and parishioners, the confiscation of secular property from priests and monks, the punishment of public sin, and the free preaching of the word of God.[15] This last meant that one didn't need to be a priest or have a license to preach.

The main group of Hussites was made up of educated university men or upper nobility. These people wanted church reform but within the system. But allowing free speech meant that all sorts of ideas about religion could be in the air and in the marketplace and taverns, not just castles and classrooms. The Hussites spawned a "radical left" that held both political and religious views. Putting these together created a gateway to revolution.

The most radical splinter group became known as the Taborites. They held their services on hilltops in imitation of the hill from which Jesus ascended into heaven. A fourth-century tradition said that this place was called Mount Tabor.[16] Soon the Hussites became two distinct sects.

The Hussites had tossed around the word *Antichrist* pretty much the way most medieval reformers did. It was anyone who actively worked against the Christian spirit. The Taborites took the term much more seriously. There was only one antichrist for them and they were determined to identify and destroy him. For the first time in Europe since the fall of Rome an apocalyptic Christian sect turned into a political revolutionary movement.[17]

Part of this was the fault of the Czech Catholic rulers, especially the new king, Sigismund. After negotiating with the moderate Hussites in the autumn of 1419, he called for a crusade to suppress them entirely. The scholars in Prague, who had been preaching nonviolent resistance, felt forced to agree that taking up arms in the defense of the truth is an acceptable act.

In 1419, a Taborite prophecy declared that the Second Coming would happen at some time during Carnival season—that is, between February 10 and 14 of 1420. The "elect" were to go to one of five cities in Bohemia to await the end and to be safe during the breakdown in society caused by the biblical tribulations. The anticipation of the event was intense. They seem to have imagined a sort of opposite to the Rapture. The preacher Koranda told the Taborites, "One day we'll get up and find all the others lying dead with their noses sticking up in the air."[18]

When the date passed without incident, there must have been many who drifted from the faith and back to the less-radical Hussite beliefs. But enough stayed that it was possible to form Taborite cities. King Sigismund laid siege to them and eventually caused the Taborites to flee. Finally they established a city of their own, which they named Tabor (of course). It was well fortified, and there, in March 1420, they set up their society, still hoping that Christ would arrive soon.[19]

By September 1420, the Taborites were beginning to wonder if Christ was going to show up at all. At this point, their leaders realized that they had been mistaken. Christ had come, but "like a thief in the night." The signs were all around. The Millennium had begun, and it was up to all the Taborites to help cleanse the earth. "The Taborites in this time of punishment are angels. . . . [T]hey are an army sent by God through the whole world to remove all scandals from the kingdom of Christ, which is the Church Militant, and to expel the evil ones from the midst of the just and to take vengeance . . . on the nations of the enemies of the Law of Christ and against their cities, villages and fortified places."[20]

This free pass to slaughter and destroy was taken up by the Taborites with frightening ferocity. They went forth from their cities, killing without mercy or even bothering to find out the religious views of the victims. They also burned towns and looted provisions for their common storehouse. The violence was all the more dreadful because, like the crusaders who took Jerusalem in 1096, they were on a mission from God; therefore, in their minds all their actions were sanctioned.

The Taborite armies were promised by their leaders that soon the world would be ready for Christ to come in all His glory. The saints and martyrs would rise, "and this would happen soon, in a few years, so that some of us now living would see the saints of God resurgent and among them Master John Hus."[21]

Once this occurred, the Taborites would be able to turn their bloody swords into plowshares and live in a world without sin or pain or even death.

The violence caused a crusade to be established against the Hussites and Taborites, strongly supported by King Sigismund, who still hadn't been able to be formally crowned due to political disputes. But after nearly fifteen years of fighting, the crusade hadn't yet succeeded, mostly due to the strength of the Taborite armies and the unwillingness of the Hussites to fight. In 1436, an agreement was made between the moderate Hussites and the orthodox Catholic forces. The Hussites were allowed to take communion as both bread and wine in their churches. After that, the two groups combined forces and finally defeated the Taborites.[22]

One sect of the Hussites, under the leadership of Peter Chelchiký, developed a new theology of personal salvation. Chelchiký preached equality, pacifism, the choosing of priests for their moral character, the "taking up of the cross" and living a life in imitation of Christ. He wrote against the excesses of the Taborites in 1421. His teachings became the basis of *Unitas Fratres* (Unity of the Brethren). In 1467 they met and chose their own priests by lot, unconnected with the Catholic Church.[23]

The Church of the Brethren is still active today.

The Hussites were not the only group that attempted to establish theocratic city governments. Geneva under John Calvin is the classic example. One of the many other Protestant groups of the sixteenth century was that of the Anabaptists. For outsiders, their main points of difference with other Protestants were their insistence on adult, rather than infant, baptism and their opposition to tithes, something they shared with English Puritans.

The Anabaptists began in Germany as a sort of second wave of Protestantism. They weren't rebelling against the Catholic Church but that of the Calvinist Zwingli.[24] From 1533 to 1535, the Anabaptists established a Kingdom of Christ in the city of Münster, before they were defeated by secular military forces.

It was only when the new sects converted the rulers of principalities that Protestantism became a long-lasting state religion, as with the success of Lutherans in Germany and Scandinavia. The English took somewhat longer to come to terms with being a quasi-Protestant country and decided to do away with the monarchy. Setting up a government without a king was harder than it looked, as Oliver Cromwell and the Fifth Monarchy Men discovered.

1 Edward Peters, ed., *Heresy and Authority in Medieval Europe* (Philadelphia: University of Pennsylvania Press, 1980), 292.

2 Howard Kaminsky, *A History of the Hussite Revolution* (Berkeley: University of California Press, 1967), w5–40.

3 J. K. Zeman, "Restitution and Dissent in the Late Medieval Revival Movements," *Journal of the American Academy of Religion* 44, no.1 (1976): 11.

4 Bernard McGinn, *Visions of the End: Apocalyptic Traditions in the Middle Ages* (New York: Columbia University Press, 1979), 259.

5 Charles-Joseph Hefele and H. Leclercq, *Histoire des Conciles Tome VII Première Parti.* (Paris: Letouzey et Ane, 1916), 253.

6 Ibid., 258.

7 McGinn, 263.

8 Ibid., 265.

9 Ibid.

10 Ibid., 299.

11 Ibid., 305–306.

12 Ibid., 329. The Church was not allowed to impose a death sentence, and priests could not be executed by the civil authorities; thus Hus had to be made a layman again, and the council had to give him to laypeople to be killed. It was just a formality.

13 Ibid., 331.

14 Peters, 139–164.

15 Peter Brock, Cornelis H. Van Schooneveld, *The Political and Social Doctrines of the Unity of Czech Brethren in the Fifteenth and Early Sixteenth Centuries* (The Hague: Mouton, 1957), 12.

16 Howard Kaminsky, "Chiliasm and the Hussite Revolution," *Church History* 26, no. 1 (1957): 44, n. 3.

17 McGinn, 263.

18 Quoted in Kaminsky, *A History of the Hussite Revolution*, 330. The preacher doesn't say what they'll do with all the bodies, but he implies that anyone who wants can get a new house.

19 Ibid., 329–359.

20 Quoted in ibid., 346.

21 Quoted in ibid., 348.

22 Richard Kieckhefer, *Repression of Heresy in Medieval Germany* (Liverpool: Liverpool University Press, 1979), 84–86.

23 Zeman, 21–24.

24 James M. Stayer, *The German Peasant's War and the Anabaptist Community of Goods* (Montreal: McGill-Queens University Press, 1994), 63.

CHAPTER TWENTY

Savonarola and Decadent Florence

I never disclosed the manner and great number of the visions and many other revelations I had. . . . Now necessity compels me to write down the coming events I publicly preached about.

—Savonarola, "The Compendium of Revelations"[1]

At the height of the Renaissance, the city of Florence was home to some of the finest artists in the world. Under the rule of Lorenzo de Medici, known as Lorenzo the Magnificent, Leonardo da Vinci, Botticelli, Verrochio, and Michelangelo lived and worked in Florence. It was also, at the end of the fifteenth century, a city rife with corruption and rapidly facing bankruptcy. Into this contradiction walked a Dominican monk with a gift for preaching. His name was Giralamo Savonarola. If the portraits of him are near to accuracy, he was tall and thin with penetrating eyes and a nose one could hang umbrellas on.

Born in the town of Ferrara in 1452, Savonarola seems to have been concerned about sin and the end of the world from his youth. In 1472, even before he became a monk, he wrote a poem in which he lamented that the world was upside down, Rome had abandoned its moral leadership, and the end was coming.[2] Of course, at twenty, many people feel this way, but Giralamo didn't grow out of his gloom.

Savonarola. *Erich Lessing / Art Resource, New York*

After becoming a monk, he was sent to Florence from 1482 to 1486 before going on to San Gimignao, where he began his apocalyptic preaching career. One of his earliest sermons had for its subject: "Do penance, for the Kingdom of God is at hand."[3]

In 1490, Lorenzo di Medici called Savonarola back to Florence and installed him as abbot of the Medici monastery of San Marco. As abbot, Savonarola encouraged the monks to create works of sculpture, paintings, and architecture. He even hired Sienese nuns to illuminate manuscripts.[4] Despite his insistence on penance and austerity before the arrival of the Apocalypse, Savonarola had an appreciation for the importance of art that fit in with the times.

His preaching over the next few years continued to dwell on the need for penance. He may have coined the phrase *bonfire of the vanities*, when, in February 1497, he convinced many Florentines to burn their wigs and other finery in an orgy of renunciation. His visions of the end were modeled on those of Joachim of Fiore but added to from visions of his own, which he was understandably reluctant to tell his followers about, at least at first.

When the French king Charles VIII invaded Italy in 1494, many in France and Italy hoped that he was actually the reincarnation of his distant ancestor Charlemagne, making his promised return as the New World emperor.[5] Savonarola at first believed that Charles was more of an Antichrist, or at least his helper, on his way to punish sinful Florentines. He changed his mind when Charles withdrew from Florence. "The Florentines began to see themselves and their city as divinely chosen to be a new elect to lead the world to salvation."[6]

This view was helped considerably by Savonarola. During the crisis of the French invasion, Lorenzo's son, Piero de Medici, had panicked and given King Charles two Florentine towns. He and his brothers then fled the city, and when they tried to return, they were blocked by angry citizens. At the same time, Savonarola was part of a city delegation to Charles and he managed to convince the king that the French and the Florentines should be allies. When he returned to Florence, he became the de facto leader of the city. All of his sermons of coming disaster were fresh in the minds of the Florentines. They recognized Savonarola as a prophet as well as a diplomat. In the ensuing weeks, Savonarola moved from believing in an imminent apocalypse. Instead he began to think that the New Jerusalem could be established in Florence with the Millennium to follow.

Savonarola told the Florentines that they were a chosen city, something they already may have believed. In a sermon from December 1494, he preached, "God has everywhere prepared a great scourge, nevertheless, on the other hand, he loves you, . . . Mercy and Justice have come together in the city of Florence."[7]

A republic was established in Florence, something Savonarola had not preached or expected but which he welcomed.[8] Like the later Fifth Monarchists, he thought that there should be no king but Christ. In a more earthly vein, he suggested that they form a government on the Venetian pattern, with checks and balances and a rotating leadership.[9]

Savonarola's visions became more spectacular, as is seen in the *Compendium of Revelations*, which he wrote to defend himself from the accusations of heresy that had reached Pope Alexander. The work is in the form of a dream vision, a prophetic literary form of great antiquity. In this dream, after several debates with the Tempter, in which he explains his own actions and that of Florence, Savonarola arrives in heaven. There he ascends through the nine choirs of angels to the throne of the Virgin Mary and announces that he is "the legate of the Florentines to the throne of the Queen of Heaven." He begs her to ask God to grant the people of Florence just rulers and the ability to live according to the Divine Laws. Jesus then approaches and gives Savonarola a ruby that symbolizes his Passion, "So that mercy and grace might be given to the people of Florence."[10]

With that sort of patronage, it would be hard for anyone to contradict Savonarola.

In one area, however, the prophetic reformer went too far for even the radical Florentines. In a sermon made at the height of his influence, on March 18, 1496, Savonarola suggested that women be allowed to decide reforms that they would be affected by. Within a few days, he was convinced to make a retraction and nothing more was heard of the plan.[11]

He cautioned the people of Florence that the Fifth Age, of the Antichrist and conversion, was beginning. He predicted the conversion of the Turks within the next few years. He also hoped for the Joachite coming of the Angelic Pope who would renew the corrupt Church of Rome. Now, Pope Alexander VI was, among many other things, the father of Cesare and Lucrezia Borgia. While I think that many of the stories about his orgies at the Vatican and incest with Lucrezia are probably greatly exaggerated, Alexander certainly used the papacy as a private fief, handing out property to his family and having his enemies mysteriously vanish. Savonarola, who had supported Alexander's strongest adversary, the French king, and had preached against the excesses of Rome, soon arrived at the top of the papal hit list.

The cynic and admirer of Cesare Borgia, Machiavelli, wrote that he thought Savonarola a charlatan. Of course, Machiavelli was a friend of the now-exiled Medici family.[12] But he had a number of other problems with the reformer. Some had to do with Savonarola's ideas of the running of a Christian state in Florence and the fact that Machiavelli had lost a seat on the city council to a supporter of Savonarola. Another matter that offended Machiavelli was Savonarola's determination to wipe out homosexual behavior. While not gay himself, Machiavelli saw nothing wrong with being so and felt that Savonarola was intruding into people's private lives.[13] It is not surprising that Savonarola was homophobic; toleration in any form was not part of his Christian city. He also called for the expulsion of prostitutes and Jews from Florence.[14]

Savonarola had his defenders, too, among them the writer Pico della Mirandola. The first printing press had appeared in Italy ten years before and was put to good use in what became a war of pamphlets between supporters of the pope and those of Savonarola.

But the issue boiled down to one inescapable fact. Pope Alexander had ordered Savonarola to come to Rome and answer his accusers. The preacher decided that this would not be a good career move. Instead, he had sent the pope a pamphlet. Because Savonarola was a Dominican friar, his disobedience was grounds for excommunication. Added to this was his "preaching of false doctrine." This was enough of an excuse for Alexander. On May 13, 1497, the pope declared Savonarola no longer among the community of Christians.[15]

This put the citizens of Florence into a serious quandary. They could either rally around Savonarola and risk being condemned with him or they could turn their backs on their prophet. Some in Florence were already disillusioned and glad of a reason to back out, but many of his devoted followers continued to protest his innocence with another round of pamphleteering. It was pointed out in these that Alexander had bought the office of pope, something widely known but politely not mentioned. This opened another can of worms, the longstanding debate about whether sinful clerics could perform valid sacraments.[16]

In February 1498 Savonarola defied the papal ban on preaching. After several weeks of tension, it was decided that he would undergo the ordeal by fire on April 7, 1498, to prove the righteousness of his teaching. He apparently forgot the appointment. His nonappearance was seen as an admission of guilt and the next day the Monastery of San Marco was raided by supporters of the pope. Savonarola and two of his staunchest followers were arrested, tried and, on May 23, hanged and their bodies burned. Worried that his followers would claim the ashes as relics, the authorities had the remains thrown into the Arno River.[17]

Perhaps the Florentines would have protected Savonarola longer if he had been less strict and kept the brothels open. It was said that they reopened shortly after his execution and hymns of praise were heard coming from grateful patrons as they entered the houses.[18]

But the impact Savonarola had on Florence and on the increasingly vocal dissidents in Europe could not be washed away as easily as his remains. If hymns were sung in derision, many more were hummed quietly in remembrance of the man who was now a martyr.

The Republic of Florence lasted another twenty years before the Medicis returned. If it wasn't a New Jerusalem, it at least had learned that princes weren't absolutely necessary to government.

One of the most long-lasting repercussions of the debate over Savonarola was the realization of the power of the press. Savonarola was especially canny in his use of the medium. His pamphlets, written in Latin, traveled all over Europe. They were embellished with woodcuts of the prophet preaching, chatting with nuns, and bringing down the Apocalypse on unbelievers. They were reprinted long after his ashes had floated out to sea and many still exist, as do printed copies of his sermons. The next century would see the blossoming of the seed planted in Florence by Savonarola and many more attempts to create a City of God on earth.

One of the most intriguing aftereffects of the life of Savonarola is that, despite his fight with the pope, some Catholics considered him a martyr, too. Even the saints Catarina de' Ricci and Philip Neri "revered him as a martyr and master of the contemplative life."[19] There is even today a group lobbying for his canonization.[20]

In looking at later groups that tried to create a New Jerusalem, it might be worth remembering the example of Savonarola and Florence. His preaching began by assuming that the end of the world would be any day. His attitude changed with his success; he began to hope that the world could change rather than be destroyed. He learned the hard way that Florence wasn't ready for perfection. The unanswerable question is what would have happened if all of Florence had stood with him? Would they have fought to the death or come to a compromise that would have allowed them to live as they liked? Would they have committed mass suicide, like some other religious groups, despite the fact that it was a mortal sin?

There is a subtle tipping point in a movement after which there is no turning back. The Florentines tipped toward their old lives. Many other followers of the prophets chronicled in this book went the other way.

---

1 Bernard McGinn, trans. and ed., *Apocalyptic Spirituality* (New York: Paulist Press, 1979), 192.

2 Donald Weinstein, "Savonarola, Florence and the Millenarian Tradition," *Church History* 27, no. 4 (1958): 293.

3 Loc. cit.

4 A. Hayett Mayor, "Renaissance Pamphleteers, Savonarola and Luther," *The Metropolitan Museum of Art Bulletin* new ser. 6, no. 2 (1947): 67.

5 This prophecy had been invented for Charles VI a hundred years before, but since it didn't come true, there was no point in wasting it, and the prophecy was recast for Charles VIII. See McGinn, 187.

6 Jack Fruchtman Jr. "The Apocalyptic Politics of Richard Price and Joseph Priestly: A Study in Late Eighteenth-Century English Republican Millennialism," *Transactions of the American Philosophical Society* new ser. 73, no. 4 (1983): 10.

7 Quoted in Rob Hatfield, "Botticelli's Mystical Nativity, Savonarola and the Millennium," *Journal of the Warburg and Courtauld Institutes* 58 (1995): 83.

8 Donald Weinstein, "The Savonarola Movement in Florence," in *Millennial Dreams in Action*, ed. Sylvia L. Thrupp (New York: Schocken, 1970), 188.

9 Weinstein, 297.

10 Savonarola, trans. McGinn, 262–264. Savonarola's love of art and beauty is evident in the lush way he describes all the levels of heaven.

11 Lorenzo Polizzoto, "When Saints Fall Out: Women and the Savonarolan Reform in Early Sixteenth Century Florence," *Renaissance Quarterly* 46, no. 3 (1993).

12 John M. Najemy, "Machiavelli and the Medici, the Lessons of Florentine History," *Renaissance Quarterly* 35, no.4 (1982): 52–53. His later relations with the Medici family went downhill for a time. They imprisoned and tortured him, but later they made up.

13 Marcia Colish, "Republicanism, Religion and Machiavelli's Savonarolan Moment," *Journal of the History of Ideas* 60, no. 4 (1999): 613.

14 Lorenzo Polizzoto, *The Elect Nation: The Savonarola Movement in Florence 1494–1545* (Oxford: Oxford University Press, 1992): 29.

15 Ibid., 87.

16 Ibid., 92. This debate would be at the heart of many of the Protestant movements just around the corner. It's possible that Martin Luther read some of the Latin polemics put out by the pro-Savonarola party.

17 Ibid., 95.

18 Patrick Macey, "The Lauda and the Cult of Savonarola," *Renaissance Quarterly* 45, no. 3 (1992), 440.

19 Donald Weinstein, "Hagiography, Demonology and Biography: Savonarola Studies Today," *Journal of Modern History*, 63, no. 3 (1991), 484.

20 Ibid., 487.

CHAPTER TWENTY-ONE

Nostradamus

The Antichrist will soon annihilate Troy,
His war of blood will last twenty-seven years,
The dead heretics, captives, exiles,
Blood, human corpses, reddened water, pockmarked earth.

—Nostradamus, Century VIII, Quatrain 77[1]

The French Provençal doctor and astrologer, Michel de Nostredame, is far more famous today than he was in his lifetime. He was born December 14, 1503, in the village of St. Remy.[2] The sixteenth century was one, like our own, in which the patterns of society were being turned upside down. As Michel was growing up, the Protestant Reformation began; whole countries turned from belief in the doctrines of the Roman Catholic Church; and a new populated continent was explored, destroying the geography that the Western world had believed in for millennia. It's not surprising that astrology and divination were practiced by thousands and trusted by most of society.

The family Nostredame is supposed to have been "new Christians," recently converted from Judaism. However, it appears from records in Provence that only one of his grandfathers was a convert.[3] Peyrot de Nostredame was born Guy Gassonet, a Jew who moved to Avignon in the 1400s.[4] He was baptized and changed his name to Nostredame. He married a Christian woman named Blanche. Nostradamus made no secret of his grandfather's conversion, and apart from occasional slurs by critics, no one seems to have cared.

Peyrot and his son, Jaume, were not physicians, as Michel Nostradamus said in his autobiographical writing; they were grain merchants. Jaume moved from Avignon to the town of St. Remy, where he married Renée, the granddaughter of a doctor who was also a tax collector.[5] Jaume became a notary in St. Remy and was well respected there. These were Michel's parents.

Provence had a number of Jewish families. Narbonne, on the edge of the Pyrenees, had had a large Jewish population since Roman times.[6] However, while many commentators have assumed Nostradamus's connection to the Jewish community as fact and even tried to fit his prophecies into a kabbalistic tradition, it seems unlikely. For one reason, there is no evidence that Nostradamus read Hebrew, which is essential to any study of the Kabbalah. For another, both Michel's brother, Jehan, and Michel Nostradamus' son César were very strong Catholics. César repeated the myths of the blood libel and of Jews poisoning wells in his historical work.[7] I don't think that's the sort of thing a crypto-Jew in fear of being exposed would remind people of.

According to Nostradamus, he was most influenced in his astrological pursuits by his great-grandfather Jean de Saint-Rémy. Jean may have lived with his grandchildren. He turned his house over to Jaume with the condition that he be allowed to live in it until his death. Nostradamus wrote many years later that he was still using a planisphere left to him by his great-grandfather to help in casting horoscopes.[8]

In the early 1520s, Nostradamus is said to have traveled in France and Italy and, apparently, worked as a pharmacist. His first book was not a list of prophecies but one of recipes for medicines and herbal jams.[9]

In October 1529 Michel commenced the study of medicine at the University of Montpellier, the best in France for that discipline.[10] Around 1533, Michel wrote a letter to Julius Cesar Scaliger, a renowned physician, poet, and philosopher. Scaliger invited the young doctor to come stay with him at his home in Agen. Nostradamus moved to

Agen, which is where he met and married his wife. He set up a medical practice and settled into a heady life of intellectual discussion with some of the greatest and rather radical scholars in the area.[11]

In 1538, the Inquisition came to Agen. Nostradamus was called before it but took the opportunity for a vacation in Bordeaux. No one bothered to go after him. They were really interested in Scaliger.[12]

Several authors and talking heads have stated that Michel, as a crypto-Jew, lived in terror of the Inquisition. These opinions, often cited as fact, come from a desire on the part of Nostradamus believers to think that as someone of Jewish heritage he had some secret kabbalistic wisdom that helped him see the future. As I said earlier, it's not likely that he did. The other problem with this idea is that the people who are making these claims don't understand the primary concerns of the Church at that time. The Inquisition in sixteenth-century Provence wasn't that interested in Jews. There was a more immediate threat to their religion that was consuming them.

The inquisitor sent to Agen to see Scaliger and his friends was Louis de Rochette. Upon his arrival, Rochette gave a long sermon in which he encouraged the citizens to turn in any friends who might have been spouting heresy or reading banned books. Placards were also put up, but apparently torn down in the middle of the night by "a band of armed men, dressed in black."[13] Still, there are always some people who love accusing their neighbors of crimes so, thanks to them, invitations were sent out by the Inquisition to many of the intelligentsia of Agen.

Scaliger and his circle were accused of reading books, not of magic and divination or Jewish mysticism, but those written by modern, subversive, radical authors. Among those listed were Calvin, Erasmus, Luther, and Zwingli. These were the men whose ideas had Catholics in an uproar. Nostradamus's friends were accused of denying that Purgatory existed and refusing to kneel for Communion but preferring to take the Host while standing, along with other heretical activities. Nostradamus and his friends were not suspected of being closet Jews but closet Protestants.[14] This is well documented and makes much more sense in the religious climate of the 1530s in France.

Scaliger was able to talk his way out of the charges, and when Nostradamus came back to Agen, everything had blown over. No one was waiting to arrest him.

It is at about this time that Nostradamus's wife and children died. He married when he was about twenty-four, but a few years later his wife and both his children died. It may have been from illness or accident. Some biographers have said that they died in a plague while Michel was traveling to treat others suffering from the same disease. However, they seem to be confusing that time with 1546, when he was living in Aix-en-Provence, working as a doctor for the city.[15]

He left Agen, probably because it was too painful to live in a place full of memories. He always revered Scaliger, naming the eldest son of his second marriage after the doctor.

He went to Aix-en-Provence, where in 1546 he did heroic work during a recurrence of the Black Death. The city gave him a good pension for the work he had done treating plague victims, and it was only after he left Aix that he married again. His wife was named Anna, but her last name is given several different spellings. It may have been Ponce or Poncet. Neither is it certain how many children they had. One son, André, became a monk. Another, Charles, was a poet. The best known is his son César, who wrote a biography of his father and painted his portrait. There were at least three daughters, Madeleine, Anne, and Diane. The first two married well and had children. Diane remained unmarried. Several of the children lived well into their seventies, perhaps inheriting René's longevity genes.[16]

In the late 1540s Nostradamus got the idea of publishing a yearly almanac that included astrological predictions, tips for when to plant, the phases of the moon, and what the weather would be like. The first one came out in 1550 and was a hit. He published an almanac every year after that. They contained many general prophecies.

Some time in the 1550s Nostradamus began to compose more

complicated prophetic quatrains. He says that he burned the first ones for fear that world leaders would use them to grab power.[17] But he finally decided to publish them as a group in 1555. In his dedication to King Henri II of France, he mentions that he has figured March 14, 1557, as the start of the seventh millennium. Therefore, since the enemies of Christ and his church are about to be assailed, he feels that he must let his revelations be known in order to warn the world.[18]

Nostradamus also wrote a long dedication/explanation/warning to his son César in which he rambles on quite a bit about prophecy not being for the unenlightened and how he hopes César will find a better profession than his since Nostradamus knows the gift of prophecy will not be passed on to his descendants. He reiterates that astrology is a serious study. He also tells his son that no one in the Church forbade him to publish, but he's going to make the predictions a little murky so that they can be understood only after the fact, just in case.

> *From all which, my son, you can easily comprehend, notwithstanding your tender brain, the things that are to happen can be foretold by nocturnal and celestial lights, which are natural, coupled to a spirit of prophecy,—not that I would assume the name or efficacy of a prophet, but, by revealed inspiration, as a mortal man the senses place me no farther from heaven than the feet are from the earth.*[19]

I should add that, by "tender brain" Michel didn't think César was stupid; the boy was only about five months old when this was written.

Nostradamus's book of prophecies, containing the first "century," or one hundred quatrains, was even more popular than his almanacs. France was eager for predictions of the future, especially if they contained doom for England and the Protestant countries, which many of them did.

Intellectuals of the day didn't think much of the new prophet.

Montaigne made fun of him. And his old mentor, Scaliger, wrote, "How can Nostradamus predict the future when he doesn't know what is going on at the present time?" and wondered why anyone would credit the "meaningless language of that impure idiot."[20] I think that's rather rough, but Scaliger wasn't known for his tact, and he probably suspected that Nostradamus was raking in the francs with his books.

Another early critic was fellow astrologer Pierre Vidal, who considered Nostradamus's technique sloppy and a disgrace to the profession.[21]

However, his almanacs and book of prophecies were becoming more and more popular. Letters began to come in begging him to answer questions about the future as well as help find lost articles and buried treasure. The almanacs were translated into English and read at the court of Queen Elizabeth.[22]

He certainly caught the attention of the court of France. Queen Catherine de Medici, the wife of Henri II, was an avid consulter of seers as well as being adept at astrology in her own right.[23] She was intrigued by Nostradamus's prophecies and extended an invitation to him to visit her court. Catherine already kept several astrologers on her payroll, the most famous being the three Ruggiari brothers, Bazile, Laurent, and Cosime, who supposedly predicted her marriage and children when she was still a young woman in Florence.[24] Nostradamus was a nice addition to the group, although he stayed with the court only a short time. The patronage of the king and queen added to his fame, especially after a quatrain from the first book was taken to have predicted the death of King Henri in 1557 in a tournament (century I, quatrain 35). Of course, several other quatrains from the same century seem to predict victory and long life to the king, but those probably meant some other king.

He returned to his home, now in the town of Salon, and continued to produce prophecies. In 1563, the queen and her son visited Nostradamus, a singular honor. Nostradamus died in 1566. His

Catherine de Medici consulting Nostradamus to learn her children's fate. 17th CE Location: Bibliotheque Nationale, Paris, France. *Snark / Art Resource, NY*

prophecies are more popular now than ever. However, even before his death, there were books being printed by impostors who wrote their own prophecies, attributing them to Nostradamus. After he died, this became a torrent that continues to this day. In the mid-1600s, enemies of Cardinal Mazarin published a book of prophecies, many of which were actually by Nostradamus, but that included two forgeries foretelling the fall of the Cardinal.[25]

Nostradamus has never completely lost his popularity. He has been credited with predicting the French Revolution, the rise of Napoleon and Hitler, and the fall of the Twin Towers in New York City. I think this may be due to the vague nature of the quatrains. When something happens, it's not difficult to find one that can be twisted to suit the event.

In order to get into the spirit of interpreting the prophecies, I picked one at random from the almanacs. This is from October 1555.

Venus Neptune poursuiura l'entreprise,
Serrez pensifs, trouble les opposans
Classe en Adrie, citez vers la Tamise
Le quart bruit blesse de nuict de reposans.[26]

Now, this is not all that clear for several reasons. For one thing, words are left out. The first line is: "Venus Neptune will pursue the undertaking." That might be astrological, saying that Venus and Neptune will give one success, but the verb is singular, so it might be that Venus Neptune is someone's name, and the reader should go to her for a loan. The next line is: "You will be thoughtful (masculine) trouble the opponents." But here *trouble* isn't a verb. So, either there is a verb missing or *serrez* is meant to go with trouble, except then it should be troubler. But, if it is, there is still a problem because a preposition is also missing. Will you be trouble to the opponents or will they be trouble to you?

You can see the usefulness of vagueness to a prophet.

The next line is interesting because it contains words that Nostradamus uses several times, causing debate among later expositors. "*Classe en Adrie.*" I read this as "A tumult in Adrie." *Classe* has been translated as a Greek or Latin word by some Nostradamus enthusiasts, but it's perfectly good Old French and means "tumult" or "trumpet blast," which could be a tumult as well or even a "trumpet blast to call the people together."[27] *Adrie* is a bit trickier. It could well be "Adriatic" or "Hadrian." But the rest of the line is "a city near the Thames," so I'm guessing that he was thinking of England, France's long-time enemy. Some have decided that it means Hadrian, who is Adolph Hitler, of course (?). You decide.

The fourth line seems to complement the one before it. "The quarter noise wounds the night of the sleeping ones." So everyone is wakened by a tumult or trumpet or warning siren in the night. Say! I'll bet it refers to the Blitz in World War II. Or the Zeppelins in World War I, or the bombers over Baghdad, or maybe it's a warning of an attack to come. I think I'm catching on to this interpretation thing!

Or it could just mean that people will be startled by a sound in the night. It's a pretty safe bet that this will happen at some point in history.

I think it's fun try to find a meaning in mysterious verses, especially if it means wordplay in several languages, but I don't get out much.

The real question is, did Nostradamus predict the end of the world?

Yes.

And sort of.

In the preface to his first century, Nostradamus tells his son that the work "comprises prophesies from today to the year 3797."[28] Well, that's a relief. However, just a few paragraphs later, he says that the end will come in 1999, at the end of a war that will begin in 1975. He repeats the former date in Century 10, Quatrain 72:

> L'an mil neuf cens nonante neuf sept mois,
> Du ciel viendra un grand Roy d'effrayeur:
> Resusciter le grand Roy d'Angolmois,
> Avant apres Mars regner par bon heur.

> The year one thousand nine hundred nine seven months,
> A great king of terror will come from the sky:
> To revive the great king of the Angols,*
> Before after Mars to reign through luck (or happiness).

There has been a lot of debate about the word *Angolmois*. In Nostradamus's time it probably meant the people of Angola, which was known through trade. Some have suggested that it is a sort of pig-Latin for Mongols "Angol-mois." I have no idea what Nostradamus had in mind, but he does seem to indicate a great upheaval of some sort in 1999.

So, according to Nostradamus, we either have over a thousand years to the end or it already happened and no one noticed.

But nowhere in the quatrains is there even a hint that Nostradamus thought the world would end in 2012.

1 My translation.

2 Charles A. Ward, *The Oracles of Nostradamus* (London: Leadenhall Press, 1891), n.p.

3 This biography is based on the work of Edgar Leroy in 1972. This book is almost impossible to find, showing that accuracy is not always rewarded. I have compiled this from quotes of his work in other sources. Not my favorite way of doing research.

4 Another, secondary source, says that his name was Abraham Solomon. Cf. Adolf Kober, "Jewish Converts in Provence from the Sixteenth to the Eighteenth Century," *Jewish Social Studies* 6, no. 4 (1944): 363. Kober cited general histories of Provence that are not completely reliable. To my mind, "Abraham Solomon" is such a stereotypical name that I'm inclined to doubt it. It is also the name of a court physician for King René of France in 1445, far too early to have been Michel's grandfather.

5 Ian Wilson, *Nostradamus: The Man behind the Prophesies* (New York St. Martin's Press, 2002), 5–12.

6 Salo Baron, *A Social and Religious History of the Jews*, vol. IV (New York: Columbia University Press, 1960), 45–48.

7 Kober, 365.

8 Wilson, 5–7. I would like to point out that knowing one's great-grandfather was only as unusual then as it is now.

9 Nostradamus, *Traité de fardemens et confitures* (Lyon, 1555). I'm surprised that no one has come out with a Nostradamus cookbook.

10 This is listed in several sources as being on record at the university.

11 Vernon Hall Jr., "Life of Julius Caesar Scaliger (1484–1558)," *Transactions of the American Philosophical Society* new ser. 40, no. 2 (1950): 117–118. Hall spent five years studying the Scaliger family papers that had never been examined before, certainly not by those interested in Nostradamus.

12 Ibid., 118.

13 Ibid. Hall cites the records of the Inquisition, still in existence (the records, not the Inquisition).

14 Ibid. Again from the records of the Inquisition.

15 Ward, 6.

16 Wilson, 237–238

17 "*Pource que les regnes, sects et regions seront changés si opposites.*" quoted in Hutin, 30.

18 Nostradamus, "*Dédicace,*" in Hutin, 79.

19 Ward.

20 Hall, 129.

21 Wilson, 106.

22 Benjamin Woolley, *The Queen's Conjurer* (New York: Henry Holt, 2001), 54.

23 Michael G. Paulson, *Catherine de Medici: Five Portraits* (New York: Peter Lang, 2002), 4ff.

24 Ibid., 66.

25 Wilson, 255.

26 Hutin, 337.

27 Fredéric Godefroye, *Lexique de L'Ancien Françias* (Paris: Librairie Honoré Champion, 1990), 86.

28 Translated in Jean-Charles de Fontbrune, *Nostradamus* (Paris: Rocher, 1980), xxiii.

CHAPTER TWENTY-TWO

Sabbatai Sevi

Almost the Messiah

A Girl from Galata . . . told her parents that an angel had
revealed himself to her, holding in his hand a flaming sword.
And that he had told her that the true Messiah had come and
that very soon he would appear on the banks of the Jordan.

—Friar Michel Févre, on Sabbatai Sevi[1]

It was not only European Protestants who saw the seventeenth century as the beginning of the millennium, Jews in eastern Europe
and the Ottoman Empire were also on a heightened watch for the
coming of the Messiah. Perhaps the growth of the Protestant movement encouraged them to feel the world was ripe for change. Across
the East there was much discussion about possible signs that the Messiah would appear any moment. And one man managed to convince
thousands of both Jews and Christians that he was the real thing.

Sabbatai Sevi[2] was born in the Ottoman town of Smyrna, now
Izmir, Turkey, in 1626, the son of a merchant. Sevi spent his youth
in the study of the Talmud before moving on to the Zohar and other
kabbalist writings.[3] He apparently had ecstatic visions from young
adulthood and, in 1648, announced to a few close friends that he had
had a dream that told him that he was the Messiah. In 1651, he was

expelled from Smyrna for making this public and so made his way to Gaza. There he met another Kabbalah scholar, Nathan Ashkenazi.[4]

In 1665, Nathan "fell into a trance" during a synagogue service. When he came out of it, he informed his colleagues that he had been told that Sabbatai Sevi was indeed the Messiah and that Nathan had been chosen to be his prophet.[5]

At the beginning, the two men and their few converts made little attempt to proselytize. However, using the network established by Jewish traders and travelers, word of their message soon spread throughout Jewish communities under both Islamic and Christian rule. The news of the Messiah's appearance went as far as England, Russia, Morocco, and Yemen. Sevi's father was the agent for several English Christian merchants who were also millenarians, and they took the story back with them.[6] To them this was the first sign of the approach of Armageddon.

The farther the rumors reached, the more they expanded.

Nathan tried to stem the rising tide of stories concerning the fantastic miracles performed by Sabbatai Sevi, stating that believers should accept Sevi as the Messiah without miracles. "[The Messiah] reaches the understanding of the greatness of God, for this is the quintessence of the Messiah. And if he does not do so then he is not the Messiah. Even he displays all the signs and wonders in the world, God forbid that one should believe in him, for he is a prophet in idolatry."[7]

Sabbatai Sevi finally began to travel, preaching his beliefs. It's not clear how many paid attention to him or understood his mystical ideology. He and his followers visited the Jewish communities of Cairo in 1662, where he was welcomed by the leader of the Cairo community and the chief rabbi of Alexandria, Hosea Nantawa. The community provided funds and sent word of their support to the Jews of Italy.[8] With very little proselytizing on his part, the self-proclaimed Messiah was rapidly gathering an international following.

Despite Nathan's insistence that miracles don't make a messiah, stories of the wonders performed by Sabbatai Sevi spread across the Diaspora. Some said that the lost tribes of Israel had returned and were marching across the desert. Others that Sabbatai Sevi had caused Christian churches to sink into the earth and had walked through fire without being burned.[9] The excitement was not contained within the Jewish communities. One English Puritan pamphlet reported that a ship had washed ashore in Scotland bearing the banner "These Are of the Ten Tribes of Israel."[10]

Despite Nathan's mystical explanations of the nature of Sevi as the Messiah, followers insisted on physical evidence of the validity of his role. How many of the stories of his cures and power over nature actually came from the Sabbateans is uncertain, but it does seem that they totally overshadowed the reality.

Christian millenarian hopes were kindled through reports that Sevi and Nathan were leading an army of Jews across the desert. Papers in the Netherlands and Germany reported almost daily on the progress of this phantom army, and these stories were picked up as far away as Muscovy, where it was stated that Mecca had been taken, and the Prophet's tomb had been looted.[11] In England, many felt that this was a sign that the Jews would retake Jerusalem, a belief that encouraged the remnant of Fifth Monarchists remaining under the Restoration.[12]

Eventually, Sabbatai Sevi and his followers returned to Smyrna, where, in 1665, he seems to have accepted the public duties of his position. The Messiah was foretold to be a political leader who would lead armies. He and his disciples began by taking over Smyrna. Sevi then divided the world into regions and named several of his supporters as kings.[13]

At this point, the Ottoman authorities began to take notice. Jewish employees of the government were neglecting their work and disrupting the order of the state in order to join the Sabbateans. Therefore, government officials arrested Sabbatai Sevi, imprisoned him in Gallipoli, and eventually brought him before the sultan in Istanbul. There in 1666, under pressure from the authorities, he officially converted to Islam and was released.

That should have been the end of the story. For some, it was. Many of his disciples were bitterly disappointed by his betrayal and returned to their normal lives. Some may have even converted to Christianity or Islam.

But this was an era when a large part of the monotheistic world anticipated the Messiah. A little thing like apostasy was not going to convince some of them that they had been mistaken. Christians who believed that Christ would again appear as a Jew were still willing to entertain the idea that it was in the person of Sabbatai Sevi. A preacher in the Netherlands told his congregation that the king of the Jews had appeared in the Holy Land.[14] The Christian scholar Peter Serrarius became a believer and, even after Sevi's conversion, set out for Smyrna to meet him, although he died on the way.[15]

Even those who didn't believe in Sabbatai Sevi saw the movement as a positive step toward the Second Coming, "for when these surheli, or mocksuns, appear, the Son of righteousness is not far off."[16]

Nathan was one who did not abandon the cause. He continued to preach throughout the Balkans, Turkey, and Italy that Sevi was the Messiah. Using the same logic that denied that a miracle worker was automatically divine, he pointed out that, whatever he called himself, Sabbatai Sevi was still, in his essence, the Messiah. It was possible, he argued, that Sabbatai Sevi had converted in response to a vision telling him that it was a "punishment for the fact that the Jewish people do not understand the Godhead."[17]

Most believers regretted their misplaced enthusiasm and went back to normal life. Both the Turkish government and the foreign merchants were relieved when business seemed to return to normal. The extent to which Jews had participated in the messianic movement is clear from the reaction of various merchants to the end of the movement. An Englishman in Smyrna wrote, "Here is now great hopes trade will suddenly much amend the Jewes . . . now beginning to Selle and promise to follow Tradeing as before, which they had totally neglected."[18]

But the Sabbateans continued. In Salonika, the belief in Sabbatai Sevi has lasted until the present. It has been suggested that the reason for this was due more to an economic crisis than a religious one, but it's amazing how often the two go together.[19] The Sabbateans in Turkey today are known as *Dönme* (convert). How many actually practice Judaism, believing that Sabbatai Sevi was the Messiah, is hard to say. Like the Marranos, who converted to Christianity but maintained their Jewish heritage, the *Dömne* are officially Muslim.[20]

The story of Sabbatai Sevi lasted in novels and other fiction for a long time. He became a symbol of the false prophet, along with Christian pretenders. It inspired Increase Mather, the New England Puritan, to write *The Mystery of Israel's Salvation*, in which he foresaw the conversion of the Jews.[21] On the other end of the spectrum seventeenth-century pamphleteers in Germany used the story as a cautionary tale to emphasize the deceitfulness of Jews, feeding into a new form of anti-Semitism that would lead to the Holocaust.

Sabbatai Sevi would never have become so widely known and discussed if Christians, Muslims, and Jews were not already expecting a Messiah, a Second Coming, or the Mahdi. The seventeenth century was primed for the end of the world.

---

1 Giacomo Saban, ed. and trans., "Sabbatai Sevi as Seen by a Contemporary Traveller," *Jewish History* 7, no. 2 (1993): 112.

2 Also spelled, Zvi, Tsevi, Tzevi, and so on, according to the mode of the translator of the Arabic and Hebrew script.

3 Moshe Idel, *Messianic Mystics* (New Haven, CT:, Yale University Press, 1998), 185.

4 Also known as Nathan of Gaza and Nathan Levi.

5 Stephen Sharot, *Messianism, Mysticism, and Magic: A Sociological Analysis of Jewish Religious Movements* (Raleigh:, University of North Carolina Press, 1992), 86.

6 Richard H. Popkin, "Three English Tellings of the Sabbatai Sevi Story," *Jewish History* 8, no. 1–2 (1994): 44.

7 Quoted in Idel, 197.

8 Jane Hathaway, "The Grand Vizier and the False Messiah: The Sabbatai Sevi Controversy and the Ottoman Reform in Egypt," *Journal of the American Oriental Society* 7, no. 4 (1997): 667–668.

9 Sharot, 88.

10 Popkin, 43.

11 Daniel Clark Waugh, "News of the False Messiah: Reports on Shabbetai Zevi in Ukraine and Muscovy," *Jewish Social Studies* 44, No.3/4 (Summer-Autumn, 1979) 317.

12 Bernard Capp, *The Fifth Monarchy Men: A Study in Seventeenth Century English Millenarianism*, rpt. ed. (London: Faber & Faber, 2008), 213–214.

13 Jacob Barnai, "Christian Messianism and the Portuguese Marranos: The Emergence of Sabbteanism Is Smyrna," *Jewish History* 7, no. 2 (1993), 122.

14 Richard Popkin, "Jewish-Christian Relations in the Sixteenth and Seventeenth Centuries: The Conception of the Messiah," *Jewish History* 6. The Frank Talmadge Memorial Volume (1992): 169.

15 Ibid., 170.

16 Quoted in Michael McKeon, "Sabbatai Sevi in England," *AJS Review* 2 (1977): 158.

17 Idel, 206.

18 Quoted in McKeon, 156.

19 Sharot, 111.

20 Leyla Nezi, "Remembering to Forget: Sabbateanism, National Identity, and Subjectivity in Turkey," *Comparative Studies in Society and History* 44, no. 1 (2002): 137.

21 Richard W. Cogley, "The Fall of the Ottoman Empire and the Restoration of Israel in the 'Judeo-Centric' Strand of Puritan Millenarianism," *Church History* 72. no. 2 (2003): 326.

CHAPTER TWENTY-THREE

The Russian Old Believers

Or "If It Was Good Enough for Grandpa . . ."

The Russian people, in accordance with their metaphysical
nature and vocation in the world, are a people of the End.
Apocalypse has always played a great part both among the
masses of our people and at the highest cultural level
among our writers and thinkers.

—Nicolas Berdyaev, *The Russian Idea*[1]

Seventeenth-century Russia had its own millennial movement
that has lasted, despite persecution, to the present. It began, like
many world-changing events, with a dispute that seemed to outsiders,
inconsequential. It had to do with how many fingers one uses to make
the sign of the cross.

Of course, that was just the trigger. The loaded gun rested with
the beliefs of the Russian Orthodox people, their sense of identity,
and their quasi-religious relationship with the czar. The seemingly
innocent and orthodox plans of Czar Alexander I and the Patriarch
Nikon in the seventeenth century threatened all three of these and
set in motion a schism that split the Russian Church, caused the
deaths of thousands of people, and indirectly led to the downfall of
the Romanov Dynasty.

Patriarch Nikon, who bore the brunt of the blame for the schism, was born in a peasant family near Novgorod in 1605. He learned to read and write and, at the age of twenty, became a priest. He married, but after their three children died in infancy, he convinced his wife that they should give up the world and become monastics.[2] She entered a convent, and Nikon became a monk. Thanks to the patronage of another monk, Nikon was introduced into the Russian court and eventually became an abbot.[3]

In 1649, he was made patriarch of Novgorod. The conditions of his election would later be used as an excuse to revolt against him. Rather than being chosen by other bishops, as was customary, he was selected by Czar Alexander and his confessor. This was part of an imperial plan to reform the church. It is not entirely coincidental that 1649 was also the year in which the Russian peasants were declared serfs, binding them to the land and depriving them of what little freedom they had once enjoyed.[4]

Nikon, with the approval of the czar, set about bringing the Russian church in line with the practices of the Greek Orthodox Church in Constantinople. Apparently Alexander felt that the prelates of the Greek Church looked down on the Russian clergy for their ignorance and backward ways.[5] The new patriarch was already a part of a group of reformers known as the "New Zealots." These clerics agreed with the Greeks and, using material from the church of Kiev, not yet a part of Russia, they published revised editions of liturgical books.[6]

At first the changes were cosmetic and conformed to Russian practice. It was when Nikon decided to call in some Greek and Ukrainian theologians to bring the Russian Church in line that things got ugly. The first change was in the matter of the sign of the cross. Russians used two fingers, symbolizing the dual nature of Christ, human and divine. The Greeks used three, for the Trinity.[7] Other changes consisted of "presenting five consecrated loaves instead of seven, chanting Alleluia three times instead of two, spelling Jesus *Iisus* instead of *Isus*, and moving a church procession against the sun instead of with it."[8] These abrupt changes in long-established practices created a storm of outrage, led by the archpriest Avvakum, who had once been a friend of Nikon's.

For the Orthodox Russians, like the Egyptians and others, the symbols of religions and the rituals were as important as the faith. How one worshiped mattered in terms of respect for God. Maintaining traditional patterns was essential.

Also there was the conviction among many Russian Christians that Moscow was the "Third Rome." The first was the real city of Rome at the time of the first Christians, the second was Constantinople. But both these Romes had betrayed the faith. The Catholics controlled the first and, in Constantinople, the Greek Orthodox Church existed only with the permission of the Ottoman Sultans. Therefore, Moscow was the last bastion of the true faith. "If Moscow were to fall from grace . . . it would mean not only the fall of Moscow as a state, as divine punishment, but the end of the whole world; a fourth Rome there could not be."[9] So any deviation from standard practice, especially by adopting the customs of the Greeks, would mean a global catastrophe.

There was more going on, of course. Nikon wasn't the most tactful of men in pushing his reforms through. He excommunicated the popular archpriest and preacher Neronov and exiled him. He also exiled the priest Avvakum, along with his family, to Siberia. Avvakum later wrote poignantly of their suffering there and how his daughter, Agrafena, waited at the window in case a neighbor lady came out to give them the remains of the food she gave the hens.[10]

Nikon eventually overstepped himself and was arrested, tried, and sent to a monastery/prison where he died. One accusation against him was that he was trying to set himself up as a pope.[11]

Avvakum was brought back from exile twelve years later and continued to preach against the new ways, which hadn't ended with Nikon's banishment. As a result, the priest was beaten, whipped, and sent into imprisonment in a monastery.[12] This did nothing to change his thinking.

Alexander was determined that the country would conform to his reforms. The severity of the punishments for priests who disobeyed the new laws was extreme. Many were exiled, imprisoned, and whipped. Friends of Avvakum had their tongues cut out and their right hands cut off.[13] The persecution, as happens in most cases, only increased the resolve of the believers. This division in the Russian Church was called *Raskol*, or schism. The schism never healed. The *Raskolniki*, or Old Believers, remained separate from the hierarchy of the Russian Church, attending their own services. The coming end of the world brought about by the treachery of the czars was incorporated into their belief. With each generation, their millenarianism became stronger.

For many Russians, it came down to a choice between the state and their own salvation. They had been taught that the czar was Christ's representative on earth, as much as the patriarch. Now both men seemed to have betrayed them. Where could they turn?

The decision was influenced for many by the martyrdom of the monks of the Solvetskii Monastery, "one of the holiest places of Russia."[14] The monks refused to submit to Moscow, holding out for eight years (1668–1676) against the soldiers of the czar. When the monastery fell, all the monks and everyone inside with them were killed.

Inspired by their faith and, perhaps, driven by a sense of hopelessness, thousands of Old Believer communities also chose death rather than forced compliance. The preferred method was self-immolation. An earlier apocalyptic sect, the Kapitonists, in the millennial year of 1666, burned themselves to death in a "purification by fire." Their example may have inspired the *Raskolniki* to do the same.[15]

The *Raskolniki* congregations went beyond the individual suicides of the Kapitonists. They barricaded themselves in their churches and, when the czar's army approached, set the buildings on fire. It is estimated that at least twenty thousand people—men, women, and children—died in this way. Most of these conflagrations occurred in the late seventeenth century, but they continued up until the middle of the nineteenth.[16]

Avvakum praised the suicide/martyrs, saying "And many Zealots of our creed, who shun the temptation of apostasy, gather into wooden houses, and voluntarily burn themselves to death with their wives and children that their souls be not ruined. Blessed be their willingness to die for the Lord!"[17]

Avvakum was to share their fate. In 1682, he was burned at the stake. His death did nothing to end the *Raskol* movement. What it did do was to introduce the concept of religious dissent as a crime against the state. This had been previously unknown in Russia and it would continue into the Soviet era.

The idea of the czar as Antichrist was obvious but difficult for many Old Believers to accept at first. They began by making Czar Alexander simply one of the horns of the Antichrist. But the feeling that the end of the world was approaching and that the czar, by abandoning his duty, taking power that he had never held before and introducing Western ways into the traditional Russian life, was no longer doing the work of God moved him up to the top position fairly rapidly.[18] They were certain that he was preparing them for the Apocalypse in the fateful year of 1666.

When the world didn't end in 1666, the *Raskol* movement revised their theory about the czar. It wasn't one individual man who was the Antichrist, but the whole dynasty. Thus the end of the world would be delayed until the fall of the Romanovs.[19] This may be one of the many reasons that there wasn't much support for Czar Nicholas Romanov when the Russian Revolution began in 1918, much to his surprise.

Under Peter the Great (1672–1725) the Old Believers were given some protection, providing that they paid a double poll tax, but his other innovations, like making the boyars shave their beards and wear Western clothing, only convinced the Old Believers that he was not to be trusted. They stayed in their own communities, often deliberately remote. It is ironic that their discipline and hard work, along with the network of fellow believers across the country, made some of them financially successful. Many prospered under Peter.[20]

However, like the Jews, they were always in danger of persecution. In 1738, one Old Believer community split on the question of praying for the czar and continuing to thrive or refusing to do so and risking prison. Many chose the latter and created a subsect known as the *Filippovtsy*.[21] By the 1800s, there were many splinter sects, some differing only in such things as saying or omitting the prayer for the czar, others so radical as to be unrecognizable to most Old Believers.

Even though the Old Believers began as a reaction to the introduction of foreign ideas into their religion, they seem to have embraced the Industrial Revolution. By 1848, the sect known as the Priestists, those who had created some form of hierarchy, controlled most of the east–west trade in Russia as well as shipbuilding and metallurgy.[22] Under Catherine the Great (1729–1796), many Old Believers moved from the remote towns they had established and set up their own communities near Moscow, where they engaged in many sorts of manufacture.

One custom that had been established in the early days of the sect was the pooling of funds. Members turned over all their property to the group when they entered, reserving a small amount for their personal use. The Moscow center also received donations from other Old Believers. This money was used to invest in business enterprises.[23]

These groups were a far cry from the early peasant believers; however, almost all Old Believers practiced communal living in that property was held in common. For this reason, one would think that they would have welcomed the Russian Revolution. It's possible that, in the early days, the urban Old Believers thought that the millennium had finally come with communism, but in the countryside, the people saw it as simply a change of masters.

Many Old Believers refused to send their children to state-run schools that celebrated Soviet holidays rather than Christian ones. Others blended Lenin in with their own saints, incorporating him into their worldview rather than adopting the Bolshevik one.[24] But the distrust of any government was by now ingrained in the Old Believers. Many refused to take part in the 1926 census or carry identity cards.[25]

The Soviet leaders now took on the mantle of Antichrist. During the 1920s there were many reports of miraculous warnings of the coming end times, although no specific leader appeared to announce it. With the first Five Year Plan in the 1930s, there was widespread belief that "the collective farm heralded the reign of Antichrist on earth." A letter was circulated, purporting to be from God, saying "'People no longer believe in me. If this continues, then in two years the world will come to an end. I can no longer be patient.'"[26] And who could blame him? But, of course, he must have given the Old Believers a second chance for they endured throughout the Soviet era.

Some Old Believers have emigrated. One group first set up communities in Mongolia but, with political changes there, were forced to move on. They settled in Australia, Brazil, and the United States. Some came to America at the end of the nineteenth century, in the great rush of eastern Europeans.[27] Others arrived in the 1960s and more after the breakup of the Soviet Union. There are groups in Oregon and, especially, in Alaska where the unpopulated areas have allowed them to rebuild their own collective societies.[28]

As with many of the groups that began in expectation of an imminent Apocalypse, the remaining Old Believers have managed to adapt their faith to conform to a longer wait along with creating a lifestyle that allows them to be prepared for when the day finally arrives.

---

1 Quoted in, David. G. Rowley. "'Redeemer Empire' Russian Millennialism," *American Historical Review* 104, no. 5 (1999): 1582.

2 The death of children influenced Ann Lee, founder of the Shakers in much the same way.

3 Sergei V. Lobachev, "Patriarch Nikon's Rise to Power," *The Slavonic and East European Review* 79, no. 2 (2001): 295–296.

4 Michael Cherniavsky, "The Old Believers and the New Religion," *Slavic Review* 25, no. 1 (1966): 2.

5 Catherine B. H. Cant, "The Archpriest Avvakum and His Scottish Contemporaries," *The Slavic and East European Review* 44, no. 103 (1966): 382–383.

6 Matthew Spinka, "Patriarch Nikon and the Subjugation of the Russian Church to the State," *Church History* 10, no. 4 (1941): 349.

7 Don't sneer at this. Countries have gone to war for more trivial reasons.

8 Vatro Murvar, "Messianism in Russia: Religious and Revolutionary," *Journal for the Scientific Study of Religion* 10, no. 4 (1971): 293.

9 Cherniavsky, 10.

10 Cant, 386. Avvakum wrote pamphlets, treatises, and his autobiography in eloquent, emotional prose that certainly helped in his appeal to the Old Believers to resist governmental pressure.

11 Murvar, 289.

12 Archpriest Avvakum and Henry Lanz, "Selected Texts from the 'Book of Discourses,'", *The Slavonic and East European Review* 8, no. 23 (1929): 254. Not the same monastery as Nikon. That would have been weird.

13 Spinka, 347

14 Cherniavsky, 18.

15 Thomas Robbins, "Religious Mass Suicide before Jonestown: The Russian Old Believers," *Sociological Analysis* 47, no. 1 (1986): 3.

16 Robbins, 6.

17 Avvakum and Lanz, 254.

18 Cherniavsky, 17. He adds that most attention was focused on the Antichrist; the Second Coming of Jesus was not dwelled upon.

19 Ibid., 20.

20 Ibid., 22.

21 Ibid., 23.

22 William L. Blackwell, "The Old Believers and the Rise of Private Industrial Enterprise in Early Nineteenth-Century Moscow," *Slavic Review* 24, no. 3 (1969): 409.

23 Ibid., 413.

24 Lynne Viola, "The Peasant Nightmare: Visions of Apocalypse in the Soviet Countryside," *The Journal of Modern History* 62, no. 4 1990): 753.

25 Ibid., 755.

26 Ibid., 759, 761–762.

27 Anton S. Beliajeff, "The Old Believers in the United States," *Russian Review* 36, no. 1 (1977): 76.

28 The Oregon group has been taken over by urban sprawl, but I ran across some in Alaska who still homeschool their children and live according to the priestless tradition.

CHAPTER TWENTY-FOUR

The Fifth Monarchy

We therefore freely, of a ready minde, and with a most chearful
heart . . . give up our lives and estates unto our Lord King Jesus,
and to his people, to become souldiers in the Lambs Army . . . ,
neither will we ever . . . sheath our swords again, untill Mount
Zion become the joy of the whole earth, . . . untill Rome be in
ashes, and Babylon become a hissing and a curse.

—*A Door of Hope*, Fifth Monarchy manifesto (1660), 16

O f all the millennial movements that littered the seventeenth
century, the British Fifth Monarchy men were among the
most paradoxical. They were not a religion; they were really not even
an organization. They were more a unified belief system. And that
belief was that they were destined to establish Christ's kingdom on
earth. Once they did this, they were certain that Jesus would descend
from heaven bodily and take up the crown of Britain, from which
base, his armies would conquer the forces of the Antichrist—that is,
the pope, along with Catholic countries, and the Ottoman Empire.[1]

When Charles I became king of England in 1625, his prospects
were good. He had a private income that allowed him to do much as
he liked, and the English people seemed willing to let him, within
limits. The limits were soon reached in two areas. The first was taxation without representation. Charles ran through his private income,
apparently not realizing that wars are expensive. The king had the

power of life and death over his subjects but not the right to take their money. Taxes had to be approved by Parliament.

Charles got around this at first by spending his own money and not convening Parliament. This worked from 1629 through 1640, until Charles needed an army to put down a Scottish rebellion. He was forced to call for parliamentary elections. The problem with this was that a lot of the members of the House of Commons agreed with the grievances of the Scots, who were refusing to swear allegiance to the Anglican Church. After three weeks, Charles dissolved this "Short Parliament." The Long Parliament followed, but it wasn't any better for Charles. Its members managed to pass laws that curtailed the king's power, especially in levying new taxes and, most important, in controlling the army.

In January 1642, Parliament got fed up with Charles' high-handedness and, in effect, fired the king. Charles went to Oxford, where he set up an "anti-parliament." So the English Civil War was originally between the king and the Parliament. But soon Parliament became divided between the conservative Presbyterians who wanted to make peace with the king and the Independents (in religion), who wanted to be rid of him.[2]

This is where the Fifth Monarchy comes in. In 1648, the Long Parliament was taken over by a section of the Independents, who became the Rump Parliament. Many of its members were believers in the prophecy from the Book of Daniel (2:36–45) in which Daniel interprets Nebuchadnezzar's dream to mean that there would be four kingdoms. The first, Babylon, was the Golden Age. Then would come kingdoms of silver, bronze, and iron, which were Persia, Greece, and Rome, respectively. Finally, "The God of heaven will set up a kingdom that shall never be destroyed. . . . It shall crush all these kingdoms and bring them to an end, and it shall stand forever" (Daniel 2:44).[3]

These men saw in the overthrow of King Charles the end of the Fourth Monarchy. They blended this with the belief that the Second Coming was at hand. It was their task to prepare the way for the reign of King Jesus. Charles wasn't the Antichrist; the pope had that honor, but the king was considered the little horn of the beast in Daniel's dream, "There were eyes like human eyes in this horn, and a mouth speaking arrogantly" (Daniel 7:8).

This did not bode well for Charles. In the Book of Daniel, the little horn is tried, convicted, and put to death (Daniel 7:11). In the minds of the Rump Parliament, Charles was no longer a king but an embodiment of evil. There was only one way to destroy evil. The king was beheaded on January 30, 1649. In many parts of Europe, kings were still considered to be consecrated by God, so executing one took both courage and conviction.

Many of the Puritans in England felt that the execution was divinely ordained. They were certain that now it was time for the saints to rule. Therefore, the next Parliament, which first sat in June 1653, was called the Parliament of Saints, although it has since been more familiarly known as the Barebones Parliament, supposedly after a member with the unfortunate name of Praise-God Barebone.[4]

Many of the Fifth Monarchists were in the army and had fought first for the king and then against him. One of the military leaders who played an important role in the Fifth Monarchy and in the government during the Interregnum (the eleven years between the death of Charles I and the return of Charles II) was Thomas Harrison. Harrison was both a major general in the New Model Army, under Oliver Cromwell, and a member of the Barebones Parliament.

Harrison (1606–1660) was the son of a Newcastle-under-Lyme butcher who had risen to be mayor of the city. He worked as a clerk in London until the start of the Civil War, when he enlisted on the side of Parliament. He must have been a good soldier for, by 1645, he was a colonel.[5]

He was also a staunch believer in the coming of the millennium. He argued for the execution of King Charles and was one of those who signed his death warrant. He must have been a charismatic man;

portraits show him looking very little like a conventional Puritan. His hair was long and curled, and he wore lace collars and fine suits. This did not prevent him from fighting in Parliament against immorality and the system of tithing citizens to support the clergy.[6] He seems to have been rigid and uncompromising in his faith, certain that he was one of the saints who would prepare the kingdom, with a rather touching naïveté about the possibility of success. When the Barebones Parliament was dismissed and Oliver Cromwell became lord protector, Harrison felt betrayed. That was the role of Jesus. Suddenly his hero had become another "little horn." However, Harrison did not mount a rebellion against Cromwell. Ordered to retire to his home in Staffordshire in 1654, he went, vowing to live peaceably.[7]

He seems to have done so, being held in not very close captivity until the Restoration. Charles II issued a general amnesty for many of the Puritan leaders but Harrison was not included. His name on the death warrant of the king's father condemned him. Harrison was tried and convicted. He was executed on October 13, 1660. The diarist and gadabout Samuel Pepys went to see the show and wrote, "I went out to Charing Cross, to see Major-General Harrison hanged, drawn and quartered; which was done there, he looking as cheerful as any man could do in that condition."[8]

In contrast to the elegant Harrison was Thomas Venner. Venner was a cooper who emigrated to New England sometime before 1638. He lived first in Salem, Massachusetts, and then Boston before returning to England in 1651.[9] He got a job at the Tower of London and became involved in the Fifth Monarchy movement. In 1655, he was dismissed from the Tower, allegedly for plotting to blow it up.[10] In 1657, he attempted to start a popular rebellion. In his notebook, he wrote, "Our present apprehension is, that having a convenient place providence, we fall uppon a troupe of Horse & execute their officers & all others of the guards or private souldiers that shall oppose us, and take their horses to horse our men, because the Lord hath need."[11]

Venner's insurrection was supposed to take place on April 7, 1657, but the plotters were betrayed and captured. Venner spent the next two years in the Tower, this time as a prisoner.[12]

It's a tribute to the patience of Oliver Cromwell that he did not execute Venner. Cromwell's son, Richard, let him go free after Oliver's death. The determined Venner immediately started planning another uprising in which he encouraged his followers to "take up arms for King Jesus against the Powers of the Earth."[13] However, this rebellion did not get started until 1661, a year after the return of King Charles II. Charles was not convinced that this was the time for a new kingdom. Venner was executed January 19, 1661.

It may have been noted that the Fifth Monarchy was made up totally of men. That's not entirely true. Women had a role in the movement, not as leaders or soldiers, but as prophets.

Two women were particularly well known for their visions, Anna Trapnell and Mary Cary. Little is known about Cary's life before she began publishing her visions in 1647. In 1653, she published *The Little Horn's Doom and Downfall*, a justification of the Fifth Monarchy tenets.[14] Although it was published four years after the king was executed, Cary insisted that she wrote the book before the events that are predicted therein.[15] She justified the establishment of the kingdom of God in England rather than Jerusalem because there were so many more saints already there. Also, along with many Fifth Monarchy adherents as well as other millenarians, Cary argued for the readmission of the Jews to England. They had been expelled in 1290, and many were certain that they must be allowed to return in order to be converted so that Jesus would return.[16]

Anna Trapnel, the daughter of a shipwright from Stepney, had her first visions in 1643. However, she didn't make them public until 1654. She did not write down her own prophecies, although she was literate, but delivered them in a trance for others to write, calling herself an instrument of God. The spirit speaking through her spoke both poetry and prose, all in support of the Fifth Monarchy opinions on the Book of Daniel and the way that Oliver Cromwell had fallen into tyranny.[17] Unmarried, she traveled alone. She was arrested once in Cornwall and tried, mainly for being a troublemaker, and spent time in prison. Her next pamphlet, *A Report and Plea*, tells the story of her treatment by the court and the disapproving populace.[18]

The visions of these women, accepted by many as divinely inspired, helped strengthen the resolve of the Fifth Monarchy supporters. However, by the late 1650s the English people in general realized that rule by saints was not working. For one thing, although a person could think life was hard because the king was a tyrant; it was less comfortable to say God was one, especially within the hearing of his divinely appointed lieutenants.

Charles II did not have to reconquer England, although there were military uprisings in his support. The Long Parliament had been reinstated, including the moderates who had been forced out in 1648. They voted overwhelmingly to invite the king to come back. Some even praised him as the Fifth Monarch.[19] He landed at Dover in 1660 and began the gloriously decadent Restoration.

The arrival of King Charles with no opposition from King Jesus was a terrible blow to the remaining Fifth Monarchists. Thomas Venner's failed insurrection was the last major attempt at establishing a kingdom of saints. The Fifth Monarchist believers eventually blended in with other dissenting Protestant groups. One small band evidently decided that England wasn't the place to await the Second Coming and set up a community in the German Palatinate, where they were rumored to be living according to Jewish law.[20]

The year 1666 raised the hopes of many and the horrors of the plague and the Great Fire of London made many in England feel that Armageddon was near.

While most who take part in a rebellion think that God must be on their side, few expect him to bodily lead the army. The Fifth Monarchists did. This rigid certainty as to the divine justice of their cause made them unable to compromise. It also made some of them, like

Harrison and Venner, prefer martyrdom. While the majority of the English did not support them, many admired the constancy of their faith and this was underscored when, in 1688, the Stuart kings were sent packing in favor of the strongly Protestant daughter of James II and her husband, William of Orange.

1 Champlin Burrage, "The Fifth Monarchy Insurrection," *English Historical Review* 25, no. 100 (1910): 740.
2 The preceding mini-history is my own interpretation of events, seriously condensed. It should not be used if you are studying for an exam on the Civil War.
3 New Revised Standard Bible.
4 Bernard Capp, *The Fifth Monarchy Men: A Study in Seventeenth Century Millenarianism*, (London: Faber & Faber, 2008): 64.
5 P. G. Rogers, *The Fifth Monarchy Men* (Oxford: Oxford University Press, 1961), 15.
6 Leo F. Solt, "The Fifth Monarchy Men: Politics and the Millennium," *Church History* 30, no. 3 (1961): 314.
7 Capp, p. 100.
8 Quoted in Rogers, 107.
9 Capp, 267.
10 Burrage, 723.
11 Quoted in ibid., 730.
12 Ibid., 739.
13 Ibid. 739.
14 David Loewenstein, "Scriptural Exegesis, Female Prophecy and Radical Politics in Mary Cary," *Studies in English Literature 1500–1900* 46, no. 1 (2006): 134.
15 Rachel Warburton, "Future Perfect?: Elect Nationhood and the Grammar of Desire in Mary Cary's Millennial Visions," *Utopian Studies* 18, no. 2 (2007): 122.
16 Ibid., 138. See also the section in this book on Jews and the Millennium.
17 Champlin Burrage, "Anna Trapnel's Prophecies," *English Historical Review* 26, no. 103 (1911): 5626–5635.
18 Susannah B. Mintz, "The Spectacular Self of 'Anna Trapnel's Report and Plea,'" *Pacific Coast Philology* 35, no. 1 (2000): 1–16. The use women made of visions and prophecy in a patriarchal society is fascinating but, I am sad to say, can't be explored further in this book.
19 Capp, 194.
20 Ibid., 202.

CHAPTER TWENTY-FIVE

The Founders of Modern Science

He has studied the prophetic parts of
Scripture till he has bewildered himself.

—*Gentleman's Magazine* (1795), 55

I t is popular to think of the "long seventeenth century" as a time of enlightenment, when old superstitions were thrown out and rationale enquiry was established. The basic principles of chemistry, biology, and physics were established. It was an age of reason in which apocalyptic and millennial speculations were only for the uneducated.

Well, that's not *exactly* the case.

JOHN NAPIER

John Napier (1550–1617), eighth laird of Merchiston in Scotland, is well known as the inventor of logarithms. He is also credited with being the first to design a prototype computer. "These were wooden or bone prisms each lateral face of which was divided and marked by cross lines into small squares . . . he also mentions that there is a way of mounting metal plates in a box and multiplying and dividing by means of this mechanism."[1] He also amused himself designing engines of war, including a sort of armored tank and a submarine.[2]

But this was only a part of his life. Napier was much involved in Scottish politics, particularly involving King James VI of Scotland, shortly to become James I of England. In 1593 Napier wrote a commentary on Revelation, *A Plaine Discovery of the Whole Revelation of Saint John*. He was much more famous for this book than he was for his mathematical genius. It went through twenty-one editions by 1700.[3] Dedicated to King James, the book is laid out with scientific precision. The first part consists of thirty-six propositions, followed by their proofs. The second half is his verse-by-verse explanation of the meaning of each sign described by John of Patmos.[4] It is not surprising that this Protestant Scot names the pope as Antichrist. It is surprising that this eminent mathematician had a problem making his math work in predicting the end. He figured that the last age of the world would be from 1541 to 1786. But he also believed that Christ would return sometime from 1698 to 1700. He finally explained that if the Elect were too impatient for the end that it would come ahead of schedule, "but I meane, that if the world wer to indure, the seventh age should continew until the yeare of Christ 1786."[5]

ROBERT BOYLE

The aristocrat Robert Boyle (1627–1691) was the fourteenth child of the first earl of Cork and not in the slightest danger of inheriting any responsibility. He had a private tutor and, with his elder brother, spent five years touring Europe in his early teens. He was fascinated by science and had money and time in which to indulge his interests. Although born in Ireland, he spent most of his life in England.[6] Boyle is best known for his work with vacuum pumps and for Boyle's Law, which states that for a given mass, at a constant temperature, the pressure times the volume is a constant. He also was interested in isolating elements, using colormetric analysis to find iron in the water at

Portrait of Robert Boyle (1627–1691). British chemist. Engraving. *Image Selection / Art Resource, NY*

Tunbridge Wells.[7] Finally, he was a mentor and inspiration to many younger scientists, including Isaac Newton.

Boyle was also a fervent Anglican who wrote many treatises on religion, especially noting that the clockwork universe that the New Science was proposing was so complicated that it was all the more likely to have had a divine mind to create it and set it running. He was also devoted to the conversion of the Indians of North America, the Irish, and any other pagans and papists around. He sponsored missionaries and underwrote the cost of translating the Bible into Arabic Turkish and Malayan.[8] He also wrote against the semi-Christian mystical beliefs common in the seventeenth century about secret societies, such as the Rosecrucians.[9]

During the Revolution and the time of Oliver Cromwell, England considered itself the New Jerusalem from which the armies of Christ would spread over the world to bring about the millennium. The restoration of the Stuart monarchy under Charles II in 1660 threw their expectations a curve. The radical Puritans, like the Fifth Monarchists who saw the Revolution as proof that the thousand-year reign of Jesus was about to begin, lost most of their followers, either through execution or a return to a less aggressive practice. The Quakers, for instance, dropped their militant stance and became pacifists, as they remain today.

Oddly, the Anglican Church, the state church of England, seems to have picked up the millennial flag. "A group of Anglican clergymen, led mainly by the followers of Robert Boyle, used millennial ideas in conjunction with Newtonian scientific principles to promote only those changes they thought would lead to political stability in England."[10] Perhaps made wary by the number of predictions of the end during the early 1600s, Boyle seems to have kept his millennial opinions low key. His sister, Katherine, Lady Ranelagh, with whom he lived in his last years, wrote him of their shared belief that "all this old frame of heaven and earth must pass and a new one be set up in its place."[11] In the same letter, she discussed the signs that this new world would arrive soon.

One of Boyle's followers was John Evelyn, trustee of the Boyle lectureship. His leadership in Anglican circles allowed him to bend doctrine toward the Boyle/Newton "natural religion." He employed this term in his many tracts and letters on the coming Apocalypse. Thus, although Boyle never wrote on Revelation in the way that Isaac Newton did, his determination to meld science and religion led to the formation of a view of the universe as orderly with a pattern ordained by a creator. It was a universe in which with the guidance of the Church it would be possible to establish a New Jerusalem through the continuing progress of humanity that would put off the final days indefinitely.[12]

ISAAC NEWTON

Isaac Newton (1642/3–1727) is still spoken of with reverence by mathematicians and scientists the world over. He is the man who set out to discover the rules by which nature operates. His work on gravity is legendary, and his basic laws of motion have yet to be repealed. He invented integral calculus and, in a dead heat with Leibniz, came up with differential calculus. He had the luck to have lived long enough to see his theories accepted and to be honored by his peers.

Even though in recent years, both academic and popular articles have concentrated on Newton's neuroses and interest in alchemy, his religion has been glazed over. One reason for this is that in the course of Newton's long life, his religious ideas changed or were refined. His own writing indicates that he was a devout Christian who believed that the Bible was the source of all wisdom.[13]

In his scientific works, Newton began with the supposition that there were rules governing the universe that were made by God. Everything he discovered only strengthened the opinion. It was not until near the end of his life that he took time for an in-depth study of the books of Daniel and Revelation. He acknowledged their obscurity but insisted that the symbolism must be clear to those of good will and, even more, honest faith.[14]

His book on the prophecies was not published until after his death, perhaps because his livelihood depended upon being at least publicly a supporter of the Anglican Church. The explanations in Newton's commentaries, for the most part, are not radical. He sees the Book of Daniel in terms of history that traces the fall of Jerusalem and Rome, the barbarian invasions, and the rise of the Holy Roman Empire under Charlemagne. When he arrives at the seventy weeks and the other calculations concerning the end, Newton is in his element. He scoffs at earlier interpreters who used sloppy math. He insists that they don't know where to start. They "either count by lunar years or by weeks not Judaic: and which is worse, they ground their interpretations on erroneous Chronology."[15]

Newton then consults the Jewish historian Josephus for dates of events that occurred around the time of the Crucifixion. He adds those to the information in the Bible and what he knows of Roman and Jewish festivals as well as the years when historical people are mentioned outside of the Bible. After several pages of meticulous analysis and giving reasons for each date excluded, Newton finally concludes that Jesus died on Friday, April 23, 34 C.E.[16] Unlike those who have studied the end times as foretold in Daniel, Newton never associates any of the beasts or kings of the north, or other enigmatic characters with people or institutions of his own day. He assumes that Daniel was prophesying for the people living in the first five hundred years of Christianity.

He also criticizes those who say that the Apostle John wasn't the man who received the revelations. Using both apocryphal gospels and the writings of the second-century fathers of the Church, Newton proves to his own satisfaction the apostolic source of Revelation and the date it was written.[17] Yet, even in material that he didn't expect to be published, Newton does not give any dates for the Second Coming. He tells the reader, "The follow of Interpreters has been to foretel times and things by the Prophecy, as if God designed to make them Prophets. . . . [W]e must content ourselves with interpreting what hath already been fulfilled."[18]

Newton's method of approaching the prophetic books is the same as his scientific method. He breaks each book into component parts, analyzes each one separately, and then decides how they fit together. One biographer called this work a "rambling muddle."[19] I didn't find it so, although he did make some statements that I found historically inaccurate, and I wasn't convinced by his assignments of historical figures to the horns, beasts, and so forth. What the work implies is that for Newton there was no difference between discovering the mechanics of the universe and deciphering the Bible.

Newton carried this even further in his ongoing investigation into the actual dimensions of Solomon's Temple. He felt that this was the real key to understanding the Apocalypse. He used information from the Book of Ezekiel as well as the philosophical writings of the medieval Jewish philosopher Maimonides. With these he worked out a time line, checking his findings with both mathematics and astronomy.[20] In this study he actually came up with some interesting dates. He felt that 1944 would end the tribulation of the Jews and that Christ would return in 1948. But the beginning of the idyllic millennium wouldn't begin until sometime between 2336 and 2370, with the Last Judgment occurring around 3370.[21]

Some of Newton's comments remind me of those who advocate the existence of the Bible Code. He felt that the answers were all clear but were written in imprecise language unsuitable for the masses to understand.[22] But for Newton, the book of nature and the book of God were both written in clear, mathematical terms.

JOSEPH PRIESTLEY

By the end of the eighteenth century, science and the millennium had joined forces. The end of the world and events that would precede it were being studied empirically. Joseph Priestley (1733–1804) is considered the father of modern chemistry for his discovery of oxygen and his research into the composition of air. His papers given at Royal Society meetings show that he also proved experimentally that electricity is carried by copper wire. He mentioned to Benjamin Franklin in 1769 that he was unable to use electricity to set off gunpowder. Franklin replied that he hadn't been able to manage that either.[23] Although Priestley hoped that the millennium would come peacefully, perhaps he felt it didn't hurt to be prepared for the worst.

He also was a dissenting minister in England who later founded the first Unitarian Church in America. He saw no break between religion and science, believing that "matter contained an in-dwelling force, power or spirit."[24] His was a new kind of millenarianism. It was not only based in logic, as many earlier mathematical calculations of the end had not been, but it also was more optimistic. Priestley felt that the world was progressing toward the millennium, not with sudden shocks but through gradual improvement of man and society.

In 1771, he wrote on his hope for the future:

The human powers will, in fact, be enlarged; nature, including both its materials, and its laws, will be more at our command; men will make their situation in this world abundantly more easy and comfortable; they will probably prolong their existence in it, and will grow daily more happy, each in himself, and more able (and, I believe, more disposed) to communicate happiness to others. Thus whatever was the beginning of this world, the end will be glorious and paradisiacal, beyond what our imaginations can now conceive.[25]

To this end, Priestley was at the forefront of education reform and believed strongly in republican governments. It was because of many of these religiously motivated convictions that his home and laboratory were destroyed in the Birmingham Riot of 1791. Priestley, his wife and sons were forced to move to America. He arrived in 1794. There he became friends with John Adams.

Adams was impressed with Priestley, but could not understand how such an intelligent man could be convinced that the millennium was about to begin. Adams wrote Thomas Jefferson that Priestley saw the French Revolution as a sign because the execution of Louis XVI meant the removal of one of the horns of the beast from Daniel.[26] Priestley apparently examined newspapers for a hint that the Ottoman Empire was about to fall, as this would open the way for the reclamation of Israel.[27] He saw the revolutions in both France and America as "a change from dark to light, from superstition to sound reason."[28] While the behavior of the revolutionary government of France discouraged him, the news that Napoleon had taken the Papal States gave him hope, just before his death, that the papal Antichrist had been defeated and that Napoleon would become the legendary Last World Emperor who would pave the way for the Second Coming.[29]

NAPIER, Boyle, Newton and Priestley were not exceptions among the people who laid down the rules for scientific experimentation and made some of the more exciting discoveries of the last millennium. While their religious beliefs varied, all stated at one time or another that they thought the prophetic books of the Bible were accurate if only they could be rightly interpreted. This scientific scrutiny gave support to the belief that the Bible was a source of information about the future and that the most brilliant men of the age were attempting to decipher it.

1 Robert G. Clouse, "John Napier and Apocalyptic Thought," *The Sixteenth Century Journal* 8, no. 1 (1974): 103.

2 Ibid.

3 Christopher Hill, *Intellectual Origins of the English Revolution Revisited* (Oxford: Clarendon Press, 1997). 9.

4 Clouse, 106.

5 Clouse, p. 109.

6 D. Thorburn Burns, "Robert Boyle, Analytical Chemist," *Philosophical Transactions: Physical Sciences and Engineering* 333, no. 1628 (1990): 3–4.

7 Loc. cit.

8 John F. Fulton, "The Honourable Robert Boyle, F.R.S. (1627–1692)," *Rites and Records of the Royal Society of London* 14 (1960): 130–132.

9 J. R. Jacob, "Robert Boyle and Subversive Religion in the Early Restoration," *Albiion* 6, no. 4 (1976): 278–280.

10 Hubert Seiwart, *Popular Religious Movements and Heterodox Sects* (Boston: Brill, 2003), 14.

11 Quoted in, J. R. Jacob, "Boyle's Circle in the Protectorate: Revelation, Politics and the Millennium," *Journal of the History of Ideas* 38, no. 1 (1977): 133.

12 Margaret C. Jacob, "Millenarianism and Science in the Late Seventeenth Century," *Journal of the History of Ideas* 37, no. 2 (1976): 339–341.

13 Howard Stein, "Newton's Metaphysics," in *The Cambridge Companion to Newton*, ed. I. Bernard Cohen and George E. Smith (Cambridge: Cambridge University Press, 2001), 390.

14 Ibid., 391.

15 Isaac Newton, *Observations upon the Prophecies of Daniel and the Apocalypse of St. John*, rpt. ed.(n.c.: Fillquarian, 2008): 114.

16 Ibid., 131–136.

17 Ibid., 193–200.

18 Ibid., 204–205.

19 Michael White, *Isaac Newton, The Last Sorcerer* (Reading, MA: Perseus Books, 1997),. 158.

20 Scott Mandelbrote, "'A Duty of the Greatest Moment': Isaac Newton and the Writing of Bible Criticism," *The British Journal for the History of Science* 26, no. 3 (993), 301.

21 White, 159–161.

22 Mandelbrote, 299.

23 Joseph Priestley, "Various Experiments on the Force of Electrical Explosions," *Philosophical Transactions 1763–1775* 59 (1763): 67. Franklin spent several years in London and attended Royal Society meetings. I love the idea of being able to ask Ben what he thought of electricity.

24 Seiwert, 28.

25 Quoted in John Mee, "Millenarian Visions and Utopian Speculations," in *The Enlightenment*, ed. Martin Fitzpatirck et al. (New York: Routledge, 2004), 369.

26 Clarke Garrett, "Joseph Priestley, the Millennium and the French Revolution," *Journal of the History of Ideas* 34, no. 1 (1973): 51.

27 Ibid., 57.

28 Quoted fin Garrett, 58. From a letter to Edmund Burke.

29 Ibid., 59–66.

PART FIVE:

The Millennial
Nineteenth Century

CHAPTER TWENTY-SIX

Heaven on Earth

The Bible is in free circulation—the Missionary to explain
it—the Sunday schools and tract Societies are the mighty
bolts of heaven. . . . Such are certain tokens, that a brighter son
will soon arise to set no more, till a thousand years of holy rest
to the saints shall complete the great week of time.

—Josiah Priest, *A View of the Expected Christian Millennium*, 1829[1]

Like many in America in the early 1800s, Josiah Priest saw the
new century and new nation in a hopeful, almost ecstatic, light.
The success of the American Revolution had convinced many Christians that this was where the Second Coming would occur. For many,
the Revolution itself was Armageddon, with the Antichrist, King
George III, defeated and chained.

Most American Christians of the time were postmillennialists.
They believed that they were in the thousand years of bliss of Revelation 20. This was the time when all things were possible to people of
good will. Poverty would be ended as would slavery. The world would
be converted to Protestant Christianity. Some wildly exuberant people even thought that women might someday have equal rights with
men. Progress was almost a tenet of early nineteenth-century religion.
"History would spiral upward by the orderly continuation of the same
forces that had promoted revivals, made America the model republic,
and increased material prosperity."[2]

In the first half of the century, millennial and utopian communities sprang up like mushrooms, particularly in New York State and on the frontier of Indiana. They ranged from the Millerites, who were decidedly premillennarian, to the Oneida Colony, whose founder John Humphrey Noyes (1811–1886) preached that the Second Coming had occurred in 70 C.E. and therefore people had already been saved. He taught that the job now was to become as perfect as possible before the general resurrection.

Noyes was an archetypal charismatic leader. He made it clear that God spoke to him alone, and he passed the word along to the faithful. That meant his word was divine law. His colony of Oneida was unusual not only for its unorthodox practices but in that it survived over thirty years. They practiced total communism, believing that property led to selfishness and crime. They also abolished marriage. As Noyes put it, "When the will of god is done on earth, as in heaven, *there will be no marriage*. . . . In a holy community there is no reason why sexual intercourse should be restrained by law, than why eating and drinking should be. . . . I call a certain woman my wife—she is yours, she is Christ's and in him she is the bride of all the saints."[3]

The debate about the position of women in the Oneida colony is ongoing. In some ways it was egalitarian. Women could chose their own partners and men were responsible for birth control. Women cut their hair short, wore bloomer costumes, and participated on an equal footing in all decision making. On the other hand, they weren't given an option to let their hair grow and wear skirts if they felt like it. The ideal was to make them look as much like men as possible. Also children were born on a policy of eugenics. Women and men were told when and with whom to procreate.[4]

While sex and communism were the most commented on aspects of Oneida, their primary goal was still attaining perfection as they saw it. They had meetings to admit to their own faults and discuss ways of correcting them. However unusual the lifestyle seemed to the outside world, the community was at a height of about three hundred people when disputes over authority started that led to its eventual dissolution.

The Oneidans were not the only group of the early nineteenth century to practice nontraditional familial patterns. For instance, the Mormon practice of polygamy was frowned on by the Oneidans as demeaning to women.[5]

Unlike the Oneidans, the Mormons or members of the Church of Jesus Christ of the Latter Day Saints, survived the loss of their founder and leader. Joseph Smith was a visionary prophet who provided his followers with a new testament, the Book of Mormon, which he received on tablets from heaven and translated. While Smith taught that the millennium was at hand, he also expected his followers to work to "build a premillennial kingdom, to transform history, to usher in the millennium."[6] Having a clear task at hand may have been one of the reasons that the Oneidans have vanished and the Mormons continue to grow.

There were also many utopian communities in early America. Most of them had a religious base but not all expected the millennium any time soon. This sense that more work needed doing before the Second Advent is an updating of the medieval concept. The revivalist and educator Charles Finney (1792–1875) put it most succinctly, "The earth must not be destroyed till its work is fully done."[7]

In Europe, the outlook was not so cheerful. The Continent was overwhelmed in the first part of the century by Napoleon, one of the prime candidates for the Antichrist.

COINCIDENTALLY, or perhaps not, 1844, the year predicted by William Miller for the end, was a millennial year for Shi'ite Muslims. It had been a thousand years since the occultation of the Twelfth Imam.

The reappearance of the imam was eagerly anticipated throughout the Shi'ite communities.

Islam had other apocalyptic warnings, some reflecting the uncertainty of contact with the outside world and its inventions. In 1877, a letter circulated, supposedly from a Shaykh Ahmad in Medina. In Egypt it was received as a telegram. It described a dream vision that warned Muslims that they had been neglecting their duties, drinking wine, refusing to give alms and not praying five times daily. The letter promised that "the last day, when the sun would rise from the west, was fast approaching."[8]

As the century waned, optimism began to fade. In the United States, the Civil War was a shock to all who had believed in an easy Manifest Destiny in which an Eden-like America stretched across the continent spreading Christian ideals as it went. In Europe, after Napoleon, there was the Crimean War and then the Franco-Prussian conflict. By the 1890s the feeling was that perhaps people had been too hasty when they thought they were living in the millennium. Maybe the Apocalypse was yet to come.

The twentieth century would confirm their worst nightmares.

1 Josiah Priest, *A View of the Expected Christian Millennium* (Albany: Loomis Press, 1829),. 85.

2 James H. Moorhead, "Between Progress and Apocalypse: A Reassessment of Millennialism in American Religious Thought 1800–1880," *The Journal of American History* 71, no. 3 (1984): 525.

3 Spencer C. Olin Jr., "The Oneida Community and the Instability of Charismatic Authority," *The Journal of American History* 67, no. 2 (1980): 291.

4 Lawrence Foster, "Free Love and Feminism: John Humphrey Noyes and the Oneida Community," *Journal of the Early Republic* 1, no. 2 (1981): 181–184.

5 Olin, 292.

6 Robert Flanders, "To Transform History: Early Mormon Culture and the Concept of Time and Space," *Church History* 40, no. 1 (1973): 112.

7 Moorhead, 529.

8 Jonathan D. Katz, "Shaykh Ahmad's Dream: A 19th-century Eschatological Vision," *Studia Islamica* 79 (1994) 160.

CHAPTER TWENTY-SEVEN

The Cherokee Ghost Dance of 1811–1812

The Cherokee confederation of the U.S. Southeast was both autonomous, with their own loose ties between communities, and slowly being integrated into British/American culture. From the early eighteenth century, they were pressured by the government and their white neighbors to assimilate into colonial society or move farther west. By the beginning of the nineteenth century, the Cherokee were divided between the Upper Towns of what are now North Carolina and Alabama and the Lower Towns of Georgia and Tennessee.

The Cherokee social structure was made up of matrilineal clan groups. Political decisions were made by each village independently, and financial matters were taken care of by each extended family. Leadership was divided among priests, warriors, and tribal headmen according to the situation.[1] In order to accommodate the colonial government, the Lower Towns tended to adopt European ways, establishing farms and even plantations, using iron tools, dressing in the European style, and intermarrying with the settlers. Some Cherokee also established the British form of representative government and legal system.[2]

Many of the Cherokee of the Upper Towns were uneasy about the loss of their lands and cultural identity. In 1808 about two thousand of

them moved west of the Mississippi River to establish traditional villages removed from colonial influence. For those who remained there
was continued pressure from the American government along with
the uncertainty about the worsening relationship between Britain and
the United States and which side to support should there be war.[3]

It was in this unsettled state that, in February 1811, a mixed-blood
Cherokee named Charlie, along with two unnamed women, received
a vision near Rocky Mountain in northwest Georgia. Charlie reported
this vision at a council held at Oostenally on February 7, 1811.[4]

The vision has been reported in several sources, mostly through
Indian agents, missionaries, or those who heard the story from their
elders. The one most quoted comes from the diaries of German Moravian missionaries, who heard it on February 10 from Chief Keychzae-
tel, who had been at the council. He told them that Charlie and the
women had just made camp when they heard a "violent noise in the
air, as if a storm was brewing." They went out to find out what was
happening and saw:

> a whole crowd of Indians arriving on the hill from the sky. . . .
> They were much frightened and for that reason wanted to go back
> into the house, whereupon that one [the drummer] called to them:
> "Don't be afraid; we are your brothers and have been sent by God
> to speak with you. God is dissatisfied that you are receiving the
> white people in your land without any distinction. You yourselves
> see that the hunting is gone—you are planting the corn of the
> white people—go and sell that back to them and plant Indian corn
> and pound it in the manner of your forefathers; do away with the
> mills. The Mother of the Nation has forsaken you because all her
> bones are being broken through the grinding [of the mills]. She will
> return to you, however, if you put the white people out of the land
> and return to your former manner of life. You yourselves can see
> that the white people are entirely different beings from us; we are
> made from red clay; they, out of white sand.[5]

Many of those attending the council believed in the vision and went home to tell others about it. In response, some villages reinstituted traditional ceremonies although they had never been completely abandoned, particularly the spring corn ceremony and festival.[6] This was known as the *Ahtawhhungnah* ceremony, in which a new fire was kindled, and the Cherokee were ritually purged of uncleanliness through dance and ritual purification in streams.[7]

This vision was not apocalyptic but, because of what came later, it has been included in the sequence that historians at the end of the nineteenth century called a Ghost Dance. As will be seen, the term is not accurate, but the apocalyptic feeling was part of the movement.

The next event to occur was the arrival of the Shawnees Tecumseh and his brother, shaman and visionary, Tenskwatawa. Tecumseh was attempting to create a coalition of Native Americans to form a united front to drive the settlers out of Indian Territory, if not back to Europe.[8] Convincing tribes that had long been enemies to work together was a daunting task, and it is amazing that Tecumseh succeeded as much as he did. In late 1811 he arrived in the south, where the Creeks had just learned that the United States planned to build a road through their land whether they liked it or not.[9] This governmental audacity helped Tecumseh's cause.

On September 19, Tecumseh met with Choctaw and Cherokee representatives at Tuckabtchie. The Indian agent, Hawkins, explained the situation regarding the road and then left. The agent to the Cherokees, Return Jonathan Meigs, who was not present, spoke to some of the Cherokee about what happened next.

They told him that Tecumseh had made his plea, warning the others that the United States was not about to stop its expansion. According to some accounts, he also made prophecies, including one in which he warned that, if they did not follow his advice, when he returned home to Indiana, he would "stamp the earth so that it would tremble."[10]

On December 16, 1811, the largest earthquake ever recorded in North America hit with an epicenter near New Madrid, Missouri. The

Mississippi River changed course, lakes were swallowed up, and new ones were formed. The earth split, leaving chasms running through fields. The earthquake was felt as far east as Boston and Washington, D.C.[11] The Moravian missionaries wrote: "Dec. 16, 1811: Early at three o'clock two shocks of an earthquake were felt. The house trembled and everything in them [sic] was in movement. The hens fell to the ground from their roosts and set up a pitiful cry."[12]

The aftershocks continued for months, with another major shock on January 23, 1812, and an even harder one on February 7.[13]

The disquiet caused by continual earthquakes was strengthened by the appearance of the Great Comet of 1811, which was at it brightest at roughly the same time as Tecumseh's travels. It's not clear whether Tecumseh foretold an earthquake, but he was given credit for doing so. It is at this point that the Cherokee visions became apocalyptic. A Cherokee named Big Bear told the Moravians of a vision another Cherokee had had that contained the warning, "Tugalo [formerly a Cherokee town in South Carolina], which is now possessed by white people, is the first place which God created. There in a hill he placed the first fire, for all fire comes from God. Now the white people have built a house on that hill. They should abandon the place; on that hill there should be grass growing; only then will there be peace." The Moravians thought this was all "silly" and tried to convince Big Bear that God didn't send such visions. Big Bear replied, "The white people know God from a book and we from other things."[14]

The visions predicted more disasters, particularly terrible storms with enormous hailstones that would destroy everyone but the traditional Cherokee, who must hide in the Great Smokey Mountains until the danger passed. It was reported that some did so.[15]

In March 1812, the Moravians reported that a new prophecy stated that there would be three days of darkness, "during which all the white people would be snatched away as well as all Indians who had any clothing or household articles of the white man's kind."[16]

By now the Moravians were thoroughly tired of these prophecies.

The earthquakes may have been getting on their nerves, too. They had been working among the Cherokee for several years and had made only one convert. They came to the conclusion that the visions were a "new stratagem of the Devil" and the only recourse was to pray harder.[17]

It may have been their prayers or the combined wisdom of the Cherokee, but the rumors of a new world without white people seemed to have died down by the spring of 1812. While this phenomenon has been called a "Ghost Dance," it has little in common with the 1890s movement among the Plains Indians. It was caused by a combination of frustration at the encroachment of a domineering foreign invader coupled with startling natural occurrences. There have been various explanations as to why the Cherokee prophecies did not take hold as did those of the Millerites and others. I suspect that there is no one simple reason. The Cherokee became involved with the immediate problems of survival. The comet faded; the earthquakes stopped. Life still held possibility.

As a side note, it was not just the Cherokees who saw a sign in the 1811 earthquake. Many who lived in the area most affected found religion. During one aftershock a Reverend James Finley "jumped to a table and shouted, 'For the great day of His wrath is come, and who shall be able to stand?'" gaining several converts at once. It was also reported that the membership in the Methodist Church in the area went up by 50 percent.[18]

The millennial movement in nineteenth-century America was off to a roaring start.

1 Dwayne Champagne, "Social Structure, Revitalization Movements and State Building: Social Change in Four Native American Societies," *American Sociological Review* 48, no. 6 (1983): 757.

2 Russell Thorten, "Boundary Dissolution and Revitalization Movements: The Case of the Nineteenth-Century Cherokee," *Ethnohistory* 40, no. 3 (1993): 364–365.

3 William G. McLoughlin, "New Angles of Vision on the Cherokee Ghost Dance Movement of 1811–1812," *American Indian Quarterly* 5, no. 4 (1979): 318.

4 Michelene E. Pesantubbe, "When the Earth Shakes: The Cherokee Prophesies of 1811–12," *American Indian Quarterly* 17, no. 3 (1993): 301.

5 Trans. Elizabeth Marx in McLoughlin, 340, from the Moravian records. The Moravians were speaking English with Cherokees and writing in German, but I think the essence of the vision is what they were told.

6 Thorten, 365.

7 Pesantubbe, 308.

8 John Sugden, "Early Pan-Indianism: Tecumseh's Tour of the Indian Country, 1811–1812," *American Indian Quarterly* 10, no. 4 (1986): 275.

9 Ibid., 284.

10 Sugden, 389.

11 Edward M. Shepherd, "The New Madrid Earthquake," *The Journal of Geology* 13, no. 1 (1905): 47. Shepherd includes firsthand accounts of the earthquake.

12 McLoughlin, 340.

13 Margaret Ross, "The New Madrid Earthquake," *The Arkansas Historical Quarterly* 27, no. 2 (1968): 87.

14 McLoughlin, 342.

15 Pesantubbe, 309–310.

16 McLouglin, 344.

17 Ibid.

18 Quoted in Ross, 100.

CHAPTER TWENTY-EIGHT

The Millerites

I was shown in a vision, and I still believe, that here was a shut
door in 1844. All who saw the light of the first and second
angels' messages and rejected that light, were left in darkness.

—Ellen Gould White, founder of the Seventh-Day Adventists[1]

O f the many religious movements of the early nineteenth century, one of the most controversial was started by a solid farmer
from upstate New York. The Millerites are of special note because of
the passionate response of the public to them and because of the after-
math to their "Great Disappointment" when the Second Coming did
not appear as they expected.

William Miller was born in Massachusetts on February 15, 1782,
the son of a Revolutionary War captain. When he was four, the family
moved to Washington County, New York, where he grew up.[2]

Miller's early religious life was typical for the time. His family was
Baptist, and his mother, Paulina, the daughter of a minister, encouraged him to read the Bible. In his memoirs, he states that he always felt
the need for a personal connection with God, but he seemed ambiva-
lent about religion in his youth, even considering himself a Deist. In
1805, he married Lucy Smith, and they began farming and producing
children. He fought in the War of 1812, becoming a captain, like his
father. He was active in civic affairs and a member of the Masons.[3]

Then, in 1816, in response to his war experiences, Miller became deeply concerned about the afterlife. This led to his determination to prove logically that the Bible was accurate and understandable, providing clear answers to life's questions. He embarked on a fifteen-year odyssey through the scriptures in search of those answers. "I found everything revealed that my heart could desire, and a remedy for every disease of the soul," he later wrote.[4]

During this time, he became aware of the millennial movements that were springing up all over the Northeast. Many of them taught that the millennium would be a time of universal brotherhood and peace, after which Jesus would return. This bothered Miller. He felt that this belief, called postmillennialism, had it backwards. In Miller's interpretation, first Jesus would return in his Second Advent, and then the millennium would begin with Christ as ruler.[5] In his statement of faith, sent in a letter to his brother, Miller wrote:

> *I believe that the Scriptures do reveal unto us, in plain language, that Jesus Christ will appear again on this earth, that he will come in the glory of God, in the clouds of heaven, with all his saints and angels; that he will raise the dead bodies of all his saints who have slept, change the bodies of all that are alive on the earth that are his, and both these living and raised saints will be caught up to meet the Lord in the air.*[6]

Miller followed with his understanding of what would happen to those left behind.

> *And while this is being done in the air, the earth will be cleansed by fire, the elements will melt with fervent heat, the works of men will be destroyed, the bodies of the wicked will be burned to ashes, the devil and all evil spirits, with the souls and spirits of those who have rejected the gospel, will be banished from the earth, shut up in*

the pit or place prepared for the devil and his angels, and will not
be permitted to visit the earth again until 1000 years.[7]

Through his belief that the Bible was clear and definite to those who studied it properly, Miller joined the corps of those who tried to work out the time of the Second Coming through mathematical calculations. Like most of the others, including Isaac Newton, he started with the Book of Daniel. He began his computations with the old favorite, Daniel 8:14: "Unto two thousand and three hundred days; then shall the sanctuary be cleansed."[8] From that and using other clues in Daniel, Miller was startled to discover that the Second Coming would be around March 23, 1843.

Miller pondered this revelation for some time, confiding it to a few friends. He seems to have known well that most people would laugh at his conclusions. Slowly, however, he began to tell others, prompted, he said, by a sign from God that he could not ignore. Nevertheless, Miller's preaching remained low key until he ran into an evangelical firebrand, then in his late twenties, named Joshua Vaughn Himes.

Himes was the minister at Boston's Chardon Street Chapel. He was a strong supporter of the abolitionist movement, working with William Lloyd Garrison.[9] Himes met Miller when the latter spoke in Exeter, New Hampshire. In 1839 he invited Miller to preach in Boston at his church. Himes became convinced that Miller was correct and that his message needed to be brought to as many people as possible before the end, which was fast approaching.

By now, thousands of people in New England and eastern Canada had heard Miller preach. Ministers from many different denominations had asked him to speak to their congregations. Miller was a good draw, and after hosting him, church leaders generally found they had new members. Miller had no intention of starting his own religion. Why bother, when the millennium was nearly upon us? So Baptist, Methodist, and Congregationalist pastors generally felt that his message would not cost them adherents. Many of them were converted to Miller's cause and began preaching it themselves.

Joshua Himes did his part by publishing a series of journals. Starting with *The Signs of the Times* in March 1840, followed by *The Midnight Cry*, first published in New York City in late 1842. Others took up the cry and began printing magazines and pamphlets as far west as Ohio, often brought out to coincide with Miller's speaking engagements. As a consequence, thousands of people accepted Miller's prophecy and began to prepare their souls for the millennium.[10]

Although Miller had many enthusiastic supporters, most of America, particularly the press, found his prophecies either irritating or laughable. As the spring of 1843 began, newspapers began reporting on Miller and the crowds that attended whenever he spoke. From this, they moved to stories about the antics of Miller's followers. Several cases of insanity and suicide attempts were laid at his door. The penny papers, or tabloids, wrote the wildest tales, such as that of the night watchman at Spring Gardens, in Philadelphia, who "heard three groans which he was certain were Gabriel's preparatory blasts."[11] The same paper told its readers that there was a bill in the Pennsylvania State House to prohibit "Millerites, Mormons, assemblymen, [and] locomotives . . . from riding the tails of comets."[12] This was probably occasioned by the appearance in early March of an extremely bright comet that could be seen even in the daytime. It was described as having two tails.[13] This set off apocalyptic fears even among nonbelievers.

However, comets and other outward signs were not of concern to Miller. It was the proof he found in the Bible that established his conviction. He believed that anyone who took that time to study would come to the same conclusions. He even provided a list of terms used that he considered "figurative" or allegorical to help in understanding. Adultery and blasphemy were both simply forms of idolatry. "Woman" could both mean the church and the anti-church. (This is not an uncommon conclusion among male theologians). "Israel" stood for the Christian church.[14]

Other than his certainty that the world was about to end, there was little new or radical in Miller's teaching. This may have been part of his appeal.

For complicated reasons, April 23, 1843, was the eventual date that many Millerites believed would bring the end. As the day approached, Miller and his followers preached to huge crowds. Even conservative newspapers became concerned, feeling that many people were failing to plant crops or provide for a future they didn't believe in.[15]

When the world didn't end on April 23, Miller was disappointed but not daunted. He went back to the Bible and recalculated. He believed he had made a mistake in using the Christian year instead of the Jewish one. Therefore, his new end date was revised to the spring of 1844.

As the new date approached, the number of faithful continued to grow. The Millerites bought an enormous tent that could accommodate over two thousand people. They took this through upstate New York and out to Ohio. The newspapers, which had lost interest after the failure of the 1843 Apocalypse, began to take notice of the Millerites once again. One topic that fascinated them was the rumor that Miller's followers were preparing "ascension robes," long white gowns to wear as they were assumed into heaven. "Some . . . persons, . . . were up all night, with their 'ascension robes' on, and their lamps trimmed and burning—ready, at a moment's warning, to be 'taken up.'"[16] These robes were considered a mark of the lunacy of the Millerites, and later Adventist historians and others have doubted that they ever existed. After reviewing the literature, I believe that Miller never suggested that his followers wear anything specific for their ascension. However, the idea of the robes was so widespread that I think many believers could have assumed that it was part of the ceremony and made them for themselves and their families.[17]

However, March 21, 1844, came and went with no Second Coming.

Miller refused to be discouraged. He wrote to Himes, "The time, as I have calculated it, is now filled up, and I expect every moment to see Our Savior descend from heaven."[18]

Miller thought that perhaps the day of reckoning would finally occur in the fall, but he set no firm date. At a camp meeting in Exeter, New Hampshire, in August, it was suggested, by S. S. Snow that Yom Kippur, the Jewish Day of Atonement, was "a day of judgment for Israel, in which the sanctuary was cleansed."[19] The next Yom Kippur, the tenth day of the seventh month, according to the Hebrew calendar, would be October 22, 1844.

This date was seized upon by the Millerites, although William Miller had his doubts. He eventually was convinced that Snow was right and wrote Himes, "I see a glory in the seventh month which I never saw before."[20]

During this period, many of the churches that had opened their doors to Miller's preaching shut them again. Part of this is because many Millerites felt that one reason for the first disappointments was the resistance of the Baptists, Congregationalists, and Methodists to joining the movement.[21] They never considered converting Catholics or Episcopalians, assuming that they were too far gone to save except by a miracle.

The absolute faith of the Millerites might have caused even the most skeptical to feel a twinge of nervousness on the eve of the twenty-second. But, sadly, Jesus did not appear that day, either.

This was the final Great Disappointment. Most of the Millerites went home and pieced their lives together. Miller and Himes undertook to raise money to support farmers who hadn't harvested and workers who had left their jobs and given away all their possessions. Some followers proposed that the date was, again, wrong. Others thought that Jesus had come, but secretly. There were many explanations but, in essence that was the end of the Millerites.

It was not the end of the millennial movement, though. Some Millerite Adventists came to believe that they had misunderstood the message. The sanctuary was not on earth, but in heaven, and it was being cleansed for the faithful. This belief, coupled with a realization that Christians had been ignoring the fourth commandment of the Decalogue by observing the Sabbath on Sunday rather than Saturday, led to the establishment of what was to become the Seventh Day Adventists.[22]

William Miller, although devastated, continued to believe that the Second Coming would happen any moment until his death on December 20, 1849. The year before, he had lost his sight, and it was only then that he gave up preaching.[23]

Joshua Himes is really the more interesting of the two leaders of the Millerites. It was his determination to publish newspapers, articles, books, and tracts and get them to the largest possible audience that spread the prophecy of William Miller. He was the object of the more vitriolic of the attacks in the press. Many assumed that he was embezzling donations from gullible followers.[24] He defended himself in his journals and his finances don't indicate an elaborate lifestyle. Most of the money donated probably went to the cost of the voluminous printings, the majority of which were given away to those who attended meetings or were mailed to be handed out as far away as England and Hawaii.

Himes lived well into his nineties. He continued with the Adventist movement, listing himself in the 1860 census as an Adventist clergyman. Like many after the Civil War, he moved west. In 1870, he was in Buchanan Village, Michigan, where he and his son, William, published an Adventist paper, the *Advent Christian Times*.[25] But, sometime around 1880, Himes decided to return to the Episcopal Church. He was ordained a minister and given a parish in Elk Point, South Dakota, where he lived the remainder of his days.[26]

It is useless to speculate as to why Himes left the Adventists. He seems not to have regretted his time as a Millerite. He met and corresponded with James and Ellen White, among the founders of the Seventh Day Adventists, until shortly before his death from cancer in 1896.

The Millerites remain the most dramatic of the many millennial groups of the early nineteenth century. They also have had the longest echo in American literature and popular culture. In Miller's own time, Nathaniel Hawthorne mentioned him in several stories. In one, "The New Adam and Eve," he records "good Father Miller's interpretations of the prophecies to have proved true. The Day of Doom has burst upon the globe and swept away the whole race of men."[27] Several other writers of the time commented on the Millerites, usually in serious tones, as opposed to the sensationalism of the papers. Late-nineteenth-century novelists generally used the Millerites for comic relief or as a warning against fanaticism.

The stories of white-robed Millerites standing on hilltops, waiting to be beamed up to heaven, had a much longer lifespan than the actual movement. In the end, Miller may have been doomed by his own publicity. In his attempt to convert as many people as possible before the coming advent, he set himself up for ridicule. When the world neither ended nor changed in any appreciable manner, William Miller was relegated to the realm of crackpot millenarians, even though his was far from being the most unusual movement of that decade of religious fervor. The movement continued sporadically for many years. In 1875, William C. Thurman, a Millerite Adventist from Boston, apparently announced that the world would end on April 19. A number of Millerites gathered in Chicago to prepare for the Rapture. A newspaper report on April 20 stated that "they now acknowledge that they have no way of determining when the world will come to an end."[28]

1 Quoted in, F.. M. Wilcox, *Testimony of Jesus: A Review of the Work and Teachings of Mrs. Ellen Gould White* (Peekskill, NY: Review & Herald Publishing, 1934), 76.

2 Jerome L. Clark, *1844: Religious Movements.* (Nashville: Southern Publishing, 1968), 18.

3 Paul A. Gordon, *Herald of the Midnight Cry* (Boise, ID: Pacific Press Publishing, 1990), 14–22.

4 Sylvester Bliss, *Memoirs of William Miller* (1853), 67.

5 Clark, 22. Note that this is much the same idea as that of the Fifth Monarchists, although it's doubtful that Miller ever heard of them.

6 Joshua V. Himes, *Views of the Prophecies and Prophetic Chronology Selected from Manuscripts of William Miller with a Memoir of His Life* (Boston: Dow, 1841).

7 Ibid.

8 King James version.

9 Gary Scharnhorst, "Images of the Millerites in American Literature," *American Quarterly* 32, no. 1 (1980): 25.

10 Clark, 30–31.

11 A. Spencer Braham, "The Philadelphia Press and the Millerites," *The Pennsylvania Magazine of History and Biography* 78, no. 2 (1954): 194.

12 Braham, 195.

13 *The New York Times*, March 7, 1880. The article was a retrospective on the comet, and the expert interviewed stated that the comet had been expelled from the sun.

14 Himes, 25–31; Clark, 40.

15 Braham, 195.

16 *Bay State Democrat* (Boston), March 17, 1843, quoted in Ira V. Brown, "The Millerites and the Boston Press," *The New England Quarterly* 16, no. 4 (1943): 593.

17 Frances D. Nichol, "The Growth of the Millerite Legend," *Church History* 21, no. 4 (1952): 298, notes that this is mentioned in a New Hampshire paper.

18 Quoted in Gordon, 87.

19 Clark, 46.

20 Quoted in ibid., 48.

21 Nichol, 297.

22 Clark, 66–71.

23 Gordon, 112.

24 Brown, 610–613.

25 U.S. Census 1870, Berrien County, MI, 23; B. Cowles, *Berrien County Directory and History* (Niles, MI, 1871), 266.

26 US Census 1880, Union County, SD, 48; Doane Robinson, *Encyclopedia of South Dakota* (Pierre, SD, 1923), 352–353.

27 Quoted in Gary Scharnhorst,: 22–23.

28 *The Milwaukee News*, April 20, 1875, 1.

CHAPTER TWENTY-NINE

The United Society of Believers in Christ's Second Coming

The Shakers

The Angels are sounding on their golden trumpets
They sound and resound from the heavenly shore.
Inviting all nations, all kindred and people
To come, come to Zion and wander no more.

—Maria Butler, Shaker hymn (1846)

The Shakers today are known for their meticulous craftsmanship, which has made antique Shaker boxes and furniture highly sought after, and for their music, some of which was used by Aaron Copeland in his symphony *Appalachian Spring*. But in the first half of the nineteenth century, they were considered a radical and possibly dangerous sect that broke up families and preached the equality of women.

The Shakers had their origin in 1847 in Manchester, England, where a couple, Jane and James Wardley, had left their own churches and formed a group in which the worship consisted of prayer and personal revelation. This took the form of trances, "singing, shouting and shaking."[1] They were dubbed the "Shaking Quakers" although it's not clear that they were ever affiliated with the Quakers.

The sect remained small and relatively unknown until 1758, when they were joined by a young woman, Ann Lee. Lee was born on February 29, 1736, in Manchester. She was the daughter of a blacksmith and may have been working in a textile factory at the time of her conversion.[2] She was then married to a blacksmith named Abraham Standerin (often mistakenly listed as "Abraham Stanley").[3]

During her time with the Shaking Quakers, Lee expressed serious doubts about sex. She came to believe that all sex was sinful, even in marriage. The deaths of her four children, either stillborn or in infancy, confirmed this conviction. After the death of the fourth child, in 1766, Jane Wardley advised Lee to give up relations with her husband.[4] Ann apparently followed this advice. Whatever Abraham thought about this, he stayed with her for several more years and came with her to America.

During the 1770s Lee's theology was beginning to develop, aided by a number of dreams and prophetic visions. The renunciation of sex and marriage was the starting point in her belief. This would free women, particularly, to have more time to contemplate the nature of God. In a series of revelations, Ann Lee came to understand that godhood was made up of God the father and God the mother. "They were one in essence but possessed two natures—masculine and feminine, each of which was distinct in function yet one in being."[5]

This concept was far from new, but it was also far from popular. When she began to publicly preach, Ann Lee was mocked, attacked, and eventually jailed for disorderly conduct when she tried to break up services at Christ Church in Manchester.[6] While imprisoned, she received a vision telling her to go to America. Upon her release, she made preparations to emigrate. She arrived with her husband, brother, niece, and five other followers, on August 6, 1774.[7]

This was not the best time to come from England with news of a radical new religion. Lee and her party were sometimes suspected of being British spies. At best, they were considered oddities. They made few converts. It was not until after the American Revolution ended in 1781 that people had the energy to look into alternative religions.

Now living on land the group had bought in a town near Albany, New York, Lee and her brother, William, made a proselytizing trip through New England. While they were still greeted with ridicule in most places, the religious climate had changed to be more favorable to the Shakers. In the midst of the Revolution and just afterward, a movement had spread through New England known as the New Light Stir. This was a follow up to the Great Awakening of the 1740s. While not specifically millennial, this movement was grounded in the Protestant belief that "God visits ordinary people with the 'New Light' of transfiguring grace and revelation."[8] One disillusioned New Lighter, who had expected the end of the world in 1779, was Joseph Meacham. Meacham found hope in the Shaker philosophy and became Ann Lee's "first born son in America."[9]

By the time of Lee's death in 1784, there were eleven Shaker "families," households of men, women, and children under the direction of an Elder and an Eldress. Apart from a belief in the approach of the millennium and strict celibacy, it's not clear what the theology of the Shakers consisted of. Lee could not read or write and had forbidden her followers to write tracts. However, after she died, the sect had been the subject of sensationalist books by former disciples. Joseph Meacham decided that the life of Mother Ann and the history of the group should be compiled in their own defense. Lee was being represented as a "pretended 'Second Christ', a fortuneteller, a drunkard, a false prophet or miracle worker and a 'woman in authority over men.'"[10] Considering that homemade whiskey was the main form of central heating in colonial America, the charge of drinking may have had some base. She might also have pled guilty to the last charge, but not to its being a bad thing.

This is the point in the story at which the historian has to walk carefully. All of the information we have on what Ann Lee believed herself to be comes from the memories of those who knew her. In line with the popular belief in personal revelation, she seems to have felt that Christ was with her at all times. She apparently referred to him as her "husband" and "lover," something any medieval nun would have understood.

In the years after her death her followers seemed to have revised this relationship with Jesus, sometimes diminishing it. In Meacham's 1790 statement of the principles of the church, he stated that the Shakers were the "fourth dispensation" and that Christ had not returned in the flesh but in spirit to the Shaker community as a whole.[11] He gives the date for this Second Coming as having begun in 1747, with the Shaking Quakers, James and Jane Wardley.[12]

However, by the early 1800s, a number of Shakers were convinced that Ann Lee had not just walked with Christ, but was Christ reborn in a female body. The preface to the 1816 book of reminiscences of Mother Ann begins, "When the time was fully come, according to the appointment of God, Christ was again revealed . . . in the person of a female. This extraordinary woman, whom her followers believe God had chosen, and in whom Christ did visibly make his second appearance, was Ann Lee."[13]

This divine presence was expressed in various ways by Lee's followers. One, Benjamin Young, was the first Shaker to write that God was dual in nature, He stated that there was a Holy Mother Wisdom who co-existed with the Creator Father.[14] The First Advent was the male side of God; therefore, the second would logically be female.

Even more, like Jesus, Ann Lee was poor, persecuted, and never wrote down her teachings. She let her apostles spread and preserve the Word.

Some Shakers were firm in their belief in Lee's divinity. Others worked around the concept in various ways. Some said that Lee was merely the "first witness" of the Second Coming. The 1827 *Testimonies* gives the doctrine of male and female in one god and states that Ann Lee is the spirit of Christ in female form. Yet they also add that they "reject the doctrine of the Trinity, of the bodily resurrection, and of an atonement for sins. They do not worship either Jesus or Ann Lee, holding both to be simply elders in the Church, to be respected and loved."[15] Clearly, the question of Lee's nature was one that varied according to the believer. It also changed over time, being downplayed by the end of the nineteenth century.

The Shakers also spoke of Ann Lee as "the woman clothed with the sun" of Revelation 12. As several modern scholars have pointed out, she was glorified by the Shakers as a woman rather than as the mouthpiece for a male god.[16] This has led some to feel that the Shakers were proto-feminists. Of course, they could also be considered proto-communists and early practitioners of modern dance. I think it's better to understand people in their own time rather than to force them into ours. It is certain that women were given an equal say in the running of the community. However, in the division of labor, women did cooking, cleaning, laundry, canning, and lacemaking whereas men were blacksmiths, farmers, broom makers, and mechanics. Work was assigned along traditional gender lines, but it appears that both women's and men's work were given equal value. Perhaps taking sex out of the mix allowed a more balanced view.

One constant in Shaker theology is that they believed that they were living in the last millennium. For this reason, once they had become full members of the community, Shakers felt that they must live sinless lives, as there could be no second chances given to back sliders. They were the final church and it was their duty to see the world through to the Final Judgment. The 1806 *Testimony*, written by a member of an Ohio Shaker community, states "He that commiteth sin is of the devil, & God must reject such a one for xt.s [Christ's] sake, because xt [Christ] and belial [Satan] can have no concord."[17]

They hoped that they could bring about a heaven on earth by convincing the rest of the world to join them. When all lived sinless lives, without reproduction, then it would be a world of saints, ready for the Last Judgment and eternal life in heaven.[18]

As time passed the Shakers became more accepted. They were

Currier, Nathaniel (1813–1888). Shakers dance near Lebanon. Lithograph. Location: Private Collection. *Giraudon / Art Resource, New York*

known for their hospitality, taking in and feeding strangers as a duty. Their craftsmanship and practical inventions were much admired.[19] They were clean, thrifty, and honest in their business dealings. The marching and dancing during their services became quaint rather than bizarre. Later evangelical movements had made ecstatic shouting and speaking in tongues more commonplace in the American religious experience.

The high point in Shaker population occurred around 1840 with about five thousand members. After that, the communities began a slow loss of members. Not enough people joined the group to keep the numbers up. Children adopted by the Shakers often left when they reached adulthood. The days were strictly regimented to prayer and work. Life as a Shaker required faith and discipline, although for many the fellowship of the community was an important factor. They tried to live as saints with tolerance for the quirks of others.[20]

As of 2006, there was one Shaker community left, one of the oldest, in Sabbathday Lake, Maine. There are four members, two men and two women. They try to maintain the Shaker way of life in the midst of tourists and encroaching developments.[21] They are not adverse to modern technology, which makes sense considering how many devices they invented to make work easier. They even have a website.[22] In 2009, they hosted a music festival.

What hasn't changed is the essential belief of the Shakers. "It teaches above all else that God is Love and that our most solemn duty is to show forth that God who is love in the World. Shakerism teaches God's immanence through the common life shared in Christ's mystical body."[23]

The last Shakers have not given up hope that the rest of the world will come around to this belief, thereby bringing on the millennium.

1 Rosemary D. Gooden, "The Shakers: A Brief Historical Sketch," in *Locating the Shakers: Cultural Origins and Legacies of an American Religious Movement* ed. Mick Gridley and Kate Bowles (Exeter, UK: Exeter University Press, 1990), 1. See also Edward Deming Andres, *The People Called Shakers: A Search for the Perfect Society* (New York: Oxford University Press, 1953); and Stephen A. Marini, *Radical Sects of Revolutionary New England* (Cambridge, MA: Harvard University Press, 1982).

2 Jerome L. Clark, *1844*, Volume I, *Religious Movements* (Nashville, TN: Southern Publishing, 1968), 331.

3 Gooden, 1.

4 Op. cit.

5 Clark, 333.

6 Tisa J. Wenger, "Female Christ and Feminist Foremother: The Many Lives of Ann Lee," *Journal of Feminist Studies in Religion* 18, no. 2 (2002): 6.

7 Gooden, 2.

8 Charles Sellers, *The Market Revolution: Jacksonian America, 1814–1846*, (Oxford, Oxford University Press, 1991), 30.

9 Gooden, 3.

10 Jean M. Humes, "'Ye Are My Epistles': The Construction of Ann Lee Imagery in Early Shaker Sacred Literature, *Journal of Feminist Studies in Religion* 8, Nn. 1 (1991): 87.

11 Clark, quoting from the 1808 manifesto *The Testimony of Christ's Second Appearing*, 337–338. The other three dispensations were the antediluvians, the Jews up to Jesus, and from Jesus to Ann Lee.

12 Wenger, 10–11.

13 Quoted in Marjorie Procter-Smith, "Who Do You Say That I Am?: Mother Ann as Christ," in *Locating the Shakers*, ed. Gridley and Bowles, 84–85.

14 Humez, 86.

15 Clark, 338.

16 Procter-Smith and Humez both discuss this. Wenger argues that the elevation of Mother Ann was intended to establish authority among her successors but also notes the emphasis on the feminine.

17 Stephen J. Stein, "'A Candid Statement of Our Principles': Early Shaker Theology in the West," *Proceedings of the American Physical Society* 133, no. 4 (1989): 517. This reproduces the document with all its idiosyncratic spellings. One interesting thing about this is that Ann Lee is nowhere mentioned in it.

18 Clark, 338.

19 Among other things, they invented the clothespin (Clark, 342).

20 Arthur T. West, "Reminiscence of Life in a Shaker Village," *The New England Quarterly* 11, no. 2 (1938): 343–360. This presents a nostalgic view of life by a man who was raised by the Shakers and then left and later came back to teach for a time.

21 Stanley Chase, "The Last Ones Standing," *Boston Globe,* July 23, 2006. Available at www.boston .com/news/globe/magazine/articles/2006/07/23/the_last_ones_standing. Accessed November 2009.

22 See www.shaker.lib.me.us. Accessed November 2009.

23 "About the Community." Available at www.shaker.lib.me.us/about.html. Accessed November 2009.

CHAPTER THIRTY

The Mummyjums

Their dress is very singular, long beards, close caps and
bear skins tied around them. The writer believes
them a set of deluded enthusiasts.

—*Sussex Register* (Newton, New Jersey, September 15, 1917)

Mummyjum sounds to me like such a cute group, tubby little teddy bears with honey on their fur. The reality is far from my comfortable image. The name was given them by the Shakers of New Lebanon, who offered them what little hospitality they would accept. The Shakers were quite used to speaking in tongues, but their visitors' constant repetition of "my God, my God, my God, my God, What wouldst thou have me do—Mummyjum, mummyjum, mummyjum, mummyjum," must have gotten on even their tolerant nerves.[1]

They called themselves "the Pilgrims" and were led by a red-bearded man named Isaac Bullard. His followers called him Prophet, and he governed them as an absolute monarch, receiving direction directly from heaven.[2] Bullard apparently came from Canada, near the Vermont border, and began his pilgrimage in Vermont.

As with many small millennial groups, it's hard to be certain what they believed, other than that the end of the world was imminent. All the information about them comes from letters, newspaper accounts, and reports by people who encountered them in their wanderings.

According to these reports, given over several states and years, the Pilgrims believed in a primitive life of constant penitence and fasting in anticipation of the end. They wore bearskin wraps; it's not clear if they wore anything under them. They ate gruel from a communal pot without spoons or forks and lived in rough huts or a tent.[3]

Starting out from Woodstock, Vermont, the group wandered from place to place, hunting for the perfect location in which to await the coming end and picking up converts along the way. They were generally greeted with astonishment and often disgust. They reportedly were forbidden to wash, change their clothes, or cut their hair or fingernails. When they arrived at the Shaker village of New Lebanon, New York, the official scribe wrote that "particularly the females were by traveling & fasting, reduced to great weakness . . . and the whole company were very dirty & filthy."[4] One of the Pilgrims, Fanny Ball, later wrote of her belief that "God was now about to establish his kingdom on earth."[5]

The Mummyjums passed into Ohio, now dressed in patchwork clothes and mismatched shoes. In Xenia, they were again lodged by Shakers, who did not succeed in converting, or even bathing, them. By now the Pilgrims numbered about fifty-five people, including a former minister, Joseph Ball, and his wife. Fanny.[6]

Semistarvation, penitential self-punishment, and lack of good personal hygiene seem to have caught up with the Mummyjums at this point. Several died of smallpox, malaria, and malnutrition before they reached their final destination in Arkansas Territory. The Reverend and Mrs. Ball left the group at New Madrid, Missouri. Some of their family later joined the Shakers. Ball eventually admitted that "Isaac Bullard was the most terrible impostor that ever trod American shores."[7] But for a time, both he and Fanny had believed that Bullard was the key to their salvation.

On one of the stops the Mummyjums made on the Missouri River, a local sheriff, who had heard about the condition of the children in the group, brought a boatload of food for them and had to hold off the adults with his sword while the children ate.[8] What happened to the children after the sheriff left is not recorded.

Eventually deprivation and the failure of Christ to return caused most of the Mummyjums to leave the group.

Isaac Bullard ended his days sometime after 1824. Two women remained with him at least until that year, living in a hut on the Mississippi. A visitor offered them safe passage back to their families but neither would abandon Bullard.

The Mummyjums may have been only a tiny group in the midst of less radical millennial movements. However, Isaac Bullard's spiritual descendants are men like Jim Jones and David Koresh, who incorporate personal charisma with apocalyptic fears to control followers who follow them even to their deaths.

1 F. Gerald Ham, "The Prophet and the Mummyjums: Isaac Bullard and the Vermont Pilgrims of 1817," *Wisconsin Magazine of History* 56, no. 4 (1973): 294. Ham quotes from the Shaker records as well as several contemporary newspapers.

2 Op. cit.

3 A letter by the Reverend Ira Chase, printed in *The American Baptist Magazine and Missionary Intelligencer* new ser. 1, no. 9 (Boston, 1818): 1, describes an encounter with the Mummyjums in upstate New York.

4 Quoted in Ham, 295.

5 Op. cit.

6 Ham, 297.

7 A letter by Joseph Ball, printed in *Woodstock Observer* 1, no. 6 (1820): 1.

8 Ham, 298.

CHAPTER THIRTY-ONE

Chinese Millennial Movements II

Jesus' Little Brother

There is a somewhat strange peculiarity distinguishing these
insurgents. The accounts received from Mr. Meadows describe
them as Puritanical and even fanatic. The whole army pray
regularly before meals.

—Letter to the earl of Clarendon, 1852[1]

The story of Hong Xiuquan, the Heavenly Kingdom, and the
attempt to create a heaven on earth in Nanjing, China, has
often been portrayed as a classic example of Christian proselytizing
gone wrong. If only the missionaries hadn't come to China, people
said, the tragic rebellion would never have occurred.[2]

Maybe, but as we have seen with the Yellow Turbans, there was a
strong millennial trend in Chinese popular religion.[3] If Hong hadn't
heard of Christianity, he might have based his beliefs on Daoist or
Maitreyan Buddhist or even Manichaean popular religions. He did
draw on all of those traditions, but it was the chance receipt of the
Christian tract, a nervous breakdown, an inexplicable dream, and his
resentment at the failure to pass a Confucian government test that
came together to create the Taiping Rebellion.

Hong, the leader of the Taiping, was born in a village in Guan-
dong (Canton) province in 1814. His family were farmers and Hakka,

rather than native southern Chinese. The Hakka had been in the area for two hundred years but were still considered an outside group. The family were doing well enough that Hong Huo Xiu, their youngest son, was able to go to school. He excelled there and was bright enough to pass the qualifying exams that permitted him to go to the city of Canton to take the civil service test. Passing this would allow him to become a government official, something that would bring honor and a better life for his family.[4]

While in Canton in 1836 to take the test, someone in the street gave him a pamphlet of excerpts from the Old and New Testaments along with exhortations to become a Christian. This was one of the many tracts written in Chinese by Western Christian missionaries. It was called "Good Words for Exhorting the Age." Hong didn't read the pamphlet then. He took the test and failed.[5]

Hong tried at least three times to pass the test with no success. In 1837, after his third failure, he fell ill and had to hire a sedan chair to carry him home. When he arrived home, he took to his bed, believing that he was about to die. Over the next month he drifted in and out of consciousness, during which time he had a number of dream visions that he didn't understand.

The account of these visions was told to a missionary, Theodore Hamberg, by Hong's cousin, Hung Jen-Kan. "Hung Jen-Kan was an educated person who lived with Hung Hsiu-ch'uan [sic] during the period of the illness and afterward; he was in sympathy with the rebellion, but his account shows that he regarded his cousin as insane."[6]

The visions, which continued off and on over a period of days, began with one that derived from traditional Chinese symbolism. Hong saw a dragon, a tiger, and a cock. All three of these can be seen as symbols of strength and victory, especially the dragon in its representation of "the *yang* force of the east, the strength of sun and light."[7]

Hong seems to have felt that he was being taken through the Chinese version of hell, as described in the Buddhist-inspired *Jade Record*.[8] After passing through the underworld, Hong was carried in a sedan chair to a beautiful palace. There he met an elderly woman, who took him to a river and washed him clean of defilement. He was then given a new heart and finally brought before an old man, who was dressed in black with a flowing golden beard. The man told Hong that he was sad because, although he made humans and provided them with sustenance, they didn't worship him but, "take my gifts and worship demons."[9] He warned Hong not to be like them.

The old man gave Hong a sword to kill the demons, a seal to overcome evil spirits, and golden fruit to eat. He then led Hong to a place from which he could see the iniquities of the world. He told Hong that he must fight against this evil. "Do thy work: I shall assist thee in every difficulty."[10]

At this point, it is said that Hong woke enough to tell his parents that a "venerable old man" had promised him power and wealth. They put him back to bed.

As his vision continued, Hong was told to drive the demons out of the thirty-three levels of heaven. Confucius was blamed for their entry into heaven, and Hong had the satisfaction of seeing the sage soundly whipped for it. With the help of the old man and his middle-aged son, Hong drove out the demons and was given the title Taiping Heavenly King, Soverign Ch'üan of the Great Way (*T'aip'ing T'ien Wang ta-tao chün-wang Ch'üan*).[11]

During this vision, Hong apparently leapt from his bed, slashing the air as with a sword, shouting "Slay them, Slay the demons!" He also told visitors that he had just become emperor of China and preferred them to use his title. If they refused, he called them demons.[12]

Hong remained in this state for forty days. He finally recovered enough to resume his studies. At that time, he said, he hadn't read the Christian pamphlet. It was only after his fourth and final attempt to pass the exam in 1843 that he began to read it.

"Good Works for Exhorting the Age" was written by a Chinese convert to Christianity named Liang Ah-fa. The work consists of parts of the Bible, not given in order. It begins with the Gospel of

John followed by Paul's letter to the Romans, Ecclesiastes, and then Genesis. Added to this are commentaries and essays by Liang containing more biblical citations. These are more concerned with the role of Jehovah, rather than Jesus. Liang also seems to have implied that the Heavenly Kingdom was both heaven and the congregation of the faithful on earth, something that Hong would attempt to realize.[13]

When he came to read the "Good Works" carefully, Hong's visions became clear to him. The man with the golden beard was Jehovah, and the middle-aged man, his son, Jesus. By reading the many places that the character for his name "Huo" appeared, he realized that God was not only speaking to him, but that he was the second son of Jehovah, sent to earth to rid it of demons. The sword had been given to him for this purpose. With it he would create a new age of great peace (Taiping). The Heavenly Kingdom would be in China, not Jerusalem.[14]

It is not surprising that his friends and neighbors were not convinced by his logic. However, he did find some followers, including his cousin Hung Jen-Kan and another relative, Feng Yuen-Shan. In 1844, they decided to go to the Hakka region of Guangxi to preach. There they had much more success. Calling themselves the "God Worshipers," they preached moral standards of behavior from the Ten Commandments, adapting them to include the prohibition of drinking, gambling, and smoking opium. The last was particularly important. Opium had been introduced by the British to the Chinese a few years before and was a major problem in China. The Opium Wars had begun in 1839 and were still going on at the same time as the Taiping Rebellion.

The Hakka living in Guangxi had suffered from the war, crop failure, and bandits. The new religion gave them hope. Hong and his friends made thousands of converts. In 1845, Hong returned to his teaching job in his village, but Feng stayed to continue the work in Guangxi. He was apparently a charismatic preacher and the movement continued to grow.

Up until this point, Hong had been relying on the original pamphlet from Canton to form his theology. In March 1846, he and Jen-Kan went to Canton, where they met an irascible fundamentalist missionary named Issachar Jacox Roberts. Hong studied with Roberts for a couple of months and was about to be baptized when, apparently through a misunderstanding, Roberts decided that Hong wasn't ready.[15] Despite this, Roberts and Hong remained friends and, when the Taiping had taken the city of Nanjing, Hong invited the minister to join them.

In August 1847, Hong returned to Guangxi, where things were going well. Feng had almost two thousand converts. They even included landholders who had money to help support the movement. The group grew bold enough to destroy idols and paint slogans on temple walls. This brought them to the notice of the authorities, and eventually Feng was jailed.[16]

Hong went to Canton to negotiate for Feng's release. While he was gone, a new twist developed among the God Worshipers. One of the converts, Yang Xiu Qing, a Hakka charcoal burner, fell into a trance during which God the father, spoke through him. On his return, Hong accepted this as a true connection to the divine. Later, Yang would become one of the kings under Heavenly Kingdom. A few months later, another convert began channeling the Elder Brother, Jesus, who sent messages to Hong and the faithful, including the information that Kwan Yin, the goddess of mercy, also lived in heaven.

After this the trances came thick and fast for a while, along with omens and prophecies of military victory.[17]

By 1850 these prophesies seemed to be coming true. The God Worshipers, now several thousand strong, had met the forces of the local government in battle and won. They now controlled Guangxi. In 1851, after winning more battles, Hong declared the arrival of the Heavenly Kingdom of Great Peace and named himself the Tien Wang (heavenly king). Over the next two years, the Taiping army moved across China. Although they had some defeats, they won many of their battles, gaining followers along the way, until, by 1853, their force was reported to be over half a million.[18]

In March, the Taiping took over the city of Nanjing, where Hong announced that the Heavenly Kingdom would be established. The God Worshipers are told that it is from here that they will be saved when the Apocalypse comes.

In convincing people that a new order had come, Hong was helped by a non-Christian prophecy. A French chronicler living in China in 1850 noted that "Among the higher and middle classes of Pekin there is a firm belief in the prophecy diffused over China a century ago, that the reigning dynasty will be overthrown in the commencement of the 48th year of the present cycle, and this fatal year will begin on the 1st February next."[19]

Hong instituted rules for his followers: Everything was to be held in common, they were to obey the Ten Commandments as he had revised them, and they were to obey their officers "in a harmonious spirit" and never retreat in battle until ordered. The last rule was that men and women were to stay celibate and apart, the women fighting in their own units.[20]

It was clear that Hong was preparing for a removal to the real heaven once his people were purified enough. But the twelve years of the Heavenly Kingdom were much like those of the British Interregnum under the Puritans. Added to the obvious problem that most people are not saints was the growing paranoia and arbitrary behavior of Hong. He often ordered executions for trivial offenses, something that always seems to go with absolute power. What was more worrying was his reliance on divine protection, rather than force of arms. When asked about creating defenses against a siege, he replied, "I, the truly appointed Lord, can, without the aid of troops, command great peace to spread its sway across the whole region."[21]

After several attempts, Issachar Roberts finally arrived in Nanjing, eager to start Christian schools there. He found Hong installed in oriental splendor. The Heavenly King explained to his old teacher that he had received new information directly from heaven. He expected Roberts to go out among the Westerners and preach the faith according

Brass cash coin of the Taiping Rebellion (1850–1864). China, Qing dynasty, ca. 1850.
The inscription on the front of this coin reads "Tai ping Tian guo." ("Taiping Heavenly
Kingdom"). The inscription on the back of the coin reads "sheng bao" ("sacred treasure").
This Heavenly Kingdom on earth was to be short-lived. The Taiping rebels were defeated
by combined Chinese and European forces in 1861. Location: British Museum, London,
Great Britain. © *The Trustees of The British Museum / Art Resource, NY*

to Hong. Roberts was horrified. It took him only a short time to realize that this was only a shadow of Christianity and that Hong could
not be convinced of his errors. Bitterly disappointed, Roberts returned
to America where he died later of leprosy, contracted during his earlier
work at a leper colony in Macao.[22]

At the end, as the Heavenly Kingdom crumbled, Hong seems to
have lost all contact with this world. In a poem penned in February
1861 he wrote:

> *Now there were four tigers, but all were killed and cast away,*
> *And throughout the world, the officials and people rejoice at my*
>   *victorious return.*
> *To Heaven the road is open; the devil tigers are exterminated;*
> *The oneness and unity of heaven and earth is arranged by Heaven.*[23]

For Hong, the millennium had arrived, and he had achieved divinity. He also wrote, "The Father, the Elder Brother, myself, and the Young Monarch [Hong's son] sit in the Heavenly Court; peace reigns over all the world, and the heavenly omens are fulfilled. The old, the young, men and women, all see the heavenly omens, and the Heavenly Elder Brother's earlier proclamations have now been realized."[24]

Instead of this idyll, the city was taken by Imperial forces. Hong committed suicide along with some of his followers. Several of the leaders were captured and made to write long confessions in which they detailed the makeup of the Heavenly Kingdom and their beliefs, but because the confessions were definitely intended to stave off execution, or at least make it less painful, they are sprinkled with negative adjectives.[25]

The Taiping armies won followers in many provinces. For the most part, these converts joined for social and political reasons, rather than religious. But the core of the believers in Nanjing seem to have had a developed theology. They published a number of their own tracts, which still exist. These mainly stress the goodness of the Heavenly Father and his younger son, Hong. But they also dwell on the evils of the day: the oppression of the peasants; the problems with opium; the state of lawlessness; and the rule of the Manchu, foreigners who make men shave their heads in front as a sign of subservience. The people of China were offered the hope of change packaged in a way that promised happiness in this life and the next.[26]

Perhaps if Hong had been more in touch with the world around him, the rebellion would have succeeded. The goals of equality among the faithful, land reform, and freedom from exploitation were the same as those of many revolutions that resulted in a permanent transfer of power, including that in China a hundred years later.

The Taiping armies were not a small regional force. They threatened Beijing and besieged Shanghai. The twelve years of war cost the lives of millions, either in battle or from disease and starvation. The winners were not the Chinese, but the Europeans, particularly the British, and the Americans, who sold guns to both sides but eventually decided to support the emperor in return for numerous trade concessions. In 1860, as their reward, the French and British took Beijing, burning the Summer Palace and looting the city. The French empress Eugenie was later presented with a pearl necklace from the collection of the empress of China.[27] Queen Victoria received a gold and jade scepter and the first Pekinese dog ever seen in Europe. She named it Lootie and kept it until its death in 1872.[28]

The Taiping Rebellion has all the marks of a millenarian movement; a charismatic leader, a doctrine of spiritual salvation, the physical salvation of the elect, a radical change in the structure of society, and a strict set of rules to be followed for the believer to prove genuine conversion. In the beginning, Hong had plans for building a real heaven on earth. This may have been thwarted by his increasing madness or it may have been that earth and heaven were just too far apart.

---

1 Vincent Y. C. Shih, *The Taiping Ideology: Its Sources, Interpretations, and Influences* (Seattle: University of Washington Press, 1972), 20.

2 In the course of this article, the Chinese names are spelled in different ways in the quotations, reflecting changes in standard ways of rendering them in English. So, Hong Xiuquan is the same as Hung Hsiu-ch'uan, for example.

3 See the section on The Yellow Turbans.

4 Jonathan D. Spence, *The Taiping Vision of a Christian China 1836–1864* (Waco, TX: Baylor University, 1996), 6.

5 Jonathan D. Spence, *God's Chinese Son* (New York: Norton, 1996), 33–50.

6 P. M. Yap, "The Mental Illness of Hung Hsiu-Ch'uan, Leader of the Taiping Rebellion," *The Far Eastern Quarterly* 13, no. 3 (1954): 289.

7 Spence, *God's Chinese Son*, 37.

8 Ibid., 38–39.

9 Quoted in Yap, 291.

10 Ibid.

11 Vincent Y. C. Shih, *The Taiping Ideology: Its Sources, Interpretations, and Influences* (Seattle: University of Washington Press, 1972), 13.

12 Yap, 292.

13 Philip A. Kuhn, "Origins of the Taiping Vision: Cross-Cultural Dimensions of a Chinese Rebellion," *Comparative Studies in Society and History* 19, no. 3 (1977): 352.

14 Yap, 294.

15 Yuan Chung Teng, "Reverend Issacher Jacox Roberts and the Taiping Rebellion," *The Journal of Asian Studies* 3, no., 1 (1963): 56.

16 Franz Michael, *The Taiping Rebellion: History and Documents*,vol. 3 (Seattle: University of Washington Press, 1971), 1574.

17 Spence, 107–108.

18 Michael, 1580–1581. Hakka women were much more liberated than other Chinese women of the time or women in the west.

19 Shih, 402.

20 Jack Beeching *The Chinese Opium Wars* (New York: Harcourt, Brace, Jovanovich, 1975), 186.

21 Quoted in Yap, 295. Yap concludes that Hong may have been suffering from schizophrenic paranoia.

22 Teng, 64–66.

23 Translated in Michael, 933.

24 Ibid., 931.

25 Several of these are translated in Michael, 1351–1542.

26 One of the tracts, "A Hero's Return to Truth," details these promises, along with the reiteration of the divine nature of the Heavenly King Hong. See Michael, 799–832.

27 Beeching, 321.

28 Ibid., 331.

CHAPTER THIRTY-TWO

The Doomsealers

An old lady on Dwight way, Berkeley, has sold her property
for $3000 ($1500 below value), because of the predictions of
the Oakland doomsealers. She will leave for the mountains in
the course of a few days. Her neighbors are highly elated
because they have been greatly annoyed by her midnight
prayers and songs.

—*Oakland Tribune* (March 12, 1890)

During the winter of 1889, a charismatic preacher arrived in
Oakland, California, to conduct a tent revival meeting. Mrs.
Maria B. Woodworth was already known as an evangelical preacher
in the Midwest, coming from near Muncie, Indiana.[1] She was one of
the forerunners of the Pentecostal movement. Although not affiliated
with any particular church, her revivals were sponsored by Methodist, United Brethren, and Churches of God congregations in the areas
where she preached.[2]

She encouraged those who attended the meetings to open themselves up to divine wisdom. On January 25, 1890, one of the attend-
ees was a twenty-nine-year-old Norwegian immigrant named George
Erickson. Responding to Woodworth's exhortations, he fell into a
trance during which he had a vision of a great earthquake and tidal
wave destroying Oakland and San Francisco on April 14 of that year.[3]

Shortly thereafter, others had the same vision, with a Mrs.

Gifford, giving the exact time of the earthquake as 4:45 P.M. In the next few days, the prophecy was expanded to include the destruction of Chicago and Milwaukee.[4]

As with the Millerites, the newspapers had a great time making fun of the Doomsealers. The *Oakland Tribune* was particularly eloquent: "The day of wrath, that dreadful day when the waters shall come up to thirty-sixth street and beyond has been officially fixed for April 14 prox. . . . For the followers of Mrs. Woodworth have said it and so it must come to pass." The article concludes: "Notice of the flood will duly be sent out to all those who affiliate with the Woodworth converts, and Mr. Bennett will spread the tidings from his bicycle."[5] According to Hayes, Bennett did indeed fulfill his task. He "mounted his bicycle and rode up and down the city streets and the country roads, crying aloud, "Flee! Flee! Flee! Flee to the mountains!"[6]

In early April, Maria Woodworth was supposed to have gone ahead to Santa Rosa, in Marin County, to prepare shelter for those who sought refuge from the coming cataclysm. The newspaper accounts are somewhat confusing, but she seems to have departed for the East, instead. She might have stayed until it was clear that the catastrophe wasn't about to happen, but that isn't certain.

Before the day of the predicted disaster, a number of believers did go to higher ground. They went up into the Berkeley Hills, perhaps in imitation of those who fled the opening of the sixth seal of the Apocalypse and "hid in caves and among the rock of the mountains" (Revelation 6:25). Papers all over the country had picked up the story. *The New York Times* insisted that sensible Americans were not fooled and that most of the believers were either "colored" or recent immigrants.[7] It's not clear where this information came from for the Oakland paper gave names of a number of local citizens who were leaving for the mountains, including a prominent doctor and his wife.[8]

The day passed without incident, and the Doomsealers started to return to their homes. An account of an interview with A. H. Wood, a member who did not flee, stated that "he knows of people who put faith in the prophecy whose names, if made public, would create surprise. He does not think that those who left will hasten back, but will drop in town quietly. The reasons given later by some of the Doomsealers for their flight—such as that they were leaving for their health, or business of other causes—were fictitious, and they were really afraid for their lives."[9]

Oddly, there was a minor earthquake on April 20 that caused a number of the Doomsealers who had returned to the city to reconsider their doubts. One paper reported:

> *John Philipson announces that he had a revelation in regard to the prophecy. Thursday morning's shock, he says, was merely the first symptom of the upheaval that is sure to come. He says that God will not now reveal the time for the destruction of the cities, and that the only way to escape is to leave San Francisco and Oakland, and never return.*[10]

Poor George Erickson, who had received the first vision, was unable to flee with the others. He had been arrested the month before, and sent to the insane asylum in Stockton.[11] I have not been able to find out what happened to him.

The disappointment in Oakland did not damage Maria Woodworth's credibility as a revivalist. However, for some time afterward newspapers in towns she visited continued to assume that she was a fraud. A year after her Oakland meetings, it was reported that she was conducting revivals in St. Louis and "has left that city mysteriously, taking with her $600.00, which had been subscribed to the cause."[12]

Woodworth wrote a number of books about her life and career as an evangelist. She seems to have believed that the visions had by Erickson and others were genuine and that they were part of a millenarian outpouring of messages from heaven. In her view, "signs and wonders" were happening every day, if one remained open to them.

She wrote, "Instead of looking back to Pentecost, let us always be expecting it to come, especially in these last days."[13]

The Doomsealers are interesting to me because they encapsulate the history of many such movements. William Miller arrived at his apocalyptic belief through a study of the Bible and careful mathematical calculations, as did Isaac Newton and many others. The Doomsealers bypassed scripture and relied on personal revelation. These two strands run through all the Christian millennial groups that I have studied. And yet, the source of the prediction seems to make little difference to those hearing the message. Believers are converted by some other means than recognized authority. Whether they respond to personal charisma in the preacher, emotional need, their own logic, Divine grace, or a combination of all of the above is not clear. Only the effect can be documented.

1 *Indiana Critic*, September 27, 1885, reports on a large revival that Woodworth conducted near Muncie, noting that she was a native of the area.

2 Wayne Warner, "Maria B. Woodworth-Etter and the Early Pentecostal Movement," *Assembly of God Heritage*, winter 1986–1987, 11.

3 D. A. Hayes, "A Study of a Pauline Apocalypse," *The Biblical World* 37, no. 3 (1911): 171. Hayes had been in the Bay Area at the time of the prediction and was giving his account of the events, comparing them to apocalyptic panics in Thessalonica in the first century. He adds that he was also in San Francisco for the earthquake of 1906 and no one came forward to predict that.

4 Ibid., 172. The tidal wave must have been expected on Lake Michigan.

5 *Oakland Tribune*, March 5, 1890, p. 1.

6 Hayes, 173.

7 *The New York Times*, April 12, 1890, p. 2.

8 Oakland *Tribune*, April 10, 1890, p. 1.

9 *San Francisco Chronicle*, April 18, 1890, p. 1.

10 *San Francisco Chronicle*, April 20, 1890, p. 1.

11 *Oakland Tribune*, March 12, 1890, p. 1.

12 *Logansport Review*, April 27, 1891, p. 2.

13 Maria Beulah Woodworth, *The Life, Work and Experience of Maria Beulah Woodworth* (St. Louis, 1894), 437–438, quoted in Warner, 12.

PART SIX:

Doomsday Just Around the Corner

The Nervous Twentieth Century

CHAPTER THIRTY-THREE

The New Apocalyptic Age

Some say the world will end in fire
Some say in ice.
From what I've tasted of desire,
I hold with those who favor fire.
But if it had to perish twice,
I think I know enough of hate
To say that for destruction ice
Is also great
And would suffice.

—Robert Frost

Like most people alive today, I was born into a world that knew it could destroy itself with no help from gods or nature. But even before the invention of the atomic bomb, the twentieth century already had a strong tradition of apocalyptic thinking. Both world wars spawned novels and films detailing the end. Art also reflected concerns about the end of the world that were not always described in religious terms.

In the last quarter of the twentieth century a number of apocalyptic movements seemed to have sprung up. All the ones that I have studied were started or rejuvenated by a charismatic leader. All expected an end of the world as we know it, and most were determined to be the only survivors. For instance, the Church Universal and Triumphant

(CUT) bought twelve thousand acres of land in Montana near Yellowstone National Park and stocked up on provisions and semiautomatic weapons to wait for the end. Of course, when the projected end date of March or April 1990 didn't happen, and the group's leader Elizabeth Clare Prophet was diagnosed with Alzheimer's, the group dwindled.[1]

The CUT combines several of the usual aspects of a doomsday cult: strict rules for living, constant supervision, separation from the outside world, and devotion to the leader. Its beliefs reflect the broadening of knowledge about non-Christian beliefs along with world mythology. Elizabeth Clare Prophet wrote words of wisdom that she channeled from people as disparate as St. Thomas More, King Arthur, the Buddha, and some lawyer from Atlantis.[2] The CUT is a cross between survivalism and New Age philosophy. The followers spend much of the day in rapid-fire chanting to clear their minds for enlightenment but live in bunkers to fight off anyone threatening their utopia.

Even without Elizabeth Clare Prophet, the CUT continues, operating in several countries. They emphasize spiritual growth through knowledge attained from "Ascended Masters" and offer "etheric retreats" to be taken by the soul, just as it was once possible for the citizens of Atlantis to attend in the body.[3] While they state that Prophet did foresee a number of things, the Apocalypse is no longer mentioned.

Another, sadder, apocalyptic group with some of the same traits as the CUT is the one known as Heaven's Gate. The group had not been familiar to most people, although it was on law enforcement cult watches. The leader was a man named Marshall Applewhite who had experienced a life-changing epiphany at the age of forty-five and came to believe that a spaceship was coming to bring him and his followers to a new and better world, where they would live in bliss forever. He and his group were computer programmers and in other tech-related fields. They were steeped in science fiction. Apparently they heard on

Meidner, Ludwig (1884–1966) © Copyright Apocalypse. 1914. Black ink and pencil on paper, 47.4 x 36.5 cm. Inv. SZ 6. Photo: Joerg P. Anders. © Ludwig Meidner-Archiv, Juedisches Museum der Stadt Frankfurt am Main. Location: Kupferstichkabinett, Staatliche Museen zu, Berlin, Germany. *Bildarchiv Preussischer Kulturbesitz / Art Resource, NY*

a late-night talk radio program that the Hale-Bopp comet, predicted to arrive in late March 1997, would be followed by a spaceship, hiding in the comet's tail.[4] At the end of March, the bodies of thirty-nine men and women were found at the Heaven's Gate home in Rancho Santa Fe, California. They had committed suicide in an orderly fashion, each dressing in new shoes, packing a small bag, and then lying in bed with a small cloth covering his or her face.

Although most people felt the tragedy of these deaths, there was also a great deal of ridicule of Applewhite and his group. How could intelligent people believe that they were on their way to life on another planet? In the sensation of the deaths and titillating revelations about self-castration, the actual beliefs of Heaven's Gate weren't much discussed.

The last website created by Heaven's Gate was still in place when I was researching this book. Reading through Do's (Applewhite's name in the group) manifesto, I found nothing that other groups throughout history had not said.

He saw Jesus as having been inhabited by a "member of the kingdom of Heaven" at the moment of his baptism by John. This is known as *adoptionism* and was one of the heresies of the early church that resurfaced from time to time. Applewhite saw the teaching of Jesus as that of preparing other people to be inhabited by angels and eventually, in those bodies, to ascend to heaven.[5]

However, after establishing his credentials as being in the tradition of Jesus, Applewhite diverged totally from Christian teaching, following more in the tradition of Gene Roddenberry, creator of *Star Trek*. He states that in 1975 an "Admiral" and his "Captain" began collecting an "away team" with other beings from a higher level. Using meetings and public statements, they chose the human bodies worthy of being inhabited. The next seventeen years were spent in seclusion, training the human bodies to fit into the Next Level. Then in 1995, Heaven's Gate took out an ad in *USA Today*, to let people know that the ship was coming soon. Through that, as well as trips all over the United States, the away team were able to find their missing crew members.[6]

The website includes their final statement, dated March 22, 1997. Titled "Heaven's Gate 'Away Team' Returns to Level Above Human in Distant Space," it begins: "By the time you read this, we will be gone." It ends with Revelation 14:13: "Blessed are those that die in the Lord."[7]

The release explains that their human bodies were only borrowed and no longer needed. An earlier page on the website assures the reader that they are not a suicide cult. They would rather take their bodies with them when they go. However, as at Masada and Waco (discussed in the section on the Branch Davidians) circumstances may necessitate abandoning them. They didn't consider it suicide, but moving on.[8]

One woman summed up her reasons for going in her video message made just before the mass suicide. "Maybe they're crazy for all I know. But I don't have any choice but to go for it, because I have been on this planet for 31 years and there is nothing here for me."[9]

Thousands of people have sacrificed themselves in the firm belief that they were going to a heaven. The early Christian martyrs are one example, and the authorities in their own time thought they were as crazy as Heaven's Gate was seen in ours.

One can't help but hope that they found the world they were seeking.

As Christian and Muslim influences were adapted into established religious beliefs in other cultures, the New Age groups, largely in Western countries, blended Eastern religious teachings to their original, usually Christian or Jewish, upbringing. As with the Taiping in China and the cargo cults (see the section on missionaries), groups such as the Church Universal and Triumphant and Heaven's Gate, took what they needed from the other religions without really understanding the dogma and history of them. Of course, in forging a belief system that fits ones own needs, I suppose accuracy doesn't really matter.

Fundamentalist Christians have remained a constant in apocalyptic thought and preaching. Some have made an excellent living at it. Like William Miller, Hal Lindsey has predicted the end several times. In his 1970 book *The Late Great Planet Earth*, he told us that the New World Order under the Antichrist would be established by 1988. When that didn't seem to happen, he wrote *Facing Millennial Midnight*, telling of the apocalyptic horrors that would occur in the year 2000 (see the section on Y2K). When that fizzled, he was not discouraged. He continued to produce books, insisting that the time was ripe, the signs were there, and the end of the world was coming soon. Enough people agreed with him to make Lindsey a very rich man.

Most evangelical Christians do not set a date for the Parousia. But they do feel that they're living in the end times. How they react to this varies with each person. Some expect to avoid the whole business by being raptured up to heaven. Others have stocked up on provisions to survive the years of tribulation. Many try to convince others to convert to their faith, either directly or through donations to missionary efforts.

The last groups who are expecting the end of the world are not usually religiously motivated, although many belong to established religions. These are the most frightening of all because they do not rely on biblical exegesis or visionary experiences. They use scientific observation, statistics, and computer modeling. From these, we have learned to fear global warming, an asteroid or meteor hit, the melting of the ice caps, global freezing, or the eruption of a super volcano. It is odd that the old standbys of nuclear power plant meltdowns and all-out atomic war are losing popularity. I'm not saying that none of these will happen. I'm certainly trying to reduce my carbon footprint just on general principles. But by adding all of these together, I think that we have to conclude that the twentieth and, so far, the twenty-first centuries have the honor of being the most apocalyptically inclined in all of human history.

1 Paul F. Starrs and John B. Wright, "Utopia, Dystopia and Sublime Apocalypse in Montana's Church Universal and Triumphant," *The Geographical Review* 95, no. 1 (2005): 102. Considering that Yellowstone is supposed to be a super volcano on alert, the Apocalypse might have started right under their feet.

2 Sally K. Slocum, *Popular Arthurian Traditions* (Bowling Green, OH: Bowling Green State University Press, 1992), 105–108.

3 The Summit Lighthouse at www.tsl.org, the website for the Church Universal and Triumphant. Accessed July 2009.

4 Janja A. Lalich, *Bounded Choice: True Believers and Charismatic Cults* (Berkeley: California University Press, 2004), 25–30.

5 Marshall Applewhite, "Do's Intro, Purpose, Belief." Available at http://heavensgate.com/misc/intro.htm. Accessed July 2009.

6 Jenody—A Student, "Overview of Present Mission." Available at http://heavensgate.com/misc/ovrview.htm. Accessed July 2009.

7 Available at http://heavensgate.com/misc/pressrel.htm. Accessed July 2009.

8 Available at http://heavensgate.com/misc/letter.htm. Accessed July 2009.

9 Allen Hall, "The Nutty Professor Who Led Flock to Their Death; MASS SUICIDES: Cult Brainwashed by 'Gospel' about UFO," (Glasgow, Scotland) *Daily Record*, March 29, 1997, p. 4. This title expresses the media take on the event.

CHAPTER THIRTY-FOUR

Modern Mahdi

The Guided One in World Islam

And of mankind are some who say, we believe in Allah and the
Last Day, when they believe not. They think to beguile Allah
and those who believe, but they beguile none but themselves:
but they perceive not.

—Mansur Al Yaman, *al-Baqara*, II:8–9[1]

With the spread of Islam across the world, the Shi'ite concept
of the Mahdi, one sent to re-create a "just society," is one
aspect of the religion that was most prone to being adapted to the
circumstances of the already established culture. This section looks at
some of the many forms of the Mahdi in the nineteenth and twentieth
centuries. Some of these Mahdi inspired new sects of Islam. Most of
them are considered heretical to Sunni Muslims. Some go beyond
Shi'ite beliefs as well. But they all have their roots in the teachings of
Muhammad.

One of the most enduring of the modern Mahdi is Mirzam
Gulam Ahmad. He was born in the Punjab, in India in 1839. He came
from a Sufi Muslim family and, as a teenager, had become acquainted
with Scottish missionaries and debated religion with them. He was
somewhat sickly, suffering from diabetes and vertigo.[2]

He passed his early adult life as something of a recluse, but in 1880, because "god's command was imperative," he published the first two parts of his treatise, *Barahin-i-Ahmadiya* (Ahmadiya Proofs) in which he announced that he was the Mahdi for the fourteenth century (fourteen hundred years after the *hegira*). It was not until 1889 that he began to have a small group of followers. Two years later, he told them that he was not only the Mahdi for the century but the final one, sent to usher in the end of days. After that, he became increasingly active in substantiating this claim, which was denied by Muslim, Christian, and Hindu clerics. The Mullahs of India condemned him and his teaching but, by his death in 1908, there was a group of a few hundred people who supported him.

After Ahmad's death, the leadership of the sect was contested. One group, known as the Qadiani, after Ahmad's home town, was led by Ahmad's eldest son. The other side followed Maulvi Mohammad Ali. The two groups split into separate sects shortly after 1914. Both groups were fervent missionaries, preaching throughout the world. Ahmad wrote tracts designed to appeal to Christians. In one, he reminds them that he is both the Mahdi and the Messiah. "Ye Christians of Europe and America!" he proclaims, "and ye seekers after the Truth! Know it for certain that the Messiah that was to come has come, and it is he who is speaking to you at this moment!"[3] He proved his claims with the usual millennial count, stating that he was the savior prophesied to come at the beginning of the seventh millennium.

Ahmad also reminded his readers that the signs of the end as predicted in the Qur'an had occurred in India in his lifetime; an eclipse of the sun and the moon, both in the month of Ramadan, and plague sweeping the area.

While not many were converted through this, the Ahmadiya did make converts because of their belief in Ahmad as the Mahdi and also because the sect followed conservative Sunni theology and practice.[4]

Missionary work is one of the most striking aspects of the Ahmadiya. One of many reasons they reach out to other cultures might be that in Pakistan, where Ahmad's town is since the partition, the members of the sect are forbidden to call themselves Muslims.[5] They are especially active in Africa, despite the animosity of the majority of Sunni Muslims, who accuse them of translating the Qur'an into the Kiswahli language, changing certain parts to fit their own doctrines.[6] In Nigeria, despite dissension due to personality conflicts, the Ahmadiya have succeeded because of their support of education for both men and women, allowing women to participate in Friday prayers and preaching in English or Yoruba.

They also have mosques in Fiji, England, Australia, and the United States. The millenarian aspects of the sect have been toned down as they have entered the world stage. An Ahmadi scientist, the theoretical physicist Abdus Salam, even won the Nobel Prize in physics a few years ago.[7]

In Nigeria, belief in the imminent arrival of the Mahdi was part of the pre-colonial Sokoto caliphate. But the arrival of the British colonial powers caused many Muslims to believe that Gog and Magog were upon them and that they were living in the end times.[8]

As the *Wakara Nasara*, the "Poem on Christians," written about 1900, says:

> *The hour of the day of judgment is fast approaching,*
> *Among the conditions is the advent of the Christians.*
> *The hold of Gog and Magog would be the next to bring its ills,*
> *They will fill the world more than the Christians.*[9]

Even when it had been decided that the coming of the British was one of the signs of the end, Nigerian Muslims were of different opinions as to what the Mahdi would do when he arrived and what the faithful should do to prepare. These ranged from forming an army to support the Mahdi in throwing out the invaders to going into seclusion to prepare oneself for judgment. The poem continues:

> Our remedy is to depend firmly on God,
> We should rely on Him to prevail upon the Christians.
> Even if no one heeds, I have done my part to admonish.
> I am with the Almighty, and not with the Christians.
> Salvation in the hereafter will not be in the hand of humans,
> Hence no one could condemn me to hell-fire.

> It is from God that I seek salvation, and [also] from the Messenger,
> Who had been granted the right of intercession on our behalf.
> We beseech you, God, to let us die with our faith,
> For apart from the Christians, more frightful events are yet to come.
> The day of dying and the day of judgment—
> These should frighten any human more than the Christians.
> Here I conclude this poem, thanks be to God,
> With the power of the one who created us and the Christians.[10]

This defeatist attitude was not the only alternative to war. Others saw this time of tribulation as a call to renew the faith and follow the law of Islam more devoutly. In a bizarre twist, in 1925 the British governor sent to Mecca for a ruling against those in Nigeria claiming to be Mahdi. The court issued one on the grounds that the signs of the end had not been fulfilled; therefore, anyone saying that he was the Mahdi or Isa (Jesus) and all who followed him, were infidels.[11]

The British also asked that the same ruling apply to India, indicating that they were having trouble there, possibly from the Ahmadiya. The pronouncements from Mecca do not seem to have dissuaded the African Muslims.

* * *

IT wasn't only European colonial powers that caused Mahdi to appear. The advent of the Mahdi Muhammad Ahmad ibn Adhallah in the Sudan in 1881 was directed against the rule of the Egyptians. Muhammad Ahmad was a Dunqulawi, living on an island in the White Nile, a man known for his Sufi piety and ascetic life. When he announced that he was the Mahdi, his intent apparently was to remove the Turkish-Egyptian government because it was corrupt and did not follow strict Islamic law.[12]

While some of his followers shared his desire to make a just society, others who joined Muhammad Ahmad included slave traders who were being forced out of business by the Egyptians and small farmers and landholders crippled by the onerous taxes of the Egyptian government.[13] Forming a coalition, the army of the Mahdi spent three years battling the Egyptians and their British allies. With each win, more Sudanese tribes joined the cause. The climax came on January 26, 1885, when the army of the Mahdi attacked and took the city of Khartoum. Two days later, a British relief force arrived to find Muhammad Ahmad in control of the city.[14]

For many Sudanese, the revolt proclaimed the time of peace and justice before the end. The tribes of the Sudan had proved they could unite and drive out the colonial powers. But the death of Muhammad Ahmad in 1886 brought an end to that unity. Without the Mahdi, the world returned to its imperfect state. In 1898, the British General Kitchner defeated the successors of Muhammad Ahmad.[15]

But the organization founded by Muhammad Ahmad continued, and in 1945, it established a political party, the *Umma*, whose religious leader was Sayyid 'Abd al-Rahman al-Mahdi, the son of Muhammad Ahmad.[16] Sayyid, born after his father's death, had been watched closely by the British colonial government. During World War I, Sayyid aided the British by convincing the Sudanese to fight on their side in opposition to the Ottoman Turks. In the 1920s, Sayyid was trying to organize a subtle power base. This wasn't helped by a local holy man, who announced that the British council was the Dajjal (Antichrist) and that Sayyid was the *Nabi Isai,* or the Second Coming of Jesus.[17] During the 1920s and 1930s the millennial expectations of his followers were high, but in the end, Sayyid decided to work for independence within the system.[18] Although Sayyid died in 1959, his grandson Sadiq al-Mahdi led a Mahdi-inspired revolt against President Nimieri in 1976. After it failed, he followed his grandfather's lead in continuing peaceful opposition and, in 1986, won a political victory.[19]

The most intriguing part of the history of these two movements is that, although Shi'ite teaching states that the Mahdi must be descended from one of the two sons of Fatima and Ali, the Prophet's daughter and cousin, this was not a consideration, for either Ahmad or Muhammad Ahmad. It also didn't seem to make a difference to their followers. Islam had spread far beyond those of Arab descent. A savior could henceforth come from any among those faithful to Islam.

1 Quoted in Jassim M. Hussain, "Messianism and the Mahdi," *Expectation of the Millennium: Shi'ism in History,* ed. Seyyed Hoossein Nasr et al. (Albany: State University of New York Press, 1989), 13.

2 Unless otherwise stated, the biographical information is from James Thayer Addison, "The Ahmadiya Movement and Its Western Propaganda," *The Harvard Theological Review* 1, no. 22 (1929): 1–32. It should be noted that there are two Ahmadiya sects that have nothing to do with each other. The first was established in Arabia in the late 1700s and is not particularly millennial.

3 Addison, 6.

4 Jamal J. Elias, *Islam* (London: Routledge, 1999), 63.

5 Shahid Javed Burki, Craig Baxter, Robert Laporte Jr., Kamal Azfa, *Pakistan under the Military* (Boulder, CO: Westview Press, 1991), 170.

6 Arye Oded, *Islam and Politics in Kenya* (Boulder, CO: Reinner, 2000), 18.

7 Theoretical physicist Abdus Salam, winner in 1979.

8 Mohammad S. Umar, "Muslims' Eschatological Discourses on Colonialism in Northern Nigeria," *Journal of the American Academy of Religion* 67, no. 1 (1999), 61.

9 Ibid., 68.

10 Ibid., 69.

11 Ibid., 71–72.

12 P. M. Holt, *A Modern History of the Sudan, from the Funj Sultanate to the Present Day* (New York: Grove Press, 1961), 76–78.

13 Hassan Abdel Aziz Ahmed, "The Turkish Taxation System and Its Impact on Agriculture in the Sudan," *Middle Eastern Studies* 16, no. 1 (1908): 106.

14 Holt, 88–90.

15 Nicole Grandin, "*A près le Mahdi: La politique coloniale chez les pasteurs arabes soudanais*," *Cahiers d'Étdes Africaines* 18, no. 17/18 (1978): 124.

16 Harold F. Gosnell, "The 1958 Elections in the Sudan," *Middle East Journal* 12, no. 4 (1958): 413.

17 Awad al-Sid al-arsani, "The Establishment of Neo-Mahdism in the Western Sudan, 1920–1976," *African Affairs* 86, no. 344 (1987): 390.

18 Ibid., 403.

19 Ibid., 404.

CHAPTER THIRTY-FIVE

Cargo Cults, Messiahs and the End of the World

Millennial Activity in Melanesia

Identifying Cargo Cults with madness and the unhealthy
products of the irrational unconscious mind has no doubt
served the prevailing discourses of colonial and Western powers.

—Professor Michele Stephen (1997)[1]

The so-called Cargo Cults of Melanesia, particularly New Guinea, are not really millennial in the sense that they expect a violent battle or disaster followed by a thousand years of peace, ending with a final judgment. But the basic themes of millennial beliefs are there, and with the arrival of Pentecostal millennial missionaries, these beliefs have become more in line with that of Western movements, with the addition of traditional Melanesian attitudes toward the afterlife.

At one time it was thought that these cults were caused by contact with the outside world and, particularly, Christian missionaries. Now, it's understood that the apocalyptic tendency was already present in many Melanesian cultures. The intrusion of Western trade, religion, and colonialism was just the spark that caused them to explode.

In most of the societies of Indonesia, New Guinea, Java, the

Celebes, and other parts of Melanesia, people believe that ancestors are not gone forever or even very far. The dead become spirits who continue to help their families and bring them gifts from the other world. This idea of gifts from the dead caused one of the first misunderstandings between the Christian missionaries and the people of the Yangoru of Papua New Guinea. This happened when the European priests arrived in the Yangoru village in 1912. At first they were greeted with delight and respect. One of the priests, Father Limbrock, wrote, "the word missionary has a good sound here." What he didn't understand was that the Yangoru thought that these pale people were "kamba, spirits of the dead, who had returned to visit their living relatives."[2]

This was the first of many cases of what anthropologists call "cognitive dissonance," in which two cultures operate from entirely different basic belief systems that meet at only a few places. Therefore, each group interprets information and events differently, often without realizing that the difference exists.[3]

This is one reason that the tribes of Papua New Guinea took so rapidly to Christianity. They embraced the beliefs that made sense to them from the preachers' stories. One of those beliefs was the idea of an apocalyptic event, followed by a new and better order. But for the people of New Guinea, newly colonized and introduced to twentieth-century goods and technology, this "millennial" world meant that the Christians would take the place of the ancestors and share the wealth.

The Apocalypse would for them be a violent overthrow of the colonial powers. The millennium wasn't exactly understood as the thousand years of peace and harmony either. The new Christians assumed that accepting the religion meant they would receive all the things that the colonials had. From this grew what is known, somewhat inaccurately, as "cargo cults."[4]

The classic image of the post–World War II cargo cult is that of natives bringing offerings to rusting airplanes in the anticipation that the gods would send more goods. The reality is much more sophisticated. As early as the 1800s, the missionaries, both Catholic and Protestant, simplified the message of Christianity to make it understandable to "simple natives." So they stressed the rewards of heaven if one accepted Jesus' teaching and the pains of hell if one did not. They proved this by giving presents from mission boxes to the converts. It was natural for the natives to assume that this was part of the deal attached to the religion. When more and more people came to church, however, the boxes were too soon emptied. So the latecomers felt cheated.[5] The missionaries weren't living up to their side of the bargain.

What the missionaries didn't understand was the relationship of the people with their ancestors, which was not diminished by conversion. The ancestors were not an article of faith but real beings with whom they interacted. Sometimes they appeared in human form or that of birds. They provided good crops and sufficient rain as well as protection from disease and enemies. In return, their descendants honored them, performing rituals of thanks and caring for their bones.

When the missionaries came, they explained that the people should throw away the bones of their ancestors because now God would provide for them.[6]

In response, many people threw out the bones and other ritual objects and put the responsibility for their welfare on Jesus. They expected him to give them even more than their ancestors had because, according to the missionaries, he was so much greater. In order to clear the way for the coming savior, "the villagers destroyed their gardens, food reserves, and killed their livestock in the hope of thus hastening the day of the coming new cargo."[7]

Even though they stopped performing the religious rites to propitiate ancestors, the belief in them remained and many were certain that the Euro-Australians, Americans, and other foreigners were either the spirits themselves or knew how to contact them. This again led to expectations that the wealth would be shared. Even those who didn't believe the white people were spirits wanted to send letters via the missionaries and anthropologists to their dead relatives, hoping that those spirits would return with the proper reciprocal gifts.

In his study of this phenomenon in another group in Papua New Guinea, Stephen Leavitt concluded: "[The] Bumbita interest in Europeans' relations with the dead presupposes that we all live in the same moral universe, not that the Europeans are somehow fundamentally superior."[8] This is one point of view. In other cases, natives were made to feel that they were not as good as the colonizers. If they were, they would have received the same opportunities for wealth.[9] This impression strengthened the need for an Apocalypse after which the situation would be reversed or at least equalized.

So throughout the nineteenth and especially the twentieth century, the people of Melanesia were both encouraged to accept Christianity and disappointed when the promised rewards and protection failed to appear.

Then, in the late 1970s, more decisively apocalyptic bands of missionaries came to New Guinea. They were Seventh Day Adventists, Baptists, charismatic Catholics, and others. These Pentecostal and charismatic Christians made great inroads into changing religious practice. In places where old and new beliefs had co-existed for decades, the traditional ceremonies were abandoned and the sacred spaces reused for crops.[10]

By the 1990s, the belief that the millennium would arrive in 2000 led many who had been sitting on the fence to decide to be born again. "The inevitability of Jesus' return and the last judgment put pressure on people to be ever prepared for these events by becoming righteous Christians."[11]

Most evangelists did not stress the actual date of the Second Advent, and after Y2K passed without incident, the Pentecostal movement still continued to grow, spread by the converts themselves, some of whom were trained at workshops in New Guinea and others who had gone to Australia for a religious education. Today, this form of Christianity is the major religion of Papua New Guinea.

* * *

THE people of Java, on the other hand, began with a very different worldview from those of New Guinea. The central creed in Javanese society was balance. The traditional phrase for this is *tata tenteram*, or "peace and order in harmony."[12] Like the Maya and many others, traditional Javanese concepts of the world are cyclical and astronomical. "[T]he affairs of the men and the event of the sky are both directed by elemental forces that recur over and over again."[13] At some points in history, the balance is too far off to repair in the usual fashion, and then there is a period of apocalyptic change, after which a "new cosmic order will prevail."[14]

In the early centuries of the Common Era, Java was heavily influenced by Hindu religion. From this, the people adopted the idea of a series of ages that grew increasingly dissolute with each change. The Javanese found this easy to incorporate into their worldview. It is thought that at about this time the concept of the *ratu adil*, or "just king," became popular. This was a quasi-messianic leader who would appear in desperate times to restore cosmic harmony. This fully Javanese messiah had aspects of the Hindu–Buddhist *Erucakra*, or one who restores order.[15] When Islamic rule came to Java and Indonesia in the sixteenth century, most Javanese added the Mahdi to the titles for the *ratu adil*. In the early nineteenth century a prince-religious leader, Dipanagara, was called by all three titles. Even after his defeat, there were many who continued to believe that he was the savior whose coming had been foretold.[16] The Indonesian leader Sukarno was thought by some to be the *ratu adil*, and he didn't object. The prophecy *Babad Kadhiri* stated that the *ratu adil* would give "justice after a long period of oppression."[17]

Although Christianity did not attract many converts in Java and Indonesia, the missionaries who had some success did so by explaining that Jesus was the expected *ratu adil*.[18]

So both the people of Papua New Guinea and Java retained their basic outlook on life and the universe while accepting beliefs from outside cultures that fit with this outlook. In both cases, there was already a thread of belief in the destruction of the world and the coming of one who would save the deserving. In Java, the need for order and balance outweighs all others. In New Guinea, the system is based on a reciprocal agreement with the ancestors or, if they are abandoned, with the religion that replaces them.

Especially in the case of New Guinea, the encouragement of Pentecostal Christian missionaries to replace old beliefs and rituals with Christian ones has led to extreme behavior, like the destruction of property to make way for the riches promised by the Second Coming and subsequent millennium.

The international spread of evangelical preachers from both Catholic and Protestant millennial sects has caused a mind-set of approaching doom in societies that had previously established systems for keeping the universe running. The new beliefs either are totally opposed to the old, creating tension in the culture, or are altered to fit into traditional worldviews. Either way, the Apocalypse has taken on a life far removed from the teaching of John in Revelation.

1 Michele Stephen, "Cargo Cults, Creativity, and Autonomous Imagination," *Ethos* 25, no. 3 (1997), 335.

2 Paul B. Roscoe, "The Far Side of Harun: The Management of Melanesian Millenarian Movements," *American Ethnologist* 15, no. 3 (1988): 517. Most of the examples here are from Papua New Guinea. It seems to have been more overrun with anthropologists than other places.

3 Actually, this happens in most human interactions; it's just more pronounced here.

4 Jean Guiart, "Conversion to Christianity in the South Pacific," in *Millennial Dreams in Action*, ed. Sylvia L. Thrupp (New York: Schocken, 1970), 122–123.

5 Ibid., 125–127.

6 Roger Ivar Lohman, "The Afterlife of Asabano Corpses: Relationships with the Deceased in Papua New Guinea," *Ethnology* 44, no. 2 (2005): 202.

7 Justus M. van der Kroef, "The Messiah in Indonesia and Melanesia," *The Scientific Monthly* 25, no. 3 (1952): 163.

8 Stephen Leavitt, "The Apotheosis of White Men?: A reexamination of Beliefs about Europeans as Ancestral Spirits," *Oceania* 70, no. 4 (2000): 309.

9 Ibid., 309.

10 Joel Robbins," Becoming Sinners: Christianity and Desire among the Urapmin of Papua New Guinea," *Ethnology*, Vol. 37, No. 4 (Autumn, 1998), 302.

11 Richard Ewes, "Waiting for the Day: Globalisation and Apocalypticism in Central New Ireland, Papua New Guinea," *Oceania* 71 (2000): 351.

12 Justus M. van der Kroef, "Javanese Messianic Expectations: Their Origin and Cultural Context," *Comparative Studies in Society and History* 1, no. 4 (1959): 300.

13 Ibid., 301.

14 Ibid., 305.

15 Michael Adas, *Prophets of Rebellion: Millenarian Protest Movements against the European Colonial Order* (Durham: University of North Carolina Press, 1979), 98.

16 Ibid., 99.

17 Martin Ramstedt, *Hinduism in Modern Indonesia: Between Local, National and Global Interests* (Florence, KY: Routledge-Curzon, 2003), 16–17.

18 Kroef, "Javanese Messianic Expectations," 311.

CHAPTER THIRTY-SIX

The Fifth World

Hopi Prophecy and 2012

It is time for the end times here, that was prophesized
and through the dreams that were given to us also.
Through those dreams we are learning that we are
getting very close to the end times.

—Grandfather 2, radio interview with Art Bell (June 15, 1998)

Among the many examples put forward by those who think
that the world will end in 2012, the Hopi Fifth World is often
mentioned. Since the 1960s, the idea of the Fifth World has drawn the
interest of many non-Hopi people, with the result that fragments of
the stories have entered into the mix that makes up New Age beliefs.

A historian of religion who has studied the Hopi language and
culture for many years compiled several versions of the Hopi Emergence story, which is essential to understanding the Last Day end of
the world prophecy.[1]

The main story of the Emergence explains that the Hopi are now
living in the Fourth World. The first three that were given to them,
one after another, became unlivable. Each time, people were neglecting the old ways and, particularly, being sexually promiscuous. The
few people who still lived according to the Path sent a bird to find a
hole in the sky so that they could climb a reed up to it and into a better

world. They then made the journey to this world, the fourth, which was at that time untouched by evil. They thought they had been careful to kick the reed ladder away before the corrupt ones could climb up after them. However, soon after their arrival, the chief's (*kikmongwi*) child became ill and died. Death should not have existed in the Fourth World, so the people realized that somehow a wicked person, a witch, had come up with them. They discovered the witch and were about to throw it back down to the Third World. But the witch convinced the chief to look back down the hole, where he saw that his child was alive and happy in the afterlife. So, the witch was allowed to stay. Nevertheless, this act allowed evil to enter the Fourth World.[2]

Because evil became part of the new world, death and corruption soon followed. Some believe that the signs say it is time to ascend to the Fifth World. This is based on moral and ecological observations. The belief that the tipping point has passed in our exploitation of the earth is one that resonates with many people. The feeling is that the old world must be destroyed and the few righteous need to be ready to move on.

The variations on this basic story are many. Hopi scholar Geertz found at least twelve, and Lomatuway'ma gives fragments of more.[3] In some, the reed grows to break into the Fourth World rather than finding a hole already there. In some the child is a girl, in others a boy. Likewise, the witch can be male or female. Sometimes the witch is a relative of the leader. The decision to allow the witch to remain is sometimes that of the chief; in others the entire community is responsible.[4] The story as a whole is much more complex, including the creation of the sun and moon, arrangements made with the gods and the ancestors, and the migrations of the Hopi. Again, each version is different. They were collected, mainly by Indo-Europeans, over the past 120 years from a variety of sources.

THE apocalyptic scenario of the Hopi people has become, in many ways, an explosive subject. It entails rights of societal privacy, appropriation of cultures, and debates within the Hopi community. It also has become part of another tradition altogether, one that has nothing to do with the Hopi people or their beliefs.

As I researched this subject, I soon realized that, with the exception of a few serious scholars, most people have come across the Hopi prophecies through the writing of Euro-Americans. Some of these non-Hopi authors have heard English versions from Hopi informants. Others get the story secondhand or thirdhand through books and magazine articles. Many more know of the prophecies through television or the Internet.[5]

Therefore, this section deals more with what use has been made of these prophecies and what need they fill in non-Hopi people, than the actual story. The many variations in the tale indicate that there isn't one original prophecy. The differences are not as important as the collective spiritual and emotional impact. I have concluded that, if one doesn't speak Hopi and hasn't grown up in a traditional Hopi environment, there isn't much chance of understanding the prophecies in the correct context.

Due to the lack of oil, gold, and fertile soil, the Hopi lands of the American Southwest were not overrun by settlers in the nineteenth century. This allowed the Hopi and other nearby tribes, particularly the Navaho, with whom the Hopi have ongoing boundary disputes, to preserve their language and way of life much longer than Native Americans living in other areas. For many years into the twentieth century, the Hopi were mainly of interest only to students of languages and ethnology.[6]

The Hopi continue to live on their ancestral land near the Four Corners, in Arizona, on three mesas. Each of the mesa communities has its own distinct characteristics. The Oraibi village on the third mesa was, until recently, the largest and has been the focal point for many outsiders who follow the prophecy of the coming end of this world that has been created through a blend of traditional and New Age beliefs. The village of Hoteville, Arizona, also on the third mesa, is a base for those Hopi who are offended by the appropriation of their beliefs by outsiders.[7] Hoteville was founded after a split in the Oraibi community. There is no one universal Hopi opinion on the coming of the Fifth World and the interest in it by non-Hopi.

The first difficulty in understanding the Hopi prophecies is one of language. Hopi is an Uto-Aztecan language, nothing like Indo-European-based ones. One can't make a direct translation from Hopi to English, only an approximation. This is true of translations from any language but even more so with one so different from that of the translators.

In Hopi, an exact, literal translation makes little sense in English, needing to be translated once again into colloquial speech. For example, in a study of Hopi lullabies, the authors freely admit that even with something as universal as a mother's song to her children, the "exact duplication of the poems in English was impossible . . . Often the implicit meanings accessible to Hopis appear cryptic in English."[8] The implicit meanings of speech are determined by the culture one lives in. In any language even native speakers can become confused if a story refers to experiences that the listener doesn't share.

Therefore, any prophecy that is read in a language other than Hopi has already been interpreted by the translator, even if that person is a native Hopi speaker.

The other stumbling block is the idea of what a prophecy is. Western tradition has it as something foreseen, sometimes under divine inspiration, by one person. A prophecy is set in stone. It doesn't appear that this matches the Hopi concept. The same basic story may be told differently according to the clan of the teller, the person hearing the story, or the time in which it is told. That does not make any of these invalid.

The mistake that early scholars made was to insist that there must be one Ur-myth, a place where all the stories began. And they believed that, if they could find it, they would find the truth. This belief was common among early biblical scholars and collectors of European folk

Awa, Tsireh (1895–1985) Hopi pattern: Eagle with Snake, c.1925–1930. Watercolor and ink on paper, 11 1/4 x 14 1/4. Smithsonian American Art Museum, Washington, DC, U.S.A. *Smithsonian American Art Museum, Washington, DC / Art Resource, NY*

tales as well. Recently, researchers have come to the conclusion that stories in the oral tradition are all valid in their own way and that it is more important to look at them individually to discover what they say about the culture of the teller, rather than to uncover the first telling.

I think that this is the attitude we must take with the end time prophecy of the Hopi. There are Hopi prophecies of the end of the Fourth World. They were not made up by outsiders. Some may be thousands of years old. Many of them are recent. That doesn't make the latter any less valid; they are modern wisdom rather than ancient.

The Hopi end of the Fourth World prophecy was first popularized by Frank Waters (1902–1995) in his 1963 work, *The Book of the*

Hopi. Waters was a life-long westerner who had a great respect for and interest in Native American society. He had previously written several western novels with strong, sympathetic Indian characters. He was part Indian on his father's side, although not Hopi. He was part of the Taos group of writers and artists in the 1940s, where he was influenced by non-Western spirituality including Buddhist and Hindu thought.[9] While visiting Hopi villages, Waters understood their belief system as a rejection of Western materialism and greed as well as being in line with Eastern spirituality. His work reflects his desire to portray the Hopi beliefs as unified with other non-Western religions in their mutual desire for peaceful co-existence with the planet.[10]

When he introduced the idea of the Fifth World to the general reader, Waters's timing was perfect. The Cuban missile crisis of 1962 had convinced millions of people that we were on the brink of nuclear war and total annihilation.[11] Waters announced that the Hopi had foreseen that the world would be destroyed in a nuclear holocaust, with only the Hopi and other disenfranchised people surviving to mount to the Fifth World.[12]

There are prophecies among the Hopi that the Fourth World is ending. "It is firmly believed that Hopiland will become the regenerated Center of the World after the catastrophes," Waters insisted.[13] But what are these prophecies? There seem to be as many versions among the Hopi of the end as there are Emergence stories. The belief that only those who follow the Hopi traditions and rituals will be saved seems to be the only constant.

While the Hopi Third World was abandoned because of immorality, the Fourth World is in danger because of nuclear war, pollution, and lack of respect for the earth. These fall in well with the convictions of many outsiders. Several of the reported prophecies also state that the god Maasaw guided the Hopi into the Fourth World and left them to their own devices. He promised he would return at the end of the fourth cycle. Part of the prophecy seems to be that, before he left, Maasaw gave sacred prophetic tablets to two brothers. These stone tablets foretold the signs indicating that the Fourth World was about to end. One brother stayed in the west on the Hopi land. The other, White Brother, went east with a piece of the tablets. It is said that White Brother will return just before the end with the tablet fragment. When the pieces are joined, the signs will be made clear and the exodus to the Fifth World will begin.[14]

This is the part of the prophecy that appeals most to outsiders. Some Hopi ethnographers have doubted that White Brother is part of the ancient prophecy. He doesn't appear in all the stories.[15] But many thousands of Europeans and Americans have seen it as permission for them to adopt aspects of the Hopi culture.

This is where some of the Hopi part company with those who wish to participate in the Hopi religion. They feel that it isn't something that one can pick and choose symbols and ceremonies from.[16] Moreover, as I understand it, there is a firm connection between sacred sites, the Hopi ancestors, and the people. As Dr. Philip Tuwaletstiwa, a Hopi geologist explained, "[Y]ou cannot export the Hopi religion. It can exist only here, where we have our shrines, springs, landmarks, materials, animals, plants and hundreds and hundreds of years of belief and practice." He added that even Hopi can't practice their religion away from the mesas.[17]

But that hasn't stopped even some Hopi from trying to explain the religion to outsiders, warning them of a coming Apocalypse.[18] A Swedish film crew interviewed several people, some Hopi, on the coming end. Few mentioned the White Brother. None mentioned 2012. In my search through the Internet (the modern equivalent of the seventeenth-century pamphlets) I found nothing written or spoken by Hopis that gave a date for the ending of the Fourth World, only a general warning that we are ruining our planet and the time of reckoning is coming. They encourage a way of life that is in balance with nature. It sounds like good advice to me.

Many of the proponents of the Fifth World prophecy state that even non-Hopi can join the move to the next level if they follow the

Hopi way.[19] This has led to an influx of sightseers, pilgrims, and others to the Hopi lands, all wanting to become part of the Hopi culture as they understand it. I have the distinct impression that even those Hopi who are willing to share the possibility that non-Hopis will make the ascent, would rather that the outsiders follow their idea of the Hopi way somewhere else.

While some Hopi now think that the Fifth World may be metaphorical, rather than literal, should the sky open to show the Hopi the way to the Fifth World, I wouldn't blame them if they climbed as rapidly as possible, leaving the rest of us to cope with the mess we made.[20]

This time I hope that they will be careful to make sure no evil witches come with them.

1 Armin W. Geertz, "A Reed Pierced the Sky: Hopi Indian Cosmography on Third Mesa, Arizona," *Numen* 31, no. 2 1984): 216–241. See also, Geertz, *The Invention of Prophecy* (Berkeley: University of California Press, 1994).

2 I've put this together from several different versions in various sources, including Geertz and Peter G. Beidler, "First Death in the Fourth World: Teaching the Emergence Myth of the Hopi Indians," *American Indian Quarterly* 19, no. 1 (1995): 75–89.

3 Geertz, "A Reed," 215; Michael Lomatuway'ma, Lorena Lomatuway'ma, Sidney Namingha Jr., and Ekkehart Malotki, *Hopi Ruin Legends: Kiqotutuwutsi* (Lincoln: University of Nebraska Press, 1993), 77–79.

4 Peter G. Beidler, "First Death in the Fourth World," 77–84.

5 A search taken in June 2009 showed 73,000 Internet sites for "Hopi prophecy end of the world."

6 S. Ryan Johansson and S. H. Preston, "Tribal Demography: The Hopi and Navaho Population as Seen Through Manuscripts from the 1900 U.S. Census," *Social Science History* 33, no. 1 (1978): 1.

7 William M. Clements, "'A Continual Beginning, and Then an Ending, and Then a Beginning Again': Hopi Apocalypticism in the New Age," *Journal of the Southwest* 46 (2004): 3.

8 Kathleen M. Sands and Emory Sekaquapteka, "Four Hopi Lullabies: A Study in Method and Meaning," *American Indian Quarterly* 4, no. 3 (1978), 195–210.

9 Philip Jenkins, *Dreamcatches How Mainstream America Discovered Native Spirituality* (Oxford: Oxford University Press, 2004), 140.

10 Ibid., 162.

11 I don't need to cite an expert; I remember.

12 Frank Waters, *Book of the Hopi* (New York: Viking, 1963).

13 Geertz, *The Invention of Prophecy*, 422–432, gives a chronological list of the various forms of prophecy.

14 Clements, 9.

15 Geertz and Clements both have mentioned this.

16 Actually, I don't know of a religion in which that is encouraged.

17 Quoted in Susan Milius, "When Worlds Collide," *Science News* 154, no. 6 (1998): 92.

18 The late Thomas Banyacya recorded an interpretation of rock carvings that can be found at www.youtube.com/watch?v=y9Vhivi6nws. Accessed November 2009.

19 Clements, 12.

20 Geertz, on the current opinion of some Hopi, private correspondence, July 17, 2009. I wish to thank Professor Geertz for reading the first draft of this chapter and making suggestions. Any misunderstandings are totally mine.

CHAPTER THIRTY-SEVEN

The Branch Davidians

David Koresh presented the Federal authorities with a
four-page "letter from God" on Friday, citing biblical passages
and threatening the forces that have surrounded his religious
sect's compound near here for 43 days. Federal Bureau of
Investigation officials said the letter, written in the first person
as if from God and bearing no salutation, was addressed to
"Friends" and was signed "Yahweh Koresh."

—*New York Times*, April 11, 1993, section 1, p. 18

On April 19, 1993, after a siege of fifty-one days, the Federal
Bureau of Alcohol, Tobacco and Firearms (ATF) raided the
compound of the Branch Davidians, in Mt. Carmel, near Waco, Texas.
The exact events of that day are still being debated, but at the end of it
about seventy-five people inside the compound lay dead, twenty-five of
them children. The conflagration that destroyed their home was seen
on television news by millions of people all over the world. And yet
finding accurate information on the Davidians and their young, charismatic leader, Vernon Howell/David Koresh, is almost impossible.
Much of what was said after the raid was colored by the emotions of
those who told their stories, both from those in support of Koresh and
those violently against him. The news reports focused on allegations of
child abuse and molestation by Koresh and then on whether the ATF
had acted inappropriately in firing tear gas into the compound.

No one seemed interested in who the Branch Davidians were and where they came from.

The Davidians were formed in 1929 by a Bulgarian immigrant named Victor Houteff. They were originally a splinter group of the Seventh-Day Adventists. Houteff and his followers felt that the mainstream Adventist Church had drifted from its apocalyptic beginnings and was integrating too much with the modern world. In 1935, Houteff bought the land in Mt. Carmel that became the headquarters of the Branch Davidians.[1]

Houteff broke with the Seventh Day Adventists in 1942 to establish the group as a genuine sect in its own right, but the Davidians drew most of their converts from that faith. This may have been because of the stress the Davidians put on an imminent Apocalypse like the forerunners of the Adventists, the Millerites.[2]

The Davidians carried on an intense missionary program and soon had converts in Portugal, Indonesia, and the Caribbean as well as the United States.[3] I read through Houteff's books *The Shephard's Rod I & II* as well as several of the Davidian newsletters. Houteff followed William Miller's calculations that the millennium would begin in October 1844. The time since then has been occupied in the "cleansing of the sanctuary."[4] While Houteff implied that the final accounting was near, he did not give a specific date. His fiercest diatribes were against "backsliders," those Adventists who had not listened to his message.

Shortly before his death in 1955, Houteff announced that following a period of 1260 literal days, Christ would initiate His kingdom. Afterwards his wife, Florence, succeeding to leadership, identified the 1260 days as extending from November 9, 1955, to April 22, 1959. As the fateful day approached, a call was issued for the faithful to dispose of property and come to Mount Carmel Center. An estimated 800 persons arrived, many bringing the proceeds from the sale of possessions.[5]

The following disappointment caused most of the group to disband and return to their previous lives. Among those who stayed were Ben and Lucy Roden, who kept the community going, in anticipation of the end, although Ben tried to encourage the Davidians to move to Israel. According to a disenchanted Branch Davidian, Marc Breault, writing in 1991 after Ben's death in 1978, Lucy, who had received several prophetic visions, took over the leadership of the group, now named the Branch Davidians. One of the stipulations for leadership was that the leader must be a prophet chosen by God.[6] Lucy convinced the others that she was now the chosen one.

In the early 1980s, Vernon Howell appeared at Mt. Carmel. He soon became a favorite of Lucy Roden. By 1983, they were living together and traveled to Israel as a couple. In 1984, according to ex-Davidians, Howell married Rachel Perry, then fourteen.[7] Lucy seems not to have been happy about this, but by then Howell had assumed control of the group. Lucy and her son, George, were pushed aside, having lost all authority. Lucy died in 1986. It is recorded that, after Lucy died, there was a shoot-out over the Mt. Carmel property between George Roden and Howell and his followers. The resulting court case convicted Roden, who was sentenced to six months in jail.[8] Later he was convicted of murder and, in 1993, was in a penitentiary for the criminally insane.

Over the next nine years, it's not certain what Vernon Howell, now calling himself David Koresh, was thinking or doing. The reports indicate that Koresh considered himself to be, at least at first, a divine messenger. The Davidians believed that the seven angels of Revelation are meant to be the Adventist prophets, starting with William Miller. Koresh stated that he was the seventh angel. He seemed to have a gift for convincing people that his biblical interpretations were logical, including convincing parents to let him sleep with their teen-aged daughters.

The allegation is that Koresh insisted that he was entitled to any woman among the believers because God had told him that he was

the man in the Song of Solomon (Ecclesiastes) who had queens, con-
cubines, and virgins.[9] Eventually, he realized that he was the Lamb of
Revelation and therefore Jesus Christ. This meant that he should produce as many children of God as possible. When the standoff began
in 1993, Koresh was interviewed by CNN. "There are a lot of children
here . . . ," he said. "I do have a lot of children and I do have a lot of
wives."[10]

The alleged sex with underage girls aspect of life in the compound
provided the impetus for the first raid on the Davidians on March 2,
1993, but the stated reason was to serve a warrant to them for firearms
violations. The ATF agents soon found out just how much fire power
the Davidians had. Four of them died in the initial crossfire. In a
phone conversation, Koresh insisted that the agents had fired first and
killed two people, one of them his two-year-old daughter.[11]

I remember the newspapers and television reports on the siege.
There were stories of various things that Koresh had done. He was
portrayed as someone who was able to brainwash his followers into
anything. Often the reporters would mention Jonestown. The images
of the dead children in the jungle were fresh in everyone's mind. I
think there was the real fear that this would happen again that caused
people to feel that something must be done at once.

Again, the reports conflicted. Sometimes Koresh was reported as
saying that they were not a suicide cult. In others, he implied that he
might prefer death to surrender. No one knew which Koresh would
choose. On the fifth day of the siege, the *Washington Post* interviewed
one of the ATF agents at the house asking what would happen next.
The man wasn't sure. "It is my understanding," said FBI special agent
Jeffrey Jamar, "that he is still waiting for a message from God."[12]

As the siege dragged on, reports from the FBI said that Koresh
wanted an "all out fire fight." That statement wasn't corroborated by
outside witnesses. The news reporters were already questioning the
tactics of the ATF.

I don't think that Vernon Howell/David Koresh intended to

create his own private Apocalypse. One reason is that he still seemed to adhere to the Davidian belief in the signs as stated in the Book of Revelation, and he gave no indication that he thought that they had all manifested themselves. When he decided that he was Christ, he may have figured that the clock had been reset for the thousand years of peace and prosperity. The other clue that he might not have planned martyrdom is that he authorized his attorneys to try to get him a book deal for his memoirs.[13]

On April 19, 1993, ATF agents started sending tear gas into the building where the Davidians were barricaded. A few minutes later, the house went up in flames. Some of the few that escaped said that the fire was an accident, caused when a can of heating oil fell and ignited. Koresh did die of a bullet wound, but he may have shot himself rather than die in the fire.

Reading through some of the thousands of articles that were printed over the time of the siege, two things stand out. The first is that David Koresh did not seem to be eager to die for his beliefs. He put off surrendering over and over, but he never seems to have said that he wouldn't do it eventually. The other thing is that the most inflammatory comments that suggested that the Davidians were a suicide cult came from Marc Braeult, who had led the effort to break up the cult. He might very well have been giving an accurate account about everything that happened but, with Koresh and his most loyal followers dead, we'll never know.

---

1 John R. Hall, Phillip D. Schuyler, and Sylvaine Trinh, *Apocalypse Observed: Religious Movements and Violence in North America, Europe and Japan* (London: Routledge, 2000), 47.

2 Ronald Lawson, "Seventh-Day Adventist Responses to Branch Davidian Notoriety: Patterns of Diversity within a Sect Reducing Tension with Society," *Journal for the Scientific Study of Religion* 34, no. 3 (1995): 330.

3 *The Symbolic Code*, 10, no. 2 (Waco TX: Davidians, 1954). Available at www.davidiansda.org/v10sc2.htm. Accessed November 2009.

4 V. T. Houteff, "Tract No. 3: The Judgment and the Harvest" (np, 1934). Available at www.davidiansda.org/tract_no3.htm. Accessed November 2009.

5 George W. Reid, "The Branch Davidians/Shepherd's Rod—Who Are They?" *The Adventist Review* (1993). Available at www.adventistbiblicalresearch.org/Independent%20Ministries/branchdavidians.htm. Accessed July 2009.

6 Marc Breault, "Some Background on the Branch Davidian Seventh Day Adventist Movement from 1955 to the Early Part of 1991," paper presented at the Biblical Research Institute General Conference of Seventh-Day Adventist, May 1991. Available at www.adventistbiblicalresearch.org/Independent%20Ministries/branchdavidian.htm. Accessed November 2009. As someone who at the time was eager to discredit the Branch Davidians, his testimony on some aspects of the organization needs to be corroborated. However, on the early stages of the organization, his comments seem to agree with Houteff's philosophy.

7 Kenneth Samples, Ervin de Castro, Richard Abanes, and Robert Lyle, *Prophets of the Apocalypse: David Koresh & Other American Messiahs* (Grand Rapids MI: Baker Books, 1994), 40. This is also a book based on interviews with former Davidians.

8 Hall et al., 47.

9 Breault.

10 Tim Madigan and Mede Nix, *The San Francisco Chronicle,* March 1, 1993.

11 "Cult Leader Says He'll Surrender," *Chicago Tribune,* March 2, 1993.

12 Mary Jordan and Sue Anne Pressley, "Gruesome Contest to Raise the Dead Led to Koresh's Takeover of Cult," *Washington Post,* March 7, 1993.

13 *The New York Times,* April 7, 1993.

CHAPTER THIRTY-EIGHT

The Bible Code

Now that computer programs are widely available to help
nearly anyone "mine" available data, there are wonderful new
possibilities for discovering misleading patterns.

—Professor Robert E. Kass, *Statistical Science* (1999)

In 1994 a paper was published in the journal *Statistical Science*. The
authors, Wiztzum, Rips, and Rosenberg (hereafter WRR), proposed the startling idea that the Torah, the first five books of the
Hebrew Bible, contained sequences of letters that, when arranged in a
matrix, produced connected word groups that foretold major events.[1]
Well, actually, the first paper just said that the authors had found the
names and dates of a number of famous rabbis linked closely in the
book of Genesis.

The article attracted some interest among statisticians, but little
more, until a journalist named Michael Drosnin became interested
and wrote a best-selling book called *The Bible Code*. This was when the
code began to be considered prophetic, including giving the date for
the end of the world.

In reading the first article of WRR, it seemed to me that there
were a number of problems with the theory. First of all, it entailed
taking out all punctuation and laying out all the letters in order but as
if wrapped around a cylinder. The authors state, "We may think of the
two vertical edges of the array as pasted together, with the end of the

first line pasted to the beginning of the second, the end of the second pasted to the third and so on. We thus get a cylinder on which the text spirals down in one long line."[2] Okay, not the way most people read the Bible, but statisticians like to make things more interesting.

Having set up a two-dimensional grid, they then began by fixing the parameters for pairings. They decided that the letters had to be no more than a certain distance apart for a correlation to be noticed, but the words could go in any direction: backward, forward, or diagonally. Then they put in the names of famous rabbis through time, up to the present. Most of them appeared on the grid along with birth and/or death dates. Here is where I had another problem. The authors used a number of variations on the names of the rabbis such as alternate spellings and names, Moses, Maimonides and Rambam, for instance, are all names for the same person.[3] It seems to me that this would increase the chances of getting hits. Also, Hebrew numbers are also letters so one could simply decide arbitrarily to make a letter a number and vice versa.

Other statements that confused me included the authors' use of Yiddish names for some of the rabbis. These are written in Hebrew characters so that part is all right, but why use Yiddish? Every rabbi would have had a perfectly good Hebrew name as well. Wouldn't the Bible have used that? Yiddish wasn't a language until the thirteenth century at the earliest. WRR also programmed in several possible ways of writing dates. This makes the chances even better for one of them to show up in the grid. Added to this is the fact that Hebrew, like Arabic, doesn't usually include the vowels in its written form. One is supposed to understand words from context. However, when the context is taken out, groups of letters can have a wide range of vowels inserted to create words, thereby giving a wide range of possibilities. So, it would be odd if they weren't able to come up with names, dates, and events.

I have seen a couple of the television documentaries on the Bible Code, and they didn't mention any of the finer points illustrated in the article. I did hear that the fact that the authors had been published in a respected scientific journal gave their findings more credibility.

There's a problem with this, too. The editor of the journal *Statistical Science* was upset enough with the outside reaction to the theories of WRR that, in 1999, he wrote a piece explaining why he had accepted the paper. While the reviewers and editorial board had not found "anything amazing" in the paper, what intrigued them was "the difficulty of pinpointing the cause, presumed to be some flaw in their procedure that produced such apparently remarkable findings."[4] In his original introduction, the editor had only called it "a challenging puzzle."[5]

The disclaimer was followed by a paper from several statisticians, three of them from Israel, who thought they had discovered the flaw.

Brendan McKay, Dror Bar-Natan, Maya Bar-Hillel, and Gil Kalai (MNHK) took a hard look at the variables and concluded that they were too inexact. Choices for words to enter into the program were not as random as WRR thought. Some of the dates that had appeared in the grid matched their list, but turned out to be the wrong ones. But MNHK reserved most of their disputes for the methodology of WRR.

MNHK tried the control test that WRR used for their calculations. They entered a list of rabbis, slightly different from the one that WRR used, into the Hebrew Book of Genesis and also into a Hebrew translation of *War and Peace*. WRR had also used *War and Peace* as a control and found no correlations. In the MNHK experiment, the connections on the Tolstoy grid were phenomenally close. The ones for Genesis were negligible.[6]

Now, the same argument could be made for the second study, that it was biased and the data skewed, even unconsciously. However, MNHK followed this study with several more, using the same parameters, as far as possible, as WRR had done. The results still did not show any surprising connections in the texts. They tried the other four books of the Torah and found no correlations in them, either. The most important thing is that the independent readers who refereed the paper were all satisfied that MNHK had found the flaw in the work of WRR and explained it satisfactorily.

There is one other problem with the Bible Code. Which Bible? Today there is a standard text but in the beginning there were many variations on the Torah. Some added words or passages; some used different words. In the finds at Qumran (the Dead Sea Scrolls) several copies of the first five books of the Bible were found. Each one was slightly different. "[T]he Qumran scriptural scrolls . . . are characterized by extreme fluidity; they often differ not just from the customary wording but also, when the same book is attested by several manuscripts, among themselves."[7] None of these changes significantly affect the sense of the text, but when the text is torn apart and put on a cylinder to predict the future, there will be different answers according to the text used. The Bible used by Samaritans to this day is based on one of these variations.[8] Have the Bible Code scholars tried using that version?

What bothers me the most about the Bible Code is the same thing that makes me uneasy about other biblical interpretations. It presupposes that all of history has been only a buildup to the grand appearance of us. I know the ways of God are mysterious and strange, but why would he have secret messages put into Genesis that could be found only by someone with a computer and too much spare time? Didn't he care about all the other generations? Apart from all the statistical objections, it just seems extremely arrogant to assume that we are the only ones who deserve to know the "secrets."

---

1 Doron Witztum, Eliyahu Rips, and Yoav Rosenberg, "Equidistant Letter Sequences in the Book of Genesis," *Statistical Science* 9, no. 3 (1994): 429–438.

2 Witztum et al., 430.

3 Witztum et al., 431.

4 Robert E. Kass, "Introduction to 'Solving the Bible Code Puzzle' by Brendan McKay. Dror Bar-Natan, Maya Bar-Hillel, and Gil Kalai," *Statistical Science* 14, no. 2 (1999): 149.

5 Ibid.

6 Brendan McKay, Dror Bar-Natan, Maya Bar-Hillel, and Gil Kalai, "Solving the Bible Code Puzzle," *Statistical Science* 14, no. 2 (1999): 197.

7 Geza Vermes, *The Complete Dead Sea Scrolls in English*, rpt. ed. (New York: Allen Lane/ Penguin, 1997), 16.

8 Magnar Kartveit, *The Origin of the Samaritans* (Leiden: Brill, 2009), 259–309.

CHAPTER THIRTY-NINE

Jews, Israel, and the End of the World

Evangelical leaders have declared that support for Israel has moved to the very top of their agenda. Christian groups are spending millions on everything from armored school buses for Israeli children to halogen lights for the army's emergency-rescue service. There are e-mail chains, prayer ministries and grassroots efforts to get the word out that the U.S. must stand united with its ally in the war on terror.

—Nancy Gibbs, *Time* magazine (2002)[1]

One of the tenets of dispensationalist Christianity is the conviction that the Jews must return to their homeland before the end of the world can get started. This is an ancient belief that began with Paul's letter to the Romans in which he insists that Israel is not lost irrevocably and will one day be saved (Romans 12:25–26). In the Middle Ages this was used as a reason for allowing a "remnant" of Israel to live in Europe. If there were no Jews left to return to Jerusalem, then Jesus would not return. However, since the Church didn't want the Parousia right away, they made sure that Jews were allowed to live, even if they were not given the rights of citizens. And when Jerusalem was taken by the Crusaders in 1099, one of the first proclamations was that no Jews could enter the city. The general feeling was, the Apocalypse could come, but not yet.

Things changed in the seventeenth century when many Protestants were looking forward to the millennium. It was the Puritan millenarian Oliver Cromwell who finally readmitted the Jews into England 350 years after they had been expelled. Cromwell, along with the Fifth Monarchists, subscribed to the idea that until the Jews returned to Jerusalem, Christ would not return. However, England under Cromwell was seen as the New Jerusalem. The Jews were readmitted in 1656 and, by 1657 had a synagogue and cemetery in London.[2] This situation did not change with the Restoration of the monarchy.

Eighteenth-century scientist Joseph Priestley wrote an open letter to the Jews, telling them to prepare for the time of returning to Israel under a ruler from the house of David.[3] Priestley was eager for things to get going.

In early-nineteenth-century America, there was much insistence that the new nation was, like England, under the Protectorate, God's country. We're used to that expression, but they *really* meant it. And the New Jerusalem could not be established in America unless the Jews were converted first. "We should remember," the Worchester County Jews Society newsletter stated, "that the conversion and restoration of the Jews are most intimately connected with those glorious Millennial scenes, toward which the promises of Jehovah are now directing the eyes and hearts of his people."[4] The society, by the way, was not made up of Jews, but of Christians eager to convert them.

In 1891, Christian Zionist theologian William Blackwell tried to convince President Benjamin Harrison to support a Jewish State in Israel. On the petition he sent to the White House were the names Charles Scribner, John D. Rockefeller, and J. P. Morgan as well as those of several congressmen.[5]

It may seem a contradiction to want a Jewish state in order to convert Jews to Christianity. This had to do with the belief drawn from the Book of Revelation that the battle of Armageddon would be fought when the Twelve Tribes were united in Israel. Conversion was the main goal, but the rebirth of Israel was essential to the fulfillment of prophecy. It also struck a chord in the spirit of the people living in the New Israel—America. One person wrote, "The whole United States . . . is an asylum for the Jew. . . . The moment he lands on our blessed shores, he is safe."[6]

The problem with all this rhetoric was that before the migrations of the 1840s, there were almost no Jews in the New Israel. It also turned out that the Jews who were so well loved were Abraham, Isaiah, Ezekiel, and David, although the last wasn't always very nice. The Old Testament Jews who hadn't been contaminated by their blindness in denying Christ, who hadn't degenerated into a morally bankrupt race, those were the ones that the early nineteenth century evangelists admired.[7] Certainly they wanted the present-day Jews to convert but, until they did, they really couldn't be allowed to come to dinner with nice people. Therefore, a Jewish state was a good place for them to go.

My impression is that this dichotomy continues to the present among pro-Israel dispensationalists.

Therefore the connection between the dispensationalists and the Jews was not a sudden change in Christian teaching. Nor was it a radical new idea that America should lead the way in helping the Jews return to the Holy Land. What the new sects did was refine ideas that had been vague before.

In dispensationalism as John Nelson Darby expressed it, one of the beliefs is that after the faithful have been caught up in the Rapture, Jews from all over the world would begin to migrate to Israel. He based this on the work of earlier Protestant writers and the Old Testament prophets, which he connected with verse twenty of Revelation. Once in Israel, some would immediately convert to Christianity. The rest would live strictly by the laws of Moses and would suffer under the Antichrist until he was defeated by Christ, at which time all Jews left alive would accept him as their savior and the Last Judgment could begin.

The birth of Israel in 1948 was like a tune-up note from the Last Trumpet for dispensationalists and many other evangelical Christians.

The fact that Jerusalem wasn't included in the settlement agreement worried some, but in 1967, when the Israelis captured Jerusalem in the Six-Day War, hopes went through the roof.

The most generous and enthusiastic segment of society to support the continuation and expansion of Israel is the fundamentalist Christian movement. When the U.S.-based United Jewish Appeal refused to fund kibbutzes across the Green Line dividing Israeli and Palestinian land, money came in from evangelical foundations. It was estimated that two thirds of all Likud West Bank settlements received money from the Christian Right.[8]

The dispensationalists have little use for a secular state of Israel. The Rapture is overdue, and Israel is not predestined to be a mundane nation but the site of Armageddon. Fundamentalist Jews understand this but their immediate goals match those of the evangelicals. They want to continue spreading across the West Bank, destroy the Dome of the Rock in Jerusalem and rebuild the Temple.[9]

The dispensationalists are with them all the way. What happens afterward may prove a problem, especially if the world doesn't end.

---

1 Nancy Gibbs, "What Do End Time Prophesies Mean for Israel and Judaism?," *Time*, June 23, 2002. Available at www.time.com/time/cover/1101020701/jew.html. Accessed August 2009.

2 Benjamin Ravid, "'How Profitable the Nation of the Jewes Are': the *Humble* Addresses of Menasseh Ben Israel and the *Discorso* of Simone Luzzatto," in *Mystics, Philosophers and Politicians*, ed. Jehuda Reinharz and Daniel Swetschski (Durham, NC:, Duke University Press, 1982), 173.

3 Clarke Garrett, "Joseph Priestley, the Millennium and the French Revolution," *Journal of the History of Ideas* 34, no. 1 (1973): 57.

4 Robert K. Whalen, "'Christians Love the Jews': The Development of American Philo-Judaism 1790–1860," *Religion and American Culture* 6, no. 2 (1996), 229.

5 Don Wagner, "For Zion's Sake," *Middle East Report* 223 (1992): 54.

6 Quoted in Whalen, 230.

7 Ibid., 231–235.

8 Colin Shindler, "Likud and the Christian Dispensationalists: A Symbiotic Relationship," *Israel Studies* 5, no. 1 (2000): 155–156.

9 Wagner, 56.

CHAPTER FORTY

Y2K

Apocalyptic Technophobia

It seems we are about to witness an "autopsy" of modern
society. As one system or company fails we shall learn
what other systems, companies and countries depend on
it. The year ahead will present unique opportunities for
education, research and public service as we help the
public understand what we are experiencing.

—Dr. Stuart A. Umpleby, *Science* (May 21, 1999)[1]

The year 2000 was the first apocalyptic prediction that was
truly worldwide. It was both secular and religious. The panic
cut across educational and economic lines. Even such a short time
after the event, I'm still not sure how it all happened. However, there
are plenty of others who have spent the years since 1997 trying to
explain it.

The first note of concern about Y2K began in 1993, when a Cana-
dian computer consultant pointed out the problem in the way computers recorded dates. They only bothered with the last two years, such
as 99. Therefore, when the calendar flipped to 2000, there could be
a breakdown of computers in everything from banking to medicine
to military controls. Even serious scientists were worried, but more
about the amount of work involved in reprogramming. Few of them,

if any, thought it would be the end of the world, just a big mess caused by a lack of planning on the part of programmers, governments, and financial institutions.[2]

What wasn't expected by those working to avoid the problem was the response from average citizens, especially those who were inclined toward seeing signs that the end was coming soon. It didn't help that 2000 was a millennial year and a super leap year. For many evangelical Christians, these signs together were what they had been expecting for generations. The call went out that Armageddon was at hand.

The proliferation of books telling people how to prepare for the coming disaster was astonishing. Television programs, movies, novels, and above all, rather ironically, Internet sites, fanned the fear.

I knew people who were stockpiling cash, food, and probably guns in order to survive in the post-apocalyptic world when there would be no banks or police protection or restaurants. The magazine *Christianity Today* began to take ads for survival products. There were also carefully worded invitations to buy land in remote undisclosed sites where families and friends could create their own survival fortresses.[3]

In a letter to one millennial Christian magazine, a writer proved that the word *computer*, when given numerical values for each letter, became "666," the number of the beast in Revelation.[4]

This love-hate relationship with technology has been around since the beginning of the Industrial Revolution. Some people see technology as the answer to any problem. "If they can put a man on the moon, they can [fill in the blank]." Others believe that machines strip away our humanity and threaten individual worth. Often, according to circumstances, they are the same people.

Was the computer problem that serious? If nothing had been done there might have been a few weeks of disorganization, some systems may have failed, causing power outages and the breakdown of banking transactions. In a check of one school system, some teachers would have been given ninety-four years of pension time, score-boards wouldn't have worked, and automated machines that chlorinate pools would have stopped. However, anyone with a Mac computer was fine, because they were calibrated to 29,000 C.E.[5]

In reading through technical and financial journals from the late 1990s, I see that most experts took the computer problem seriously, but didn't link it to an end of the world scenario. In many cases these professionals spent a lot of time explaining why certain things wouldn't happen, like an automatic launching of all of Russia's nuclear warheads.[6] Those who designed and programmed computers appear to have been much more concerned with the overreaction of laypeople than anything that might occur due to a programming glitch.[7]

The Y2K bug was identified in time to figure out a solution and, despite complaints that not enough businesses and governments were making the adjustments rapidly enough, we now know that pretty much everyone did.

I didn't stockpile anything or do more than plan an end of the millennium party. But I must admit that at ten seconds to midnight, I wondered if we would all be suddenly partying in the dark. I'm pretty certain I wasn't the only one. Because, unlike most other millennial panics, this one stretched around the world. The technology that threatened us had become universal. It was hard not to feel at least a qualm in the face of all that hype.

In Papua New Guinea, a place that had only recently starting dating years by the current calendar, the message of millenarian Christian missionaries combined with rumors and news reports to create a sense of terror. This led to a rapid increase in attendance at the new evangelical churches by people "searching for their future security and for a clear picture of what was to come."[8] Some Christian groups in New Guinea practiced extreme self-denial in anticipation of "the last days (*las de*) when Jesus would return and take those who followed his law to heaven."[9]

This is an extreme example of what was happening everywhere.

Not always expressed in terms of the Apocalypse and destruction of the world, many of those who became seriously concerned about Y2K, seemed to see it as more of a symbol for all the things wrong with the planet. It wasn't necessary to believe in monotheistic apocalypses to start thinking about the fragility of civilization. Some said that the Y2K bug showed how we were replacing God with machines. Many felt that we needed to reevaluate our ideas of progress. Survivalists and conservationists were united in the feeling that technology and overdevelopment were leading humanity to its own doom without the promise of a Rapture or any last-minute savior.[10]

I think that for what was just another failed prediction of the end, Y2K had a greater impact than any previously predicted. Even those who only briefly wondered how they could survive without air-conditioning, TV, automatic tellers, or e-mail faced the possibility of a very different world than the one they knew.

What annoys me is that all this time was spent worrying about how a glitch in computer programming was going to destroy the world. We were told that the economic system was going to collapse. We'd be reduced to a primitive state and Armageddon would start. And yet, when the economy did collapse seven years later, I didn't hear one prophetic word of warning. Think of all the seers who could be saying "I told you so," but can't. It's very discouraging for those who like to be prepared.

---

1 Stuart A. Umpleby, "Y2K: An 'Autopsy' of Modern Society?" *Science* 284, no.5418 (1999): 1274.

2 Robert F. Bennett, "The Y2K Problem," *Science* 284, no. 5413 (1999): 438–439.

3 Lisa McMinn, "Y2K, The Apocalypse, and Evangelical Christianity: The Role of Eschatological Belief in Church Responses," *Sociology of Religion* 62, no. 2 (2001): 207–208.

4 Andrea A. Tapia, "Technomillennialism: A Subcultural Response to the Technological Threat of Y2K," *Science, Technology and Human Values* 28, no. 4 (2003): 493.

5 Elizabeth E. Bass, "The Bell Tolls—or Not," *Technos: Quarterly for Education and Technology* 8, (1999): 28.

6 Michael R. Craig, "Russian Roulette: The Vulnerability of Russia's Crumbling Nuclear Arsenal to Y2K Problems Poses a Global Threat," *Forum for Applied Research and Public Policy* 14 (1999): 27.

7 Tapia, 499.

8 Andrew Strathern and Pamela J. Stewart, "History, Conversion and Politics," in *Religious and Ritual Change, Cosmologies and Histories*, ed. Pamela J. Stewart and Andrew Strathern (Durham, NC: Carolina University Press, 2009), 315.

9 Joel Robbins, "Christianity and Desire among the Urapmin," *Ethnology* 303.

10 Tapia, 497–512.

CHAPTER FORTY-ONE

The Rapture

Or "If You Hear a Trumpet,

Grab the Steering Wheel"

I look upon this world as a wrecked vessel. God has
given me a lifeboat and said, "Moody, save all you can."

—Evangelist Dwight L. Moody

One of the most intriguing and relatively new twists in evangelical Christian belief is the idea of the Rapture. The notion
is that those who are already the Christian elect shouldn't have to
go through the premillennial Tribulations. Therefore, before things
get nasty on earth, all of them will be transported bodily into
heaven.

Now, this is not exactly a biblical doctrine. Only one person in
the New Testament ever rose bodily into the next world. Even the
Catholic tradition of the assumption into heaven of the Virgin Mary
comes from an early folk belief. The closest one comes to an ascension is in Saint Paul's first letter to the Thessalonians (4:16–17), who
had been having a rather rough time of it. He promises them that
at the end: "with an archangel's call, and with the sound of God's
trumpet, [Jesus] will descend from heaven, and the dead in Christ will

rise first. Then we who are alive, who are left, will be caught up in the clouds together with them to meet the Lord in the air."

Until the early 1800s, this was taken either as a metaphor or as something that wouldn't happen until just before the Last Judgment. At that time, a group was formed in Ireland and England, led by a man named John Nelson Darby (1800–1882). They called themselves the Plymouth Brethren and rejected Church hierarchy. Their meetings were open to any Christian and were purposely without an agenda so that the Holy Spirit could lead them.[1]

The Brethren believed in evangelical missionary work but otherwise in remaining separate from the world. This included participation in the military for they were totally antiwar. This was not only based on Christian pacifism but on their conviction that "'the saints' belong to no nationality: they are 'heavenly men on earth.'"[2] In their separation from the world, the Brethren acknowledged that armies might be necessary in these evil times, but that being a soldier was no job for a Christian. Several officers in the British military resigned their commissions after converting to the Brethren.[3]

The Brethren believed in premillennial dispensationalism. Dispensations are just another way of describing the old organization of the ages of the world. Darby and the Brethren added the twist that each age was culminated by a disaster, starting with Adam and Eve being thrown out of Eden. The next dispensation was Noah's flood, then the Tower of Babel. After that was the time from Abraham to Moses, ending either with the Exodus or the founding of Israel, then Moses to Jesus. The time of Christ is the current dispensation. It will end with the tribulations that precede the Second Coming. It was the Brethren who came up with the Rapture as the ultimate in noninvolvement.

The evangelical work of the Brethren crossed the Atlantic by the late 1800s and was popularized at the 1875 Niagara Bible conference and later ones.[4]

Imaging the Rapture, Charles Anderson. *With the kind permission of the Bible Believers' Evangelistic Association, Inc. Copyright 1974, www.bbea.org*

Dwight L. Moody (1837–1899) was one of the driving forces behind the spread of the beliefs of the Brethren in the United States. With his partner, Ira Sankey, he composed hundreds of popular hymns. He also was a powerful preacher who traveled throughout America and Britain, spreading the dispensationalist view of the end of the world. For most of his life, he was also active in the YMCA, soup kitchens, and relief work on the battlefields of the Civil War, in which he was a conscientious objector.[5]

Cyrus Scofield (1843–1921) also had a great deal of influence in promoting the Rapture. He wrote Bible study courses and published tracts on dispensationalism. But his most lasting accomplishment was the publication in 1909 of *Scofield's Reference Bible* by Oxford University

Press. In it Scofield interpreted the Bible in such a way as to explain the dispensationalist doctrine. It was an instant success and is still in print.

It is not clear whether William Miller had read any of the teaching of the Brethren when he developed his belief in the ascension of believers at the millennium. The Millerites expected a bodily assumption into heaven although most of the other teachings of the Brethren, such as dispensationalism, were not part of his original message.

The Rapture seems to have become part of fundamental Christian dogma among groups that do not adhere to all the teachings of the Brethren. It has also been popularized by a series of books, starting with *The Late Great Planet Earth* by Hal Lindsey. This book predicted the Rapture for 1988, but Lindsey later revised this to 2000. In his more recent books, he has declined to set any more dates but continues to state that the time is imminent. In 2009, he presented a series of television programs that also appear on his website. These explained his take on the Rapture with many biblical citations.[6]

One of the most vivid images of the Rapture is that told by evangelist Jerry Fallwell (1933–2007):

> *You'll be riding in an automobile. You'll be the driver perhaps. You're a Christian. There will be several people in the car with you, maybe someone who is not a Christian. When the trumpet sounds, you and all the other believers in the automobile will be instantly caught away—you will disappear leaving behind only your clothes and physical things that cannot inherit eternal life. That unsaved person or persons in the automobile will suddenly be startled to find the car is moving along without a driver, and the car suddenly somewhere crashes.*[7]

This is a fairly dramatic image. My initial reaction is not to let the Christian drive. As a matter of fact, it might be a good idea for those who believe in the Rapture to consider using only public transport just for the sake of those left behind.

1 Ernest R. Sandeen, "Towards a Historical Interpretation of Christian Fundamentalism," *Church History* 36, no. 1 (1967): 67–68.

2 Peter Brock, "The Peace Testimony of the Early Plymouth Brethren," *Church History* 53, no. 1 (1994): 36.

3 Ibid., 39.

4 Nancy A. Schaefer, "Y2K as an Endtime Sign: Apocalypticsm in America at the *fin-de-millennuum*," *Journal of Popular Culture* 38, no. 1 (2004): 84.

5 Randall Balmer, *The Encyclopeidia of Evangelism* (Waco, TX: Baylor University Press, 2004), 467.

6 Hal Lindsey, *The Hal Lindsey Report*. Available at www.hallindsey.com/videos/?vid=61. Accessed July 2009. More reports followed the completion of this book.

7 Quoted in Daniel Wojcik, "Embracing Doomsday: Faith, Fatalism and Apocalyptic Beliefs in the Nuclear Age," *Western Folklore* 55, no. 4 (1996): 309–310.

PART SEVEN:

Still Waiting for the End

CHAPTER FORTY-TWO

End-Time Scenarios

How might the world end? Most of the millennial movements concentrate on the warning signs. Then millenarians work on becoming part of the remnant that will either survive or get a straight ticket to heaven. The general feeling is that some sort of (super)natural disaster will take place. It might be flood, earthquake, fire from the sky, or the stars going out. For those who have trouble visualizing the end, here are a few suggestions taken from recent films and documentaries.

1. A giant meteor, comet, or asteroid will hit the earth.

If it is big enough, the impact could cause "dust clouds, changes in atmospheric chemistry, tsunami activity, climatic change with accompanying sea-level changes and possibly tectonic or volcanic activity."[1] On top of that, there could be "corrosive rain, water pollution, air pollution a thousand times worse than the harshest modern smog and airborne toxic metals lethal to any nonburrowing animals."[2]

This has apparently happened more than once in earth's history. Scientists generally agree that either one or more meteors played an important part in the extinction of the dinosaurs. It is still possible that some people might survive, living in underground facilities until the worst was over. After all, the received wisdom is that getting rid of the dinosaurs left the way free for mammals to stake a claim to be masters of the world. So this might not be the total end of the world, but it would definitely fit with the stories in many cultures in which a small group of survivors must start civilization all over again.

In most of the films about this, humankind sends up nuclear bombs that destroy the asteroid or whatever is about to fall from the skies. This is generally not considered the best idea, even though it makes for an exciting visual effect. My favorite suggestion is to hitch the object to a sail that catches the solar wind and steers it away from us. Of course, the odds are that we won't even see the object until it's too close to do anything about it.

So there's really no point in worrying about it now.

2. A super volcano will erupt, causing all of the problems of a meteor hit.

This is also a popular scenario. The caldera under Yellowstone National Park is a favorite possibility. Geologists have known for some time that there was a lake of magma underneath the area. It has caused a cataclysmic eruption at least three times already, with the last major event occurring about 600,000 years ago.[3] But Yellowstone is not the only magma caldera, even in the United States. There is at least one more at Long Valley in California, near Yosemite National Park and the popular ski resort of Mammoth Lakes. Other possible sites are Japan, New Zealand, the Andes, and Indonesia.[4]

Yellowstone is the most frequently studied of these caldera, which are what remains after a major volcanic eruption. It has been noted that the area is continually undergoing seismic activity, and it certainly will erupt again at some point. "Because another caldera-forming eruption is almost inevitable, though not imminent, a continuous monitoring program is important."[5] Sounds like a good idea.

Super volcanoes are measured both by the intensity of the eruption and by the amount of material thrown into the atmosphere. "The biggest super-eruption recognized so far produced approximately five thousand cubic kilometers of deposits, creating the so-called Fish Canyon Tuff event in Colorado.[6] By contrast, Mount St. Helens managed only one half cubic kilometer of ash. However, despite warnings that we are due for another super eruption soon, the odds are negligible that one will go off in the next one hundred years."[7]

If it should happen that one did, the result would be immediate loss of life for those in the surrounding area from suffocation and heat. The sulfuric acid emitted would weaken the ozone layer and affect breathing. Clouds of ash in the atmosphere would block sunlight and could bring about several years of cold weather with poor harvests, thus bringing about global starvation. Ash could also keep planes from flying and disrupt electric power. The eruption could trigger other earthquakes and flooding.

Would it be the end of the world? It would certainly be a challenge to civilization but, again, some people would probably survive. And, since at the moment, we can't predict super volcanoes or do anything about them, I'm checking this off my list of things to worry about.

3. The magnetic poles will reverse.

The gist of this apocalyptic prediction is that every now and then, seemingly on a whim, the North and South Poles change places. This sounded strange to me but I did some research and not only is this true, but the magnetic poles are constantly wandering about, within a certain radius, and they don't even move together! Sometimes the South Pole sets off toward Australia and the North Pole checks out Siberia. They don't move at the same pace, either.[8]

Actually, the fact that the magnetic poles wander has been known for several centuries. I just missed the memo. After reading in both scientific journals and books for general readers, I became convinced that serious paleogeologists and physicists don't understand why this happens. Those who write about this for nonscientists, on the other hand, seem to think that this flip will happen very soon, maybe by 2012, and that it will cause continents to break apart, migrating animals to get lost, and people to lose interest in sex.

Even though I can't understand much about variations in the molten iron core of the earth or lithospheric rotations, the tentative conclusions of scientists, with lots of graphs and experimental results, sound more convincing that unfootnoted warnings of doom.

In some studies, it appears that two prehistoric extinction events occurred just after a pole shift. Now, when geologists say that something happens rapidly, one has to consider the source. A shift can take between two and twenty thousand years. They also note that there was a lot of volcanic activity at those times. The question is, did the pole reversal cause the volcanoes?[9]

The answer is, no one is certain. Magnetism is not well understood. The Ulysses project, which sent a satellite to the sun, discovered a great deal about how the sun's magnetic field works, including the fact that it has polar reversals every few years.[10]

What scientists seem to agree on is that this reversal won't happen overnight or any time soon. So I'm not adding it to my panic list. But that leads to the next catastrophic prediction.

4. The sun will send a solar flare that will destroy the world.

This seems to go along with the 2012 fear that, at the time, the sun will be at "solar maximum" and be emitting all sorts of radiation, coronal mass ejections, and cosmic rays. The proponents of this theory are under the impression that solar maximums are rare. They aren't. The last one I know of was in 2003. There may have been another since.[11]

Since I keep missing them, I'm guessing that solar flares, although they can temporarily disrupt electronics, especially in airplanes, are not going to contribute to the end of the world.

So, What Might Wipe Out
Everyone on the Planet?

The natural upheavals just listed are among many phenomena that have provided fodder for doomsday prophets and filmmakers. Some of them may happen, but no one knows when and there's little that can be done to prevent them in any case. But there are two things that might destroy the world that we can do something about.

This first is my childhood terror, all-out nuclear war. There's no sense in pretending that we could survive a mass exchange of the kind of bombs we have now. But that is something that is totally in the hands of the human race. If we wind up in a radiated nuclear winter, it will be our own fault.

The second is an ecological disaster. Recently, the majority of people on earth have become aware that we are living in a complicated interrelationship with everything else on earth and that we have spent the past couple of thousand years ignoring the consequences of our actions. There are no easy solutions to this. But again, unlike meteors, gamma ray bursts (*very* unlikely), volcanoes, and a magnetic flux, in this case we can at least try to put things right.

---

1 David M. Raup, "Large-Body Impact and Extinction in the Phanerozoic," *Paleobiology* 18, no. 1 (1992): 82.

2 Gregory S. Paul, "Giant Meteor Impacts and Great Eruptions: Dinosaur Killers?," *BioScience* 39, no. 3 (1989): 164.

3 Gordon P. Easton et al., "Magma Beneath Yellowstone National Park," *Science* new ser. 188, 4190 (1975): 787–796.

4 Calvin Miller et al., "(Potentially) Frequently Asked Questions about Supervolcanoes and Supereruptions," *Elements* 4, no. 1 (2008): 16.

5 Charles Wicks Jr., Wayne Thatcher, and Daniel Dzuisin, "Migration of Fluids beneath Yellowstone Caldera Inferred from Satellite Radar Interferometry," *Science* 282 (1998): 458.

6 Stephen Sparks et al., *Super-Eruptions, Global Effects and Future Threats* (London: Geological Society of London, 2005), 6. This is a report to the government and the public, clearly written, that answers many concerns about the topic. I recommend it. Available at www.geolsoc.org .uk/index.html. Accessed November 2009.

7 Sparks et al., 9.

8 Sid Perkins, "North by Northwest: The Planet's Wandering Poles Help Reveal History of Earth and Humans," *Science News* 173 (2007): 392.

9 Vincent Courtillot and Jean Besse, "Magnetic Field Reversals, Polar Wander and Core-Mantle Coupling," *Science* new ser. 237, no. 4819 (1987): 1145.

10 E. J. Smith et al., "The Sun and Heliosphere at Solar Maximum," *Science* new ser. 302, no. 5648 (2003): 1165–1169.

11 Ibid., 1167.

WHEN WILL THE WORLD END?
PREDICTIONS THROUGH TIME

Date of Prediction	Date of the end of the World Predicted	Type	Predictor
About 800 B.C.E.	3 trillion years from now	Apocalyptic	Hindu-Buddhists
1st century C.E.	Any minute	Apocalyptic	Most Christians, some pagans
120 C.E.	172 C.E., or a bit after	Apocalyptic	Montanus, in a vision, seconded by his followers, Priscilla and Maximilla
About 184	184	Millennial	Yellow Turban movement in eastern China announced that the end had begun and they were setting up heaven on earth
190	204	Apocalyptic	Anonymous person playing around with the Book of Daniel
About 100	382 (or 442)	Millennial	some of the Lingbao Daoist texts in China
About 190	500	Millennial	Hippolytus, who thought that 204 was way too soon
200	500	Millennial	Theologians Julius Africanus and Lactantius
About 250	392	Messianic	Chinese Pure Land sects and Daoists (different messiahs, but one can't have too many)

Date of Prediction	Date of the end of the World Predicted	Type	Predictor
397	500	Millennial	Bishop Hilarianus, who was getting nervous about the near future
965	1000	Messianic	According to the Jewish scholar, Saadia Gaon, after some time wrestling with the Book of Daniel
125 AH/743–744	Around 200 AH	Messianic	Muslim folk tradition
About 1025	1068	Messianic	Jewish computers of the end, who thought it had been 1000 years since the destruction of the Temple
1170	1260, or thereabouts	Millennial	Joachim of Fiore
1100	1352	Messianic	Calculated by medieval French Jewish scholar Rashi, from the Book of Daniel
About 1120	1131	Messianic	Spanish Jewish poet Judah Ha-Levi, in response to the invasion of Spain by the fundamentalist Almoravid Muslims
1295	1295	Messianic	A Jewish prophet in Ayllon, Spain
1345	1370	Coming of Antichrist	Franciscan John of Rupescissa, from visions received while in a papal prison, waiting for a broken leg to heal, and while recovering from the plague
	1415	Start of millennium	
	2370	Last Judgment	
1388	1400	Millennial and apocalyptic	Thomas Wimbledon, preaching at St. Paul's London (he had better reason than most; it had been a year of famine and earthquakes)
Winter 1420	Carnival February 10–14, 1420	Apocalyptic	The Taborites who, when the world didn't end, set up their own New Jerusalem
	1533		Anabaptists at Munich

Date of Prediction	Date of the end of the World Predicted	Type	Predictor
March 14, 1557	1999	Millennial (start of)	Nostradamus, in one of his few clear prophecies
Before 1607	2300	Messianic and millennial	Thomas Brightman, British theologian
About 1610	1788	Millennial	John Napier, inventor of logarithms, who also thought that the elect might get an early start in 1700
1614	July 28, 1625	Millennial	Eleanor Davies, who also calculated the Day of Judgment for 1645 (she did foresee her husband's death and that of the duke of Buckingham and King Charles I)
About 1620	1648	Messianic	Some Jewish calculations for the coming of the Messiah, according to the Zohar
1627	1694	Millennial	Johannes Heinrich Alsted, Protestant theologian
About 1630	1660 or a bit later	Apocalyptic	Russian Old Believers
1642	1666	Messianic	John Archer, British Puritan
	1666 (or 1667 or 1672)	Messianic	Sabbatai Sevi
1645	1701	Millennial	Fifth Monarchy prophet Mary Cary
About 1680	3370	Last Judgment	Isaac Newton, using sophisticated math and pure reason
	1779	Millennial	Joseph Meacham and the New Light Baptists
1815	1823 or 1848	Second Coming	Dutch poet Willem Bilderdijk, after reading the Sibyl, Thomas Burnet, and the Talmud

Date of Prediction	Date of the end of the World Predicted	Type	Predictor
1843	October 21, 1844	Apocalyptic	Millerites; Miller's last try (he spent the rest of his life wondering where he had made the mistake in his math)
Early 1800s	1260 AH/1844	Messianic and apocalyptic and millennial	Shi'ites who noted that it was the 1000th year since the occultation of the 12th imam
1849	1868	Millennial and apocalyptic	J.A., who lived in London and was able to afford to print a tract on the end times
About 1870	1874	Messianic	Charles Taze Russell, in the *Watchtower*
1872	April 19, 1875	Apocalyptic	William C. Thurman, a follower of William Miller who thought Chicago was a good place to wait for the rapture
1875	1914	Messianic	Charles Taze Russell, who also predicted the Second Coming in 1918 (he died in 1916, still hopeful)
October 1889	April 14, 1890	Apocalyptic	The Doomsealers; San Francisco only, but if you lived there, it would seem like the end of the world
1887	April 11, 1901	Millennial	The Reverend Michael Paget Baxter
About 1970	1975	Apocalyptic	Some Jehovah's Witnesses
1980s	January 1, 1990	Apocalyptic (nuclear bombs)	Elizabeth Clare Prophet of the Church Universal and Triumphant
	1988	Apocalyptic	Hal Lindsey in *The Late, Great, Planet Earth*
1980s on	2000	Economic Apocalypse	Many people who didn't understand computers see Y2K, and Hal Lindsey again

Date of Prediction	Date of the end of the World Predicted	Type	Predictor
About 900 and 1986 on	2012	Some sort of change, not clear what	Perhaps the Mayas and Olmecs (or perhaps not); many television and film prophets
About 1400	2027	An undefined change	Ancient Aztec calculations, but if you miss that, it could also be 2079
20th-century science	5,000,000,000 or so	Very apocalyptic	When the sun burns out, if the asteroid doesn't hit first, or the ozone gets too thin or the poles make a quick reversal

CHAPTER FORTY-THREE

The End of the End

S o, if you made it to the end of this book, the world probably hasn't ended yet. That doesn't mean it won't happen tomorrow, or the next day, or three trillion years from now. But, looking back at all the prophecies and calculations, it seems likely that the end will come as the Bible says, "like a thief in the night," when everyone is busy with other things.

In researching this book, I read about a lot more prophets, doomsday groups, and theorists than I could possibly include. You may find the ones I've chosen a bit odd. I may have left out your favorite scenario. But the more I researched, the more I realized that the ideas about the end of the world were astonishingly similar. Almost all of them predict massive destruction of societies with almost total loss of life. This disaster is usually caused by immoral behavior on the part of people along with lack of respect and devotion for the deities. *But* . . . each story includes those who are saved: the righteous, the devout, the ones who put the secret sign over their door.

I began to realize that no one expects their world to end. People who expect the Apocalypse soon aren't preparing to die but to survive. They'll build an ark or be raptured up or hitch a ride on the mother ship. The human race is programmed for survival and even (perhaps especially) the most ardent prophets of doom know that they will be among the elect.

Even the extreme cults soon fell into a pattern. Many center around a person, not an idea. The person assumes the role of intercessor for God, sometimes becoming God. For reasons that the psychologists and sociologists are still wrangling over, the prophet collects a group of followers. They don't belong to a particular socioeconomic group; they have different education levels. The only thing they have in common is devotion to the leader and absolute certainty that he or she will keep them safe from whatever disaster is going to occur. I included only a few of these. When you've studied one sex-crazed controlling messiah, you've petty much studied them all.

So, at base, the first Christians who went eagerly to the arenas, the Taiping "Little Brother of Jesus," the Mummyjums, and the Branch Davidians are really the same. Where they differed wasn't in concept but in execution. While the differences among these groups are what make them fascinating, trying to decide which ones to focus on was almost impossible. There were and are so many really interesting individuals who have become committed to finding the time of the end and preparing for it, that it was simply a matter of choosing the ones that most intrigued me. Had I world enough and time this could have run thousands of pages. But each story would have been a variation on a theme.

One of these themes that was difficult to categorize was the revolutionary aspect of the end of the world. It's very hard to tell if a group really wants to set up a perfect society in anticipation of the end or if it has a primarily political agenda to overthrow an oppressive government or to justify territorial expansion. I tried to steer clear of politics, but sometimes the two goals are so intertwined that one can't separate them.

So I have tried to show the unity within the variety over time, space, and culture. It may seem as if everyone in history spent all their waking hours trembling in fear. That's only because the end is the focus of this book. Even though the Apocalypse is very popular, most people are more concerned with muddling through the day at hand than worrying if it's all going to go *poof!* tomorrow.

I think that this fascination with Armageddon, the Apocalypse, the Final Battle, and the Antichrist among nonreligious people is the same as that with ghosts, mutant ants, vampires, and invasions from space. Most of us don't really believe in them, but it's fun to let ourselves be scared for a while. After all, the monsters are always killed, the meteor destroyed, and just when it seems that the bad guys will win, the savior always arrives.

And, of course, the good guys always find a way to survive, right?

Glossary

Apocalypse/Revelation: Mean the same thing—a showing or revealing. *Apocalypse* is Greek; *Revelation*, Latin. However over the centuries, Revelation has come to be used mostly for the book of John of Patmos and Apocalypse both for the book and for a disaster of major proportions, probably leading to the end of the world.

Chiliasm: The Greek term for millenarianism. It comes from the Greek for one thousand. I like it; it's shorter. Of course, every time I read it, I get a craving for Tex-Mex food.

Dispensation: Another term for era. The division of the biblical history of the world into "dispensations." We are, of course, in the last one.

Eschatology: The study of the ways is which people look at the end times, both of individual humans and of the world.

Exegesis: Explanation for the meaning of what someone else wrote. This is very popular with those who study the Bible, but there are scholars who specialize in Shakespearean exegesis, too, and for any writer who might have a hidden agenda.

Latitudinarian: Someone who is easygoing about religious beliefs as long as they don't infringe on others' lives.

Messianic: A type of religious belief that a savior will arrive to clean up the mess that humans have made or to remove a corrupt or oppressive government. One can expect a messiah without the world ending. However, in many traditions, the messiah only appears shortly before the end.

Millennialism: The belief that there will be a thousand years between the beginning of Christianity and the end times. It has been stretched to imply a belief that the end is coming soon. It's also been stretched to assume that God doesn't measure time the way people do.

Occultation: In Islam, the concealment of the Mahdi, who will return when needed. In astronomy, the eclipse of a star or planet by the moon.

Parousia: Another word for the Second Coming of Jesus. It is from the Greek and is used when people want to sound classy.

Premillennialism (or millenarianism): The belief that the thousand years of peace under the rule of Jesus will be preceded by disasters, tribulations, and the reign of the Antichrist. Premillennialists tend to be pessimistic about the possibility of making the world better without divine help and hope to be raptured up to heaven before things get much worse. But many of them still believe in helping out others when there is need.

Postmillennialism: The belief that Christ's incarnation began a thousand years in which people can improve the world, convert almost everyone to Christianity, and prepare humankind for the Second Coming, which will arrive at the end of the millennium. The early 1800s saw many reform movements made up of postmillennialists, such as antislavery leagues.

Syncretism: The blending of two or more different religious beliefs to form a third, which often has elements found in neither.

Index